T0393980

"Graciana del Castillo's books have demonstrated that peace is far too difficult to leave to the generals, diplomats, peacekeepers, lawyers and political scientists. She shows that sustainable peace without economic transformation is close to impossible. This volume advances that important body of work, drawing crucial distinctions among the phases of economic transformation and proposing novel solutions to the persistent failure of the international community to play its proper role in the design and implementation of the political economy of peace."

Michael Doyle, University Professor, Columbia University and author of "The Question of Intervention" (Yale, 2015)

"From hard lessons of the past, Graciana del Castillo works to build a new paradigm for the vital economics of peace and reconstruction that applies in the critical period of transition between war and normal economic development."

Roger B. Myerson, Glen A. Lloyd Distinguished Service Professor, University of Chicago. Winner of the 2007 Nobel Prize in Economics

"Peacebuilding is much lionized, but rarely lives up to expectations. This is doubly puzzling as the UN has been engaged in peacebuilding for several decades. This excellent, admirably compact volume explains the need for active UN peacebuilding and the multiple challenges it faces. Graciana del Castillo is an economically literate, politically acute analyst committed above all to positive results on the ground. She is uniquely qualified to decode the objectives and challenges involved having been a lead actor in peacebuilding."

Dr. David M. Malone, Rector of the United Nations University and Under-Secretary-General of the United Nations

"Accessible and unencumbered by jargon, *Obstacles to Peacebuilding* is an authoritative, hard-hitting and unvarnished assessment of the UN's underwhelming record when it comes to helping countries recover from war and protracted conflict. It is an excellent and timely study, covering a broad canvas of cases and pregnant with policy implications. Of interest to practitioners, scholars and students alike, this is a contribution to the literature that deserves a very wide readership."

Mats Berdal, Professor of Security and Development,
King's College London and author of
"Building Peace After War" (Routledge, 2009)

"Much has been learned about building peace, stability and prosperity in countries undergoing security and political reform, national reconciliation, and economic reconstruction. With her critical eye, Graciana del Castillo pulls it all together in this tightly written, insightful and compelling book."

Ambassador Enrique ter Horst, former SRSG in El Salvador and Haiti
and Assistant Secretary-General in the Office of the Director-General
for Development and International Economic Cooperation

Obstacles to Peacebuilding

Combining the insights of a seasoned practitioner with the academic rigor of a meticulous policy and risk analyst, Graciana del Castillo discusses the major obstacles to peacebuilding that need to be removed before war-torn countries can move towards peace, stability, and prosperity. As Secretary-General António Guterres assumes leadership in January 2017, a top priority must be to address the bleak peacebuilding record where over half of the countries under UN watch relapse back into conflict within a decade.

While policy debate and the academic literature have focused on the security, political, and social aspects of the war-to-peace transition, this book focuses on "the economic transition" – that is, "economic reconstruction" or "the political economy of peace" – which, in the author's view, is the much-neglected aspect of peacebuilding. The book argues that rebuilding war-torn states effectively has acquired a new sense of urgency as extremist groups increasingly recruit people by providing jobs and services to those deprived of them due to government and economic failures.

Based on past lessons and best practices of the last quarter of a century, the author makes recommendations to move forward and improve the record. It will be of great use to students and scholars of peacebuilding, as well as policymakers in national governments, donor countries and international organizations involved in peacebuilding, statebuilding, and development.

Graciana del Castillo is senior fellow at the Ralph Bunche Institute for International Studies, a member of the Council on Foreign Relations and of several boards. She holds a Ph.D. in Economics from Columbia University where she was adjunct professor, senior research scholar, and associate director of the Center for Capitalism & Society. She has published extensively and is the author of *Rebuilding War-Torn States* (2008).

Álvaro de Soto (author of the Foreword) is a former Under-Secretary-General of the United Nations.

Global Institutions

Edited by Thomas G. Weiss
The CUNY Graduate Center, New York, USA
and Rorden Wilkinson
University of Sussex, Brighton, UK

About the series

The "Global Institutions Series" provides cutting-edge books about many aspects of what we know as "global governance." It emerges from our shared frustrations with the state of available knowledge—electronic and print-wise, for research and teaching—in the area. The series is designed as a resource for those interested in exploring issues of international organization and global governance. And since the first volumes appeared in 2005, we have taken significant strides toward filling conceptual gaps.

The series consists of three related "streams" distinguished by their blue, red, and green covers. The blue volumes, comprising the majority of the books in the series, provide user-friendly and short (usually no more than 50,000 words) but authoritative guides to major global and regional organizations, as well as key issues in the global governance of security, the environment, human rights, poverty, and humanitarian action among others. The books with red covers are designed to present original research and serve as extended and more specialized treatments of issues pertinent for advancing understanding about global governance. And the volumes with green covers—the most recent departure in the series—are comprehensive and accessible accounts of the major theoretical approaches to global governance and international organization.

The books in each of the streams are written by experts in the field, ranging from the most senior and respected authors to first-rate scholars at the beginning of their careers. In combination, the three components of the series—blue, red, and green—serve as key resources for faculty, students, and practitioners alike. The works in the blue and green streams have value as core and complementary readings in courses on, among other things, international organization, global governance, international law, international relations, and international political economy; the red volumes allow further reflection and investigation in these and related areas.

The books in the series also provide a segue to the foundation volume that offers the most comprehensive textbook treatment available dealing with all the major issues, approaches, institutions, and actors in contemporary global governance—our edited work *International Organization and Global Governance* (2014)—a volume to which many of the authors in the series have contributed essays.

Understanding global governance—past, present, and future—is far from a finished journey. The books in this series nonetheless represent significant steps toward a better way of conceiving contemporary problems and issues as well as, hopefully, doing something to improve world order. We value the feedback from our readers and their role in helping shape the on-going development of the series.

A complete list of titles appears at the end of this book. The most recent titles in the series are:

UN Peacekeeping Doctrine in a New Era (2017)
edited by Cedric de Coning, Chiyuki Aoi, and John Karlsrud

Global Environmental Institutions (2nd edition, 2017)
by Elizabeth R. DeSombre

Global Governance and Transnationalizing Capitalist Hegemony (2017)
by Ian Taylor

Human Rights and Humanitarian Intervention (2016)
edited by Elizabeth M. Bruch

Displacement, Development, and Climate Change (2016)
by Nina Hall

UN Security Council Reform (2016)
by Peter Nadin

International Organizations and Military Affairs (2016)
by Hylke Dijkstra

The International Committee of the Red Cross (2nd edition, 2016)
by David P. Forsythe and Barbara Ann J. Rieffer-Flanagan

Obstacles to Peacebuilding

Graciana del Castillo

**Foreword by
Álvaro de Soto**

Routledge
Taylor & Francis Group

LONDON AND NEW YORK

First published 2017
by Routledge
2 Park Square, Milton Park, Abingdon, Oxon OX14 4RN

and by Routledge
711 Third Avenue, New York, NY 10017

Routledge is an imprint of the Taylor & Francis Group, an informa business

British Library Cataloguing in Publication Data
A catalogue record for this book is available from the British Library

Library of Congress Cataloging in Publication Data
A catalog record for this book has been requested

ISBN: 978-1-138-20563-5 (hbk)
ISBN: 978-1-138-20567-3 (pbk)
ISBN: 978-1-31546-641-5 (ebk)

Typeset in Times New Roman
by Taylor & Francis Books

Contents

List of illustrations		x
Abbreviations		xi
Other abbreviations		xiii
Foreword by Álvaro de Soto		xiv
Introduction		1
1	Peacebuilding conceptual framework: From *An Agenda for Peace* and its supplement to *An Agenda for Development*	13
2	Economic reconstruction amid the multidisciplinary transition to peace	29
3	The economics of war, the economics of conflict resolution, the economics of peace, the economics of development	43
4	Economic reconstruction vs. development: evolving conceptual views	59
5	Peacebuilding at the UN – from conceptualization to operationalization	79
6	The peacebuilding record, lessons, and challenges	100
7	Specific economic issues affecting peacebuilding in selected countries	117
8	Policymaking premises for effective economic reconstruction	148
9	Moving forward: thinking outside the box	163
Bibliography		170
Index		174
Routledge Global Institutions Series		186

List of illustrations

Tables

2.1	Transition from war to peace	31
3.1	Characteristics and peculiarities	54
6.1	Performance of war-torn countries with foreign interventions	103
6.2	Aid comparison across war-torn countries	105
6.3	Case studies covering security, political, and/or social transitions in war-torn countries	111
6.4	Case studies covering security, political, social and/or economic transitions in war-torn countries	113
8.1	The economics of peace: premises for effective reconstruction and peacebuilding	150
8.2	Economic policymaking	153
9.1	Minimalist structure for reconstruction zones	166
9.2	Overall objectives of reconstruction zones (RZs) to move countries towards a path of peace, stability, and prosperity	167

Figure

2.1	39

Diagram

3.1	45

Abbreviations

ATM	Automatic teller machine
BWIs	Bretton Woods Institutions
CEPAL	Spanish acronym for the UN Economic Commission for Latin American and the Caribbean
CPA	Coalition Provisional Authority (Iraq)
CSCs	Country-Specific Configurations (United Nations Peacebuilding Commission)
DDR	Disarming, demobilization, and reintegration
DRC	Democratic Republic of Congo
ERSG	Executive representative of the Secretary-General
FARC	Spanish acronym for the Revolutionary Armed Forces of Colombia
FUNDS	Future United Nations Development System
FMLN	Spanish acronym for the Farabundo Martí National Liberation Front
GDP	Gross domestic product
GNI	Gross national income
HIV/AIDS	Human immunodeficiency virus
HDI	Human Development Index
ICT	Information and communications technology
IMF or Fund	International Monetary Fund
MDGs	Millennium Development Goals
NATO	North Atlantic Treaty Organization
NGOs	Non-governmental organizations
ODA	OECD Official Development Assistance
ODF	OECD Official Development Finance
OECD	Organization for Economic Co-operation and Development
ONUSAL	United Nations Observer Mission in El Salvador
MINUSAL	United Nations Mission in El Salvador

PBFund	United Nations Peacebuilding Fund
PRTs	Provincial Reconstruction Teams
RENAMO	Portuguese acronym for the Mozambican National Resistance
RPF	Rwandan Patriotic Front
RZs	Reconstruction zones
ERZs	Export-oriented reconstruction zones
LRZs	Local-production reconstruction zones
SIDA	Swedish International Development Cooperation Agency
SMEs	Small and medium-sized enterprises
SRSG	Special Representative of the Secretary-General
UCDP-PRIO	Uppsala Conflict Data Program; International Peace Research Institute, Oslo
UN	United Nations
UNAMA	United Nations Assistance Mission in Afghanistan
UNDP	United Nations Development Programme
UNODC	United Nations Office on Drugs and Crime
UNOMOZ	United Nations Operation in Mozambique
UNTAC	United Nations Transitional Authority in Cambodia
UNU/WIDER	United Nations University, World Institute for Development Economics Research
URNG	Spanish acronym for the Guatemalan National Revolutionary Unity
USAID	United States Agency for International Development
USIP	United States Institute of Peace
WDR	World Bank World Development Report

Other abbreviations

Architecture	United Nations Peacebuilding Architecture
Chapultepec Agreement	El Salvador's peace agreement
Commission	United Nations Peacebuilding Commission
Peacekeeping department	United Nations Department of Peacekeeping Operations
Political department	United Nations Department of Political Affairs
Support Office	United Nations Peacebuilding Support Office

Foreword

Álvaro de Soto

For 25 years Graciana del Castillo has been applying her relentless and unforgiving analytical mind to the subject of how the international community handles transitions from war to peace after intrastate conflict since the end of the Cold War. As the international community has grappled with this new challenge, del Castillo has pursued what we might call a running commentary in articles and books. Her readers will no doubt agree that flattery is not part of the portfolio of currencies in which she deals. They will also share my view that there is not much about which to dispense flattery. Her writings and the conclusions she reaches leave little room for optimism.

In fact, a casual reader might be forgiven for pigeonholing del Castillo as a UN basher. That reader would be mistaken. Indeed, she describes the UN as "the global organization responsible for the maintenance of peace and security ... ideally placed to support economic reconstruction [the economics of peace] because of its political nature and the need for impartiality." The bitter tone of her commentary is the result of deep-seated disappointment that the hope that shone briefly at the end of the Cold War, that the UN was finally coming into its own after decades of marginalization, was soon dashed. This was not just because of the inability of states, particularly those who in effect gave birth to the post-WWII collective security system, to come together consistently, but also because the secretariats of the programs and agencies that are at its centre seem incapable of adapting to the new challenges and the needs they generate.

As colleagues in the Executive Office of United Nations Secretary-General Boutros Boutros Ghali, Graciana del Castillo and I jointly took an interest in the subject in the early 1990s when we were overseeing the implementation of and compliance with the 16 January 1992 Peace Accord that brought an end to the 12-year civil war in El Salvador. The Accord was the culmination of a 22-month negotiation which I shepherded as the personal representative for the Central American peace process of Boutros Ghali's predecessor, Javier Pérez de Cuéllar. It was initialled at midnight on 31 December 1991, his last day in office. Del Castillo joined Boutros Ghali's team in 1992 as the senior economist in the Executive Office.

Del Castillo's first article, "Obstacles to Peacebuilding," *Foreign Policy*, 94 (Spring 1994) was written with me, as was the next, "Implementation of Comprehensive Peace Agreements: Staying the Course in El Salvador" in *Global Governance*, 1 (June 1995). Since then, except for a recent joint article titled "Obstacles to Peacebuilding Revisited," *Global Governance*, 22 (2016), she has written several articles as well as three books on her own. *Obstacles to Peacebuilding* is her third.

Boutros Ghali became secretary-general at a time of hope, in the wake of Pérez de Cuéllar's unprecedented—and still unmatched—string of peacemaking successes which placed the UN squarely among those who sired the end of the Cold War. The UN Security Council was able to hold its first meeting ever at the level of heads of state and government on the last day of Boutros Ghali's first month in office. They asked him to recommend how to strengthen the capacity of the UN for preventive diplomacy, peacemaking and peacekeeping.

Inspired in what had been agreed as part and parcel of ending the war in El Salvador, the UN's first start-to-finish mediation of an internal conflict, Boutros Ghali quickly understood that internal conflict would soon become the UN's bread and butter and that it would require comprehensive action rallying various arms of the UN system over prolonged periods of time. In his report to the UN membership pursuant to the Security Council summit's request, titled *An Agenda for Peace*, he set out a fourth activity alongside the preventive diplomacy, peacemaking and peacekeeping triad which he called *post-conflict peace-building* (PCPB) and defined as the activities aimed at preventing the recurrence of conflict—as opposed to preventive diplomacy which is aimed at averting a conflict's outbreak. *An Agenda for Peace* received many plaudits and, as the UN fumbled to articulate and give practical shape to PCPB, its recommendations were the subject of close examination over subsequent years.

In her first book, *Rebuilding War-Torn States: The Challenge of Post-Conflict Economic Reconstruction* (Oxford: Oxford University Press, 2008), del Castillo provided a comprehensive analysis of economic reconstruction amid the transition to peace, usually as part of a multipronged process, arguing that unless the overarching political objective of avoiding recurrence of conflict prevails at all times, peace will be ephemeral, and that policies that pursue purely economic objectives can have tragic consequences. While insisting on that main premise, which she first presented in "Post-Conflict Peace-Building: A Challenge for the United Nations," *CEPAL Review* 55 (June 1995), she did not believe that the UN, at that time, had the operational, technical and human capacity needed to discharge such a task, nor had it taken the steps needed to develop it.

In her second book, *Guilty Party: The International Community in Afghanistan* (Bloomington, Ind.: XLibris, 2nd edition, 2016), she posited that the answer to extremism, insurgency, drugs, and poverty is inclusive and sustainable growth rather than war. She focused on what went wrong with US-led intervention and what can still be done to bring peace, stability, and prosperity to the country and the region.

In *Obstacles to Peacebuilding*, del Castillo turns her attention to the economic issues that can so decisively affect conflict resolution and the maintenance of peace but which are all too often neglected in the process of negotiating the end of a conflict. She distinguishes between the economics of war, the economics of conflict resolution, the economics of peace, and the economics of development. She analyzes rigorously the different goals of each of these, the necessary policies to address the challenges in each phase, and what is at stake if the specificities of each of these phases are not understood and solutions tailored to them are not designed and implemented. In particular, she argues that the failure to address correctly the economics of conflict resolution during peace negotiations and the economics of peace in the post-conflict period continue to be a major obstacle to peacebuilding.

Del Castillo also describes the difficulties involved in moving from one phase to the other, particularly since phases often overlap and the move is rarely linear. She argues that the lack of adequate economic expertise and the tendency to neglect the crucial importance of economic reconstruction issues in peacebuilding efforts—or to treat a state navigating such a transition as if it could simply return to well-worn development patterns—have led to the disappointing record.

She analyzes how views on these issues have evolved over the years, particularly at the UN and the Bretton Woods institutions. She provides country evidence to substantiate her view—which we espoused in our 2016 article in Global Governance—that the much touted "Peacebuilding Architecture" put in place following the summit to mark the UN's 60th anniversary, including an ill-conceived Peacebuilding Commission, which has produced a lacklustre performance—in fact merely rehashed old conceptual arguments on peacebuilding while skirting the difficult issue of how to improve the policymaking and operational capacity of the UN at headquarters and on the ground to make peace sustainable.

She also uses her experience of a quarter of a century to establish basic premises for effective economic reconstruction. She argues persuasively that the application of such premises to specific situations could help national policymakers and the UN and others involved in efforts to design more effective peacebuilding strategies in order to assist the move toward peace, stability and prosperity. She also presents a minimalist structure for reconstruction zones as an example of how to apply basic premises to create a more integrated framework utilizing conflict-sensitive policies and synergies between local communities, foreign investors, governments and foreign interveners to facilitate such move.

In del Castillo's view, unless the UN starts thinking outside the box, its peacebuilding efforts will continue to fail simply because peacekeepers—those with the military capability to keep the peace—cannot be kept in a country indefinitely, nor is it realistic to rely on aid to provide the basic needs of war-torn countries endlessly.

Given the consequences of turmoil and terrorism in the Middle East, Africa, Europe, and elsewhere, and with a new secretary-general taking office in January 2017 and several silver anniversaries taking place that year, the author argues that the time is overdue to revisit and reflect on the disappointing and costly peacebuilding record, and find ways to make it better.

Introduction

- **Identification of a major obstacle to peacebuilding**
- **Obstacles to peacebuilding revisited**
- **Organization of the book**

Rebuilding war-torn states in a cost-effective, inclusive, and sustainable way has proved to be a key missing factor in peacebuilding efforts across the world since Cold War-related civil wars faded a quarter of a century ago and new conflicts arose from the disintegration of the Soviet Union and the former Yugoslavia. Since then, a large and diverse group of countries – at low levels of development and scarred by civil war or other intrastate conflicts, rather that interstate wars[1] – embarked, mostly with the support of the United Nations, on a complex and multidisciplinary[2] transition to peace, stability, and prosperity. The use of these three terms is necessary to convey the idea that the transition involves more than just moving away from the conflict and insecurity of the past; there must be also economic and social gain for it to be sustainable. Supporting such transition has provided a serious challenge for an organization unprepared to deal with the economics of peace or political economy aspects of peacebuilding.

The UN capacity in this area remains inadequate. Not surprisingly, failure at addressing the economics of conflict resolution during peace negotiations, and the economics of peace during the post-conflict period, effectively continue to be a major obstacle to peacebuilding.

The main argument of this book is that the political economy of peacebuilding requires replacing the economics of war with the economics of peace promptly and with determination. This is imperative so that countries can avoid relapse into war or violent conflict, and can eventually fully engage in the economics of development. This of course, does not preclude a reactivation of development activities as soon as feasible.

But moving directly from the economics of war to the economics of development – as if war-torn countries did not have special needs with large budgetary implications, and as if policymaking in these countries could proceed as in others unaffected by deadly conflict – has led to a most unimpressive UN peacebuilding record.

It has also led to a huge cost in terms of blood and treasure – both to host countries and to what is collectively referred to as "foreign interveners"[3] that support war-torn countries in transition. These consist of the UN system as a whole, including the Bretton Woods institutions (BWIs) – the International Monetary Fund (IMF) and the World Bank[4] – member states, bilateral and multilateral donors, and regional and non-governmental organizations (NGOs).

UN support for the reconstruction of war-torn countries, that is, for their transition to peace, stability, and prosperity – encompassing simultaneous action in the political, security, social, and economic areas – put the organization temporarily back in fashion in the early 1990s. This was not to last, partly because of failures in Angola, Rwanda, and Somalia.

The record has hardly improved since then. An overwhelming majority of the countries that embarked on the transition with the support of UN peacekeeping and peacebuilding operations – encompassing both military and civilian support in the four areas – relapsed into violent conflict within the first decade (Table 6.1). Those that managed to keep a tenuous peace often relied on long-lasting and costly peacekeeping operations or foreign troops to avoid conflict recurrence.

Moreover, with guns gone silent – either through peace agreements or following military interventions – and despite large commitments in international assistance in the form of aid disbursement and technical support, most of these countries have been unable to stand on their own feet, let alone get back into a path towards sustained prosperity for the population at large. Most gains have gone to certain elites that have benefited both from the economics of war and from the economics of peace. This has led to growing inequalities and sowed the seeds for new conflicts.

Indeed, most countries have faced serious impediments to bringing about the necessary changes needed to resume the development path interrupted by war. This has been due to a combination of misguided policies – both involving foreign interveners and national policymakers – as well as misplaced priorities that violate basic premises, including those involving the sequence of policies in the post-conflict period (Chapter 8).[5] In the process, many have failed to reactivate their economies productively and inclusively and have become highly aid dependent. Some, like Afghanistan and Liberia, have fallen into a chronic aid addiction during the first decade of the transition. Moving them out of the "aid trap" will not be easy. Afghanistan has the ominous distinction of having both relapsed into conflict and become the most aid-dependent country in the world. Liberia has only managed to keep the peace by having a large and costly UN operation in place for over 12 years. Both countries remain among the bottom 10 percent in the Human Development Index.

As Nobel Laureate Edmund S. Phelps stated in the prologue to my 2008 book *Rebuilding War-Torn States*, it could have been expected that when wars stopped, countries would have found their footing again and set about to make up the lost ground with regard to their development.[6] But rebuilding from the ashes of civil war and other internal chaos in countries at low levels of development has proved quite unnerving.

Failure at effective reconstruction has also been associated with great human suffering. Indeed, relapses into conflict have been serious and often more bloody than previous conflicts, as the experience of Angola and Rwanda in the 1990s and Afghanistan and Iraq in the 2000s well attest. The genocide in Rwanda that followed the collapse of the Arusha Peace Agreement in 1994 (with close to one million people dead) and the collapse of the agreements in Angola in 1993 and 2001 (with about 350,000 dead) are examples of the high human cost of reverting to conflict. In Afghanistan and Iraq, about 6,750 American troops lost their lives, together with troops from allied countries, and hundreds of thousands of Iraqi and Afghan combatants and civilians. Moreover, failed states create a large number of refugees and displaced populations and become incubators for terrorism, trafficking of drugs and people, smuggling, extortion, and other illicit activities.

With war raging in the Middle East and with conflicts flaring up in Africa, Europe, and elsewhere, and with the international community engaged in post-conflict reconstruction following civil wars, military intervention, and/or regime change across various continents, it is indeed the perfect time to revisit and reflect on the peacebuilding record and find ways to improve it going forward by avoiding past mistakes and failures.

With António Guterres assuming power at the UN in January 2017, and with the year marking the 25th anniversary of the creation of the Department of Peacekeeping Operations (hereafter peacekeeping department) and the Department of Political Affairs (hereafter political department), and of the signature of peace agreements in El Salvador and Mozambique, it seems like the perfect time to analyze and assess: What have we learned from the past? What has gone right and what has gone wrong? How can we think outside the box to improve the disappointing and costly record (both in terms of lives and treasure) of reconstruction and peacebuilding.

Improving the record has now acquired a new sense of urgency given multiple and growing terrorist threats to global peace and security from extremist groups such as Boko Haram, Al-Shabaab, and Da'esh/Islamic State in Iraq and the Levant (ISIL). These and other extremists groups, in particular Hezbollah, Hamas, Al Qaeda, and the Taliban, increasingly recruit members and sympathizers by providing services and infrastructure, jobs, and other basic needs to those deprived of them in countries with ineffective and corrupt governments and feeble foreign interveners. Poor governance at the national level is associated with a variety of economic failures, including from the provision of aid. Terrorist groups in turn finance themselves to a large extent by drug and other racketeering activities that thrive in insecure areas lacking alternative livelihoods.

Moreover, terrorism and drug production are closely interrelated. War-torn countries are often large producers of illegal drugs and operate as safe havens for radical terrorist groups and drug trafficking in their regions. Production, manufacturing, and international trafficking of illegal narcotics attract international criminal syndicates and terrorist groups in a vicious circle that threatens global peace and security. As UN Secretary-General Ban Ki-moon notes, "The connections between drug trafficking, organized crime, corruption and terrorism are becoming more diverse and sophisticated, and fuel insecurity and political instability globally."[7] As an example of the critical role that some of the war-torn countries play in this vicious circle, the United Nations Office on Drugs and Crime (UNODC) notes that, of global annual flows of 430–450 tons of heroin and morphine, about 380 tons are produced exclusively with Afghan opium.[8]

The renewed sense of urgency also relates to the growing global repercussions of failed foreign interventions – particularly humanitarian crises and huge flows of refugees – which are having tremendous political, security, socioeconomic, and moral repercussions in Europe, the Middle East, and elsewhere. Migration has hit neighbouring countries and donor countries alike in a variety of ways with unpredictable global consequences. At the time of writing, the June 2016 referendum by British voters to exit the European Union cost Prime Minister David Cameron his job, roiled global markets, and led to a devaluation of the pound to its lowest level in decades.

A third factor relates to the spread of infectious diseases in humans, plants, and domestic and wild animals that recognize no borders. Among those affecting humans, the most notorious are infectious diseases such as malaria, Ebola, and the Zika virus. Ebola hit countries such as Liberia, Sierra Leone, and Guinea – three countries in the agenda of the UN Peacebuilding Commission – which failed to utilize aid to improve their health systems and other basic services. Misguided reconstruction policies in these countries made them more vulnerable to disease, with serious regional and global repercussions.

Last but not least, the sense of urgency also relates to climate change, environmental sustainability, and biodiversity depletion. War-torn states have often seen the depletion of forested areas, including for the use of wood stoves for cooking and for heating during winters. Local communities and foreign transnational corporations often encroach on forested areas to convert them into plantations, to deal with population pressures, and to graze animals in forested areas, often affecting wild plant diversity and spreading diseases. These countries are particularly prone to overexploitation of natural resources, including illegal timber and other wood and medicinal plant products. Some are subject to slash-and-burn farming practices, soil erosion, and other environmental damage, often resulting from years of war, lack of investment, and illegal and unregulated exploitation of natural resources.

Because of the global repercussions of war and insecurity, war-torn countries have a disproportionately large political, security, social, and environmental impact in comparison with their small contribution to the global economy in terms of production and trade. A few war-torn countries also account for a large share of aid from donor countries, leaving others as aid "orphans," which creates its own set of problems in terms of peacebuilding efforts.

Afghanistan is perhaps the best example of a country whose political weight in the foreign policy agenda of the United States and other major donors has been incommensurate to its tiny economic share of only about one-fifth of one percent (0.02 percent) of global output.[9] In the past, this was related to the important role Afghans played as allies and main protagonists in the Cold War against the Soviets. In the new millennium, its potential for regional and global disruption was most clearly illustrated by 9/11. The country's political importance is related mainly to its geopolitical and strategic location at the crossroads of Asia and Europe on what was once part of the Silk Road, and the fact that, as M. Ishaq Nadiri remarked in 2009, "seven atomic owning nations were vying with each other in Afghanistan (Pakistan, India, China, Russia, possibly Iran, the United States, and the United Kingdom)."[10]

At the time, President Obama was deciding on the military surge, and there was ample concern that Afghan problems could have security, political, and economic repercussions well beyond its borders – particularly in nuclear-armed Pakistan, but also in the Central Asian countries – as it had after the United States had abandoned the country following the demise of the Soviet Union in the early 1990s.[11] As Moisés Naim of the Carnegie Endowment for International Peace has warned, as criminal organizations fuse with weak and corrupt governments, nuclear deterrence might become more difficult.[12]

Other war-torn countries have also had a political impact well beyond their impact on the global economy. Iraq did not start as a global problem, but it certainly became one. The U.S. invasion in 2003 led to strained relations between the United States and Europe, created a split among the permanent members of the Security Council, and often led to violent opposition to U.S. policies across the world. U.S. recognition of the unilateral independence of Kosovo in February 2008, and Russia's recognition of independence in Abkhazia and South Ossetia following the Georgian war in August of that year, led to the worst confrontation between the United States and Russia since the end of the Cold War. Russia's annexation of Crimea in 2014 following military intervention added to the polarization between Russia and the United States at the Security Council. At the present time, perhaps Syria and to a less extent Yemen illustrate best this situation.

War-torn countries have also affected the operations of the multilateral system, particularly the UN, in a major way. As Thomas Weiss noted, picking up the pieces after the dust of conflict has settled "has become the growth industry in the United Nations' conflict business."[13]

The dimension of the problem calls for an improved operational capacity at the UN to deal with peacebuilding. The 2016 *Global Peace Index*[14] compiled by the Institute of Economics and Peace, a leading think tank in this area, shows that the world has become a less peaceful place in the last year – reinforcing the declining trend of the last decade. Results also show growing inequality – with the most peaceful countries continuing to improve and the least peaceful falling into greater deadly violence and conflict.

Identification of a major obstacle to peacebuilding

In a 1994 *Foreign Policy* article entitled "Obstacles to Peacebuilding," Álvaro de Soto and I questioned the capacity of the UN to tackle the new institutional challenges as the organization was coming out of the marginalization of the Cold War in the early 1990s.[15] Multidisciplinary missions set up to support war-to-peace transitions went far beyond the military aspects of traditional UN peacekeeping and encompassed diverse civilian peacebuilding activities. The latter included economic reintegration of former combatants and other war-affected groups and involved a variety of actors from inside and outside the UN system. The main purpose of such activities was to make peace long-lasting by avoiding recurrence of violent conflict.

Countries embarking on the transition to peace in the aftermath of the Cold War were at low levels of development and emerging from civil war or other internal conflict, which required special efforts at national reconciliation. Reconciliation was imperative so that combatants from both sides could return to their villages and communities could rebuild their social fabric. The fact that they were at low levels of development made reactivation of their economies a whole new ball game. Both factors made economic reconstruction very different from the successful Marshall Plan.

In the new context, foreign interveners pressured countries to embark on a complex multidisciplinary transition to peace, and in this sense reconstruction was different from previous ones in Korea and Vietnam. While the Security Council assumed leadership in the "political" and "security" areas of this transition, the IMF and the World Bank assumed leadership in the "economic" and "social" ones.

Through their technical advice and lending conditionality, the BWIs promoted rapid and wide-ranging transformation of these countries through market-based and private sector-focused economic policies. Various other organizations in the UN system and bilateral agencies in donor countries participated in supporting roles during the transition.

The case of El Salvador was an early example of the new context in which UN-led peacebuilding would take place. As discussed by Álvaro de Soto in the Foreword, with the support of the Security Council, the UN had mediated for the first time through 1990 and 1991 an internal conflict to end the long war between the government of El Salvador and an insurgent group, the FMLN (Spanish acronym for the Farabundo Martí National Liberation Front).

Strikingly, the 1991 initialling of the peace accord on New Year's Eve at UN headquarters in New York had no effect on the approval by the IMF Board of Directors in Washington, DC on 6 January 1992, less than one week later, of an economic program that did not incorporate the financial needs of the peace agreement. On the contrary, it contained strict fiscal and external targets that deprived the government of any flexibility with respect to domestic financing in 1992.

As the year unfolded, it soon became clear that lack of financing would affect critical peace-related programs. There was an understanding between the government and the IMF that expenditures resulting from the peace agreement would have to be financed by additional public savings (including from a reduction in military out-lays), reallocation of public expenditure, or external resources (including foreign aid and borrowing).[16] Given that military expenditure during the war was largely foreign financed, this was not only an unrealistic scenario, it was oblivious of Lord Keynes' dictum following World War I that peace has high economic consequences.[17]

With its tough economic conditionality and lack of concessionality from the BWIs,[18] the IMF-sponsored economic program in 1992 became a major obstacle for the Salvadoran government to start and implement various aspects of the UN-negotiated peace agreement, including the arms-for-land program and the creation of a civilian police force, programs that were crucial to the consolidation of peace and its sustainability. Not surprisingly, as former Under-Secretary-General Marrack Goulding put it at the time, only nine months after the signature of the peace agreement in Mexico City on 16 January 1992 (the Chapultepec Agreement) the country was back on the verge of war.[19]

This experience allowed de Soto and me to identify a problem that would continue to haunt countries in the transition to peace for the next quarter of a century: the UN and the BWIs were involved in separate but simultaneous political and economic processes which most often placed them on a collision course.

While many analysts and practitioners interpreted our *Foreign Policy* article as simply calling attention to the lack of coordination between the UN and the BWIs, our message went far beyond. We argued that, in countries transitioning from war, preventing recurrence of conflict must have overriding priority over any other economic or political goal. Thus, in the absence of sufficient foreign aid, funding for critical political and security projects may have to come from "scarce domestic resources," which might create a real dilemma for the government.[20]

We asked rhetorically, "Should it [El Salvador] sacrifice economic stabilization to proceed with implementing the peace accords, or should it strictly carry out its stabilization and structural adjustment program, perhaps endangering the peace?" We posited that "[n]either path is independently sustainable. There is an overriding need to harmonize the two processes so that they support, rather than counteract, each other."[21]

De Soto and I noted that El Salvador's dilemma offered a stark example of the need for the "integrated approach to human security" that Boutros-Ghali advocated, particularly in the case of war-torn countries. We also argued that international organizations should support a country facing such dilemma to help it "avoid a collision between competing processes, insisting on the pre-eminence of peace over narrow economic objectives."[22]

The practical consequence of accepting that the "political or peace" objective should prevail at all times – including in budgetary allocations – is that, in such a process, the "economic or development" objective may be stalled, at least temporarily. Thus, national policymakers and foreign interveners must accept delays in economic stabilization and structural reform, as well as in basic development benchmarks (health, education, and infrastructure) whenever peace is at stake. They also need a different yardstick to measure "success."

Because of the "political" nature of peacebuilding activities – including those in the economic area – de Soto and I emphasized the leading role that the UN had to play vis-à-vis the BWIs and other UN agencies in setting priorities, both strategically and operationally on the ground. However, the UN never had the operational, technical, and human capacity needed for such a task – nor, we have argued, has it ever taken steps to fill that need effectively.

Obstacles to peacebuilding revisited

In May 2016, de Soto and I published a follow-up article entitled "Obstacles to Peacebuilding Revisited" in *Global Governance*. In it, we assessed how the major obstacle to peacebuilding – that is, the difficulty in integrating the political and economic aspects of the transition to peace – that we identified in the case of El Salvador in 1992 had evolved over the next quarter of a century.

Such assessment is timely in light of the bleak record with war-torn countries and peacebuilding (Tables 6.1 and 6.2), where a large majority relapses into conflict within the first decade in transition and/ or becomes dependent on peacekeeping operations to keep the peace and on aid to finance the country's basic economic and security needs. I argue that a combination of misguided policies, misplaced priorities, ineffective aid, and widespread corruption – involving both national governments and foreign interveners – lie behind the bleak record.

Countries have found it particularly difficult to move from the economics of war to the economics of peace, and the UN has not been able to provide much assistance. Failure to reactivate economies in an inclusive way from the very beginning has deprived the large majority of the population of a peace dividend in terms of improved living conditions and income-generating opportunities. This has fostered public discontent and fuelled insurgencies and illicit activities. In turn, this has impeded efforts at improving governance, the rule of law, justice, and human rights; has worsened security; and has made national reconciliation elusive.

In particular, our 2016 article analyzes whether the UN institutional and operational capacity to overcome obstacles has improved in light of the so-called Peacebuilding Architecture adopted in 2005. We found that the operational capacity of the organization to assist war-torn countries to reduce the risk that conflict will recur has not improved.[23]

Moreover, the new architecture has failed to overcome the potential clashes of competence, waste of resources, and bureaucratic hurdles that are imperative to consolidate peace in a cost-effective and sustainable way. Indeed, we found that, after ten years of existence, the architecture might have even contributed to such problems, and we made some recommendations on institutional changes that could help improve the UN capacity for peacebuilding going forward.[24]

Organization of the book

The purpose of the book is to discuss in a more detailed, rigorous, and referenced way – including through the use of relevant country illustrations and statistical evidence – many of the obstacles to peacebuilding that de Soto and I discussed in our *Foreign Policy* and *Global Governance* articles.

Because obstacles to peacebuilding relating to security stabilization, political governance, human rights and transitional justice, and social reconciliation are well discussed in the academic literature, this book will focus on the "economic transition," "economics of peace," "economic reconstruction," or "the political economy of peace" (terms used interchangeably), as a key but much-neglected aspect of peacebuilding in war-torn countries in the post-Cold War period.

The book proceeds as follows: Chapter 1 addresses the conceptual development of the term "peacebuilding," as defined in Secretary-General Boutros-Ghali's *An Agenda for Peace* and its use in contrast with the concept of "preventive diplomacy." The chapter also discusses the concept of "an integrated approach to human security" and analyzes how these concepts have evolved over time and across institutions.

Chapter 2 analyzes the path from war to peace, including the four distinct aspects of the war-to-peace transition: security (or stabilization), political (or governance), social (or national reconciliation) and economic (the economics of peace or economic reconstruction). The chapter argues that these transitions have been mostly analyzed by policymakers, other practitioners, academics, and pundits with a "silo mentality" when in fact these four transitions are closely interrelated, and failure in any one of them puts the others at risk.

Chapter 3 focuses on the economics of war, the economics of conflict resolution, the economics of peace, and the economics of development and the nonlinear connection between these phases. The chapter analyzes "the economics of peace" and argues that this intermediate phase – whose main objective is to ensure that conflict will not relapse – must not be conflated with the "economics of development," i.e., normal development in countries not affected by violent conflict. Conflation of the two has had dire effects.

Chapter 4 analyzes how the conceptual thinking about these issues evolved at the UN and at the BWIs in the 1990s and 2000s. The chapter shows how many of the ideas developed at the UN and opposed in Washington have gradually spilled over to the work of both the World Bank and the IMF.

Chapter 5 analyzes how "peacebuilding" evolved from Boutros-Ghali's conceptualization to its operationalization in the field and its actual performance. Since improved lives and livelihoods of the population at large are key factors in peacebuilding, the chapter analyzes the impact of the Peacebuilding Architecture in this area after ten years of existence, to assess whether it has improved or hindered UN efforts in this area.

Chapter 6 discusses the bleak 25-year peacebuilding record of UN operations. The chapter argues that lack of economic expertise at the UN to deal with the economic aspects of peacebuilding is a major factor behind the disappointing record.

Chapter 7 identifies critical economic issues that have affected peacebuilding in UN operations, both positively and negatively.

Chapter 8 presents basic premises for effective peacebuilding based on country experiences with economic reconstruction in the last quarter of a century presented in Chapter 7. Although every conflict is unique, the parties to peace agreements, peace mediators, and foreign interveners must consider these premises, and adapt them to their own context as they negotiate and design peace agreements or implement peace processes.

Chapter 9 proposes "reconstruction zones" as a way to overcome the difficulties of the past and think about ways of moving forward in a more cost-effective, integrated, inclusive, and sustainable way to ensure that countries can eventually stand on their own feet and move to a path of peace, stability, and prosperity.

Notes

1 All societies experiment with different degrees of conflict. Except where otherwise indicated, the book uses the term "conflict" interchangeably with "violent conflict" or "deadly conflict," as in civil war or other internal chaos.

2 The term "multidisciplinary" is preferable to indicate the different expertise needed, but the terms "multidimensional" or "multipronged" have also been used in this context.
3 The term "foreign interveners" is preferable to "international community" since not all member states participate in supporting war-torn countries.
4 The UN system includes all departments in the Secretariat as well as the UN programs and agencies. Although as agencies the IMF and the World Bank are part of the UN system, due to their specific role in economic stabilization and financing, they are also referred to as the BWIs or are included as part of the international financial institutions (IFIs), which also include the regional development banks.
5 Throughout the text, the chapter in brackets indicates that the topic is addressed in more detail there.
6 Edmund S. Phelps, Prologue in Graciana del Castillo, *Rebuilding War-Torn States: The Challenge of Post-Conflict Economic Reconstruction* (Oxford: Oxford University Press, 2008), vii.
7 UN, *Report of the Secretary-General on the work of the Organization* (New York: General Assembly document A/70/1, Supplement 1), 22 July 2015.
8 UNODC webpage.
9 Calculated by the author using 2009 data. For details, see del Castillo, *Guilty Party: The International Community in Afghanistan* (Bloomington, Ind.: XLibris, 2nd edition, 2016), 199.
10 M. Ishaq Nadiri, "Economics as a Pre-Requisite for the Stability of Afghanistan and the Region," Paper presented at the "Conference on Peace Through Reconstruction" (New York: Columbia University, Center on Capitalism and Society and Earth Institute: 23 October 2009).
11 Del Castillo, *Guilty Party*, 95–100.
12 Moisés Naim, *Illicit: How Smugglers, Traffickers, and Copycats Are Hijacking the Global Economy* (2005).
13 Thomas G. Weiss, Prologue in Rob Jenkins, *Peacebuilding: From Concept to Commission* (London: Routledge, 2013), vii.
14 All indices mentioned in this book can be found online by name.
15 De Soto and del Castillo, "Obstacles to Peacebuilding," *Foreign Policy*, 94 (Spring 1994) 69.
16 IMF, *El Salvador: Article IV Consultation – Staff Report* (Washington, DC: July 1991). For details on El Salvador, see case study in del Castillo, *Rebuilding War-Torn States*, 95–136.
17 John M. Keynes, *The Economic Consequences of the Peace* (New York: Harcourt, Brace and Howe, Inc., 1920).
18 Lending from the BWIs was at market rates rather than at concessional terms because Salvadoran per capita income was above the threshold.
19 Marrack Goulding, *Peacemonger* (London: John Murray, 2002), 241–45.
20 De Soto and del Castillo, *Obstacles to Peacebuilding*, 71.
21 Ibid.
22 Ibid., 77. See also S. Neil MacFarlane and Yuen Foong Khong, *Human Security and the UN* (Bloomington, Ind.: Indiana University Press, United Nations Intellectual History Project Series, 2011).
23 De Soto and del Castillo, "Obstacles to Peacebuilding Revisited," *Global Governance*, 22 (April–June 2016), 219–225.
24 Ibid.

1 Peacebuilding conceptual framework

From *An Agenda for Peace* and its Supplement to *An Agenda for Development*

- **Peacebuilding: conceptual definition, timing, and sequence**
- **Preventive diplomacy vs. post-conflict peacebuilding**
- **An "integrated approach" to human security and to development**
- **International financing of peacebuilding**
- **Sovereignty, policy ownership, and peacebuilding**
- **Other definitions and obstacles to peacebuilding**
- **Conclusions**

An analysis of the post-Cold War period as a whole, in Mats Berdal's view "would surely reveal, as one of its most striking characteristics, the widespread practice of external intervention undertaken with the express aim of building *sustainable peace* [emphasis added] within societies ravaged by war and violent conflict."[1] It also reveals that, although the concept of "peacebuilding" was developed early on, it evolved over time as the context in which it took place started to change in fundamental ways soon after.

This chapter addresses the conceptual development of the term "peacebuilding" in Boutros-Ghali's *An Agenda for Peace* and how it evolved in its 1995 *Supplement for An Agenda for Peace* (hereafter Supplement) and in its 1994 *An Agenda for Development*; discusses the timing and sequence of UN activities; and analyzes what his proposals for "an integrated approach to human security" and "an integrated approach to development" mean in practice.

The chapter also addresses the issue of local "ownership" of policies and strategies for peacebuilding; analyzes the arguments of the Secretary-General for the UN to be able to draw on resources of the UN system as a whole for this purpose; and presents additional points made by academics and practitioners highlighting the economic aspects of peacebuilding, which reflect mostly their own expertise and the institutional mandate of their own organizations.

Peacebuilding: conceptual definition, timing, and sequence

Upon assuming office, and "at a time when the UN seemed at last poised to play the role for which it was conceived,"[2] the Security Council asked Secretary-General Boutros Boutros-Ghali to make recommendations on how to strengthen the capacity of the UN for preventive diplomacy, peacemaking, and peacekeeping In his *An Agenda for Peace,* he added to the three traditional UN activities a new one that he labelled "post-conflict peace-building" (with the hyphen dropping later on). He defined the term as "action to identify and support structures which will tend to strengthen and solidify peace in order to avoid a relapse into conflict." The "post-conflict" qualification was designed to contrast it with "preventive diplomacy," an ongoing and fundamental UN peacebuilding activity.[3]

Boutros-Ghali's argued that "[p]eacemaking and peace-keeping operations, to be truly successful, must come to include comprehensive efforts to identify and support structures which will tend to consolidate peace and advance a sense of confidence and well-being among people."[4]

Among the post-conflict peacebuilding structures, he listed the disarmament of former combatants and the restoration of order, controlling and possibly destroying weapons, establishing and training civilian police forces, monitoring and promoting human rights, and reforming or strengthening governmental institutions and promoting formal and informal processes of political participation. As de Soto rightly pointed out, "the institutions of economic management, budget formulation, and resource allocation appeared nowhere" among the structures mentioned in *An Agenda for Peace.*[5]

After some digression, Boutros-Ghali also mentioned that the UN has an obligation to develop and provide when requested "support for the transformation of deficient national structures and capabilities, and for the strengthening of new democratic institutions."[6] In de Soto's view, the digression had the unfortunate effect of blurring Boutros-Ghali's vivid original insight. As a result, "some of us in the Secretariat were disappointed at what appeared to be a dilution of the concept as originally stated, and made it our business to highlight and flesh it out on our own, unsupported but unopposed."[7]

An Agenda for Peace was hardly an example of good organization. Before even defining the term "post-conflict peace-building," together with the other UN activities in chapter II, Boutros-Ghali posited that with the end of the Cold War, demands on the UN surged, with the security arm of the organization emerging as a "central instrument for the prevention and resolution of conflicts and for the preservation of peace." In his view, the aims of the organization were expanded "[t]o stand ready to assist in peacebuilding in its differing contexts: rebuilding the institutions and infrastructures of nations torn by civil war and strife; and building bonds of peaceful mutual benefit among nations formerly at war; and in the largest sense, to address the deepest causes of conflict: economic despair, social injustice and political oppression."[8]

For our purposes – discussing the economics of peace as a critical component of peacebuilding – it should be highlighted that, by mentioning economic despair as one of the deepest causes of conflict[9] and by linking "success" of UN peacemaking and peacekeeping activities to a sense of "well-being among people,"[10] Boutros-Ghali was implicitly recognizing the importance of economic factors – without which it will be impossible to reduce economic despair and improve people's well-being.

With the attention given by academics and practitioners alike to the major obstacle to peacebuilding identified in our *Foreign Policy* article as the UN-mediated peace agreement and the IMF-sponsored economic program were on a collision course,[11] and with the Secretary-General expressing concern about it publicly in a press conference in Bangkok in April 1993 (Chapter 4), the "economic factor" in peacebuilding activities began to be seen in a new light.

With increased evidence of the challenges, in his *Supplement*, Boutros-Ghali added the "reintegration into civilian life" of former combatants and "the coordination of support for economic rehabilitation and reconstruction" to the list of activities needed for peacebuilding.[12]

It has gone unnoticed that in *An Agenda for Peace*, Boutros-Ghali only refers to "disarming" of warring parties, without mentioning the need for "reintegration into productive activities." With the hindsight of experience, and the difficulties faced in El Salvador, Mozambique, Cambodia, and others, his *Supplement* explicitly notes that peacekeeping operations will have a mandate to launch various peacebuilding activities "especially the all-important reintegration of former combatants into productive civilian activities."[13]

By then, the Secretary-General was acutely aware of the difficulty of reintegrating combatants productively and on a sustained basis under inadequate levels of aid and with the budgetary and external constraints imposed by IMF-sponsored economic programs. The lack of productive opportunities for reintegration proved then – and continues to be today – one of the major factors behind the dismal record with UN operations in the aftermath of the Cold War (Chapter 6).

The issue of "timing" and "sequence" of peacebuilding in relation to other UN activities has led to several interpretations and even confusion. Some of the confusion resulted from subsequent work at the UN. For example, the 2000 *Report of the Panel on UN Peacekeeping* – known as the Brahimi Report – notes that "[p]eace-building ... defines activities undertaken on the *far side of conflict* [emphasis added]."[14]

Incomprehensibly, and perhaps explained by the lack of an institutional memory and competent staff at the UN, a 2010 document prepared by the Peacebuilding Support Office entitled *UN Peacebuilding: An Orientation* notes that, "[a]t the UN, 'peacebuilding' came to the forefront of intergovernmental debates with ... *An Agenda for Peace* (1992). This identified postconflict peacebuilding as one of a series of tools at the UN's disposal *following* [emphasis added] preventive diplomacy, peacemaking and peacekeeping."[15]

This obviously does not make any sense and has created confusion. Indeed, why would one need peacebuilding "following" preventive diplomacy unless the latter failed? In addition, if one leaves peacebuilding activities to be performed "following" the peacekeeping mission ended, the result would most probably be failure.

In Boutros-Ghali's conception, peacebuilding would take place throughout different UN activities. As discussed above, his *Agenda* mentioned that peacebuilding activities would have to take place during peacemaking and peacekeeping to make the two successful.[16] It also takes place during "preventive diplomacy" that "seeks to resolve disputes before violence breaks out." That this was his conception is clear from the *Supplement*, where he specifically refers to "peace-building, whether preventive or post-conflict."[17]

A distinction in terminology between the two situations is justified on the grounds that – although preventive diplomacy indeed requires a number of peacebuilding activities – for obvious reasons it excludes those that are specific to the post-conflict context, in particular disarming, demobilization, reintegration; destroying weapons; and demining.

Two additional points are worth clarifying. First, in order to be effective, post-conflict peacebuilding activities have to be carefully planned during the peacemaking phase – that is, they have to be included in peace agreements or planned carefully before military interventions such as those that took place in Afghanistan and Iraq. Otherwise, their implementation will likely fail.

Second, while the term "post-conflict" was inspired by and apposite to the Salvadoran case, the label would not apply to later operations in Afghanistan, Iraq, and the DRC, among others, where important armed groups had been excluded from the peace process and/or where large parts of the territory remained outside the control of the government. In these countries, a combination of peacebuilding and peacemaking would need to take place simultaneously, often in different parts of the country.

In defining "peacebuilding" in his *An Agenda for Development*, Boutros-Ghali strengthened the importance of the "economic factor" in sustaining peace by arguing that,

> Only sustained, cooperative work on the underlying economic, social, cultural and humanitarian problems can place an achieved peace on a durable foundation. Unless there is reconstruction and development[18] in the aftermath of conflict, there can be little expectation that peace will endure .... The most immediate task for peacebuilding is to alleviate the effects of war on the population.
>
> Food aid, support for health and hygiene systems, the clearance of mines ... represent the first peace-building tasks. ... it is essential that efforts to address immediate needs are undertaken in ways that promote, rather than compromise, long-term development objectives. As food [and other relief supplies are] provided there must be concentration on restoring food production capacities ... road construction, restoration and improvement of port facilities and establishment of regional stocks and distribution centres.
>
> ... the reintegration of combatants is difficult, but it is critically important to stability in the post-conflict period. In many conflicts, soldiers have been recruited at a very young age. As a result, the capacity of former combatants to return to peacetime society and make a living is severely compromised, thereby undermining society's prospects for development. Effective reintegration of combatants is ... essential to the sustainability of peace. Credit and small-enterprise programmes are vital if excombatants are to find productive employment. Basic education for re-entry into civilian society, special vocational programmes, on-the-job training, and education in agricultural techniques and management skills are key to post-conflict peace-building.[19]

I refer to the above arguments as Boutros-Ghali's dictum for effective reconstruction and peacebuilding. To summarize,

- Peace will not be long lasting without effective "reconstruction and development;"
- Peacebuilding includes activities such as demining, disarming, demobilization, and reintegration that are fundamentally different

from development-as-usual activities in the absence of violent conflict (and have serious budgetary implications);

- Humanitarian assistance should be accompanied from the very beginning with investment and capacity building to avoid long-term dependency; and,
- Effective reintegration requires the creation of job opportunities and a level playing field for farmers and small entrepreneurs.

With a single term in office, Boutros-Ghali did not have much time to put his dictum into practice. Much blood and treasure could have been saved had national policymakers and foreign interveners applied his dictum.

Preventive diplomacy vs. post-conflict peacebuilding

From an economics point of view – which is what this book focuses on – it is true that many of the policies and much of the expertise needed for preventive diplomacy and for post-conflict peacebuilding are the same.[20] One could also argue in favor of having the same organizations and experts addressing both situations jointly, utilizing the same pool of resources and the same set of tools.

Indeed, as Boutros-Ghali stated at the time, and it would still be hard to dispute, "social and economic development can be as valuable in preventing conflict as in healing the wounds after conflict has occurred."[21] To be sure, different kinds of conflicts, humanitarian disasters, health pandemics, and failed states could possibly be prevented through decisive action to improve the well-being of the population of the respective countries through better employment opportunities and more cost-effective provision of basic services, infrastructure, and other public goods.

It goes without saying that it is better to prevent than to cure. Not surprisingly, as a candidate for secretary-general, António Guterres rightly posited the need to improve the capacity of the organization in this area. It is indeed a must to improve the political capacity of the UN in conflict prevention. At the same time, conflict prevention using economic tools across the world would require improving living conditions in a large number of countries with billions of deprived people in them, all experiencing various conflict and natural disaster risks of different degrees. But will the funds be available? Would it be possible to redirect funding from addressing crises towards this type of prevention?

At the time I was the senior economist in Boutros-Ghali's office, I argued that prevention using economic tools is an overwhelming project and a long-term proposition that would require huge financial resources over long periods of time. Such resources were not – and would not likely ever be – available to the organization.[22] To think otherwise is deceptive.

Having worked on Latin America for many years, and having represented Uruguay (the country where I was born and raised) in economic meetings at the UN in the mid-1980s, I also anticipated the difficulties of doing so for political reasons. Governments that exhibit increasingly high conflict risk – exactly those on which the UN preventive diplomacy efforts must be focused – become particularly zealous of their national sovereignty and foreign interference in internal matters, including on the economy. As a director for sovereign risk at Standard & Poor's in the early 2000s, I had the opportunity to confirm that this was the case after observing it firsthand. At the present time, Venezuela provides a vivid example.

In terms of financing, I warned that for the UN to divert scarce resources and attention from the relatively small number of post-conflict countries that face the highest risk of reverting to conflict – or preventively from those few that are experiencing a rapidly rising risk of falling into it – would be a mistake. From a pure risk-analysis point of view, focusing limited funding on countries exhibiting the highest risks could be expected to yield a higher rate of return in terms of social welfare and would hence be a better investment of international resources to maintain peace. In expanding preventive action, the UN needs to ensure that its funding is not spread out too thinly on a large number of lower-risk countries as to be irrelevant.

An institution like the IMF, for example, that also argues that prevention of economic crises can be more effective than crisis resolution, provides precautionary financing to help prevent and insure against crises. Thus, countries that feel under stress can borrow from the Rapid Financial Instrument that provides quick financial assistance for this purpose. Would the UN be able to create a preventive fund with the amount necessary to have an impact on the many countries under conflict stress that would request it?

Clearly the UN should strengthen its preventive diplomacy capabilities, particularly in countries where there are specific risks. For such cases, the organization must sharpen its capacity (including through an overhaul of recruitment practices to replace its aging staff with new and highly-skilled talent) to be able to react through improved diplomatic and technical expertise, as well as through better early warning systems involving the UN system on the ground.

The above would require that the UN development system strengthen its capabilities to become more effective in supporting development efforts in poor countries with relatively lower risk of conflict. Because of the well-known weak performance of the system in this regard – as it is well documented in a number of surveys and reports of FUNDS (Future United Nations Development System)[23] – there is also a need to improve the cost-effectiveness and expedience with which the system provides development and peacebuilding assistance.

Economic policies and strategies relevant to preventive and post-conflict peacebuilding could also be used sometimes to strengthen "peacemaking." Efforts at rehabilitation of services and infrastructure in places like the Palestinian Territories with an immediate impact on the wellbeing of the population, or efforts at productive reintegration of low- and mid-level Taliban militants as conflict rages in at least parts of Afghanistan, are examples of economic action that could help peacemaking. In fact, the "economics of conflict resolution" has been a much neglected factor in peacemaking, just as "the economics of peace" has been to post-conflict peacebuilding.

An "integrated approach" to human security and to development

In *An Agenda for Peace*, Boutros-Ghali also argued that the addition of post-conflict peacebuilding responsibilities to the other UN activities would demand the concerted attention and efforts of an enlarged set of stakeholders involved in supporting countries in the war-to-peace transition as donors or providers of technical assistance.

Because different parts of the UN system were increasingly involved in peacebuilding, in his *Supplement*, Boutros-Ghali reiterated that "[i]f United Nations efforts are to succeed, the roles of the various players need to be carefully coordinated in an 'integrated approach to human security.'"[24]

At the same time, in his report on the work of the organization in 1992, Boutros-Ghali also argued for "an integrated approach to development." This may have been a way to reassure developing countries not affected by war that "the Organization's responsibilities and commitments in the political and security area was not going to be carried out at the expense of its responsibilities in the development field, and neither should be subordinated to the other."[25] The Secretary-General's argument for an integrated approach to development was that

> Political progress and economic development are inseparable: both are equally important and must be pursued simultaneously. Political stability is needed to develop effective economic policies, but

when economic conditions deteriorate too much ... divisive political strife may take root.[26]

Not surprisingly, these two concepts of an integrated approach to human security and an integrated approach to development put together created great expectations that UN peacebuilding activities would be able to deal with deprivation and the scourges of war over a longer-term horizon, in a more cost-effective and integrated manner.

Boutros-Ghali embarked frantically in a series of landmark conferences with the idea of creating a more comprehensive and integrated vision of development that could guide the work of the organization in peacebuilding. In 1994, before some of these conferences had yet taken place, Boutros-Ghali published his own vision in *An Agenda for Development.* In it, the Secretary-General addressed peace, the economy, the environment, society, and democracy as the five basic pillars of development. In his view, human rights – including those of indigenous peoples, women, children, and the disabled – is as integral a part of development as are peace and democracy.

In this way, the two agendas – on peace and development – are inextricably linked. Although "the economy" is one of the basic pillars of "development," it has been the much neglected one at the UN, including at the United Nations Development Program (UNDP). Moreover, the UN has failed to play a role in promoting inclusive growth, which is a *sine qua non* for effective peacebuilding (and part of Boutros-Ghali's dictum).

A number of factors acted against an effective integration of human security and development. Particularly difficult was to integrate "the economy" as a foundation for peacebuilding and long-term development. Peace mediators – defined in a broad way to include all those that bring warring parties to an agreement for peace and affect its implementation – normally have extensive experience in diplomacy and often in international relations. Some also may have experience in international law, human rights, international justice, security, or peacekeeping.

Rarely, however, do peace mediators have much experience in economic and financial issues that would allow them to analyze how those factors affect conflict and could affect the post-conflict. Neither do they have experience to analyze issues affecting risks and opportunities for the private sector to create investment, employment, and growth going forward – all critical to war-torn countries. However, while they include in their teams political, human rights, justice, and security experts, they do not usually include economic and financial experts.

This is particularly unfortunate since economic reconstruction must be a strong pillar in peacebuilding efforts. Peace agreements often include national reconstruction plans which give a critical role to market-based, private-sector-led economic policies. Such plans, if not well-designed, are likely to interfere with effective political, security, and social reforms during the post-conflict peacebuilding phase.

Moreover, as de Soto and I also noted in our 1994 article, "language differences and a paucity of communication between peacemakers and economists are a part of the problem."[27] This has affected peacebuilding efforts in a variety of ways – from conflict resolution efforts to moving away from the war economy to post-conflict peacebuilding – and has been a major deterrent to effective integration.

It was thus most unfortunate that the progenitor of the integrated approach to peacebuilding and development failed to take the small practical steps needed to put them into practice.[28] The cost of such wasted opportunity was indeed large. During the last quarter of a century, the demands on the UN to support countries coming out of war did greatly increase, but the integration of political and security issues with the socioeconomic ones remains elusive.

International financing of peacebuilding

In *An Agenda for Peace*, Boutros-Ghali went beyond the need for a simple integration of the activities of the different peacebuilding actors. He argued that the Secretary-General should be able "to mobilize the resources needed for … positive leverage and engage the collective efforts of the UN system for the peaceful resolution of a conflict."[29]

As de Soto and I clarified in our *Foreign Policy* article,

> Lest alarm bells be needlessly set off, it should be emphasized that the expression "draw upon the resources" should not be taken literally to mean that the U.N. must be granted a blank check against funds of all agencies and programs. At the present time, however, we find ourselves at the opposite extreme …[30]

The lack of timely financing in El Salvador to implement key programs was a stark example of how political, security, and socioeconomic problems had been addressed separately as it was the tradition at the UN – rather than with the integrated approach that Boutros-Ghali promulgated.[31]

In his *Supplement to An Agenda for Peace*, Boutros-Ghali went further on the issue of financing, rightly arguing that peacebuilding "can be a long-term process and expensive – except in comparison with the cost of peacemaking and peace-keeping if the conflict should recur."[32]

Specifically addressing the issue that de Soto and I had first raised in our 1994 article, Boutros-Ghali acknowledged that the organization had learned that "in putting together the peacebuilding elements in a comprehensive settlement plan, the UN should consult the IFIs [international financial institutions] to ensure that the cost of implementing the plan is taken into account in the design of the economic plans of the governments concerned."[33]

Although many of the financial restrictions on peacebuilding were real and to be taken seriously, fitting into the UN mould of blaming lack of resources for failure to carry out the organization's functions with success, Boutros-Ghali argued that "[p]eace-building is another activity that is critically dependent on Member States' readiness to make the necessary resources available."[34]

More resources alone would not suffice to improve peacebuilding if the organization keeps on doing the same things and expects different results. This book will analyze and provide evidence that, in most cases, failure at peacebuilding has been directly linked to misguided policies, wrong sequence, and misplaced priorities, and to the lack of an integrated, operational, and cost-effective approach.

Sovereignty, policy ownership, and peacebuilding

In *An Agenda for Peace*, Boutros-Ghali had strongly argued that "the foundation stone of this work [peacebuilding] is and must remain the State."[35] Because war-torn countries were engaging in the transition to peace with the support of foreign interveners, particularly the UN system at the time, this was blurring the issue of national "policy ownership." A relevant issue became "who is in charge" of policymaking – the national authorities or the foreign interveners?

As de Soto and I argued in our 1994 *Foreign Policy* article, as a general rule, it is the role of sovereign governments to harmonize policies and set priorities as they embark on the transition to peace. An "arbitrary model of nation-building" must not be imposed on reluctant, sometimes faraway countries. At the time, we envisaged transitions in which the sovereign government would be in the front seat designing and implementing policies, with the UN system, including the Bretton Woods Institutions (BWIs) in the back seat – close enough to facilitate, coordinate, and monitor the international community's technical and financial support, but without imposing the strategy.[36] This was clearly the pattern of the 1990s in countries such as Cambodia, El Salvador, Mozambique, Angola, and Guatemala.

Soon the nature of conflict and the ability to deal with it took a turn for the worse, which changed the operational nature of peace transitions. By the mid-1990s, conflicts were often interrupted through military intervention rather than negotiation. Following the human tragedies in Rwanda and Srebrenica, Boutros-Ghali's *Supplement* recognized that a new breed of intra-state conflicts presented the UN with operational challenges not encountered since the Congo operation in the early 1960s.[37]

These conflicts were accompanied by humanitarian crises and the collapse of state institutions – including the police, the judiciary, and the institutional capacity for economic policymaking and management of aid. Many became so-called "failed states."[38]

Not surprisingly, foreign intervention had to extend beyond military, humanitarian, and reconstruction tasks, to include the re-establishment of basic governance. This was the case in Rwanda and Burundi, where France, Belgium and other countries participated in humanitarian interventions in the mid-1990s, and by the turn of the century in Kosovo and East Timor, where NATO and Australia, respectively, led military interventions. The latter two became UN-led transitional administrations when the Security Council mandated the special representative of the Secretary-General (SRSG) to exercise all executive and legislative power through the issuance of regulations.

Transitions to peace confronted yet another twist after the terrorist attacks of September 11, 2001. This gave rise to the US government's "war on terror" and to US-led military interventions in Afghanistan in October 2001 and Iraq in March 2003.

At the time of our *Foreign Policy* article, de Soto and I did not envisage the type of operation in which the UN would assume extreme positions – that is a very intrusive role (transitional UN-led administrations), versus a marginal one (transitional US-led administration).[39]

The marginal role was particularly true in Iraq where the Security Council did not approve the military intervention and where the UN presence, which the Council had mandated following it, soon ended with a devastating bomb attack in August 2003. After the invasion, the US became an occupying force, with the Coalition Provisional Authority making all policy decisions on economic reconstruction until June 2004 when an interim government was formed and Iraq resumed sovereignty. But US intrusion continued in all reconstruction matters, which restricted national ownership.

Afghanistan was allowed to make sovereign decisions concerning economic matters – particularly those which foreign interveners agreed with, such as the orthodox macroeconomic framework established in

2002. However, because a large part of the huge amount of aid that the country received during the first decade was channelled outside the national budget, policy ownership of programs was quite limited.

With the US military and civilian surges starting in 2006 as security deteriorated, the United States played a much more intrusive role in Afghanistan's reconstruction. Because a large part of the economic reconstruction of both Iraq and Afghanistan was led by the US military and with resources allocated to it, it was labelled "expeditionary economics."[40]

Variations over time in the type of foreign intervention in countries in the transition to peace created a whole new set of economic challenges for national policymakers and foreign interveners. The book will address them in following chapters.

Other definitions and obstacles to peacebuilding

As Berdal noted, Boutros-Ghali's broad definition of the term "peacebuilding" acquired an even broader connotation over time at the UN and in the academic literature,[41] with the term covering "integrated and coordinated actions aimed at addressing the root causes of violence, whether political, legal, institutional, military, humanitarian, human rights-related, environmental, economic and social, cultural or demographic."[42] In his view, the term is synonymous with the "entire basket of post-war needs" in countries and societies emerging from violent conflict. While the comprehensiveness was total, what was missing was "any sense of priorities."[43] Likewise, Charles Call and Elizabeth Cousens also talked about "laundry lists and what could be called 'no agency left behind' notion of peacebuilding."[44]

The lack of priority, particularly with regard to basic economic issues, has been, and continues to be, a major obstacle to peacebuilding. Economic issues need to be addressed right away as *sine qua non* for effective and long-term productive reintegration of former combatants, which as Boutros-Ghali emphasized, is "essential to the sustainability of peace."[45] Despite the fact that reintegration should be used as a carrot to lure armed groups into supporting peace processes, donors have been reluctant to finance such programs that are not only costly but also require long-term support (Chapter 7).

The BWIs are the leading actors in the economic reactivation of war-torn countries. However, the UN lacks technical capacity to analyze some of the complex economic issues affecting these countries in a rigorous and consistent way, and is unable to communicate with the BWIs at a technical level, to find common ground on how to deal with them while addressing peacebuilding needs at the same time. This has impeded an effective and integrated approach to human security and raised questions with respect to the UN's capacity as the leader of global peacebuilding efforts.

UNDP's website notes that "UNDP helps governance institutions in countries bring constitutional reforms, organize credible elections, strengthen parliaments, and address policy and institutional options for peace, risk-reduction and development through reconciliation, empowerment and inclusion." UNDP's stated goal in this area is to bridge "the gap between humanitarian, peacebuilding and longer-term development efforts, helping countries in peaceful settlement of disputes and progress towards democratic governance." It is interesting that the development arm of the UN specifically refers to everything except the economy of war-torn countries – as if it were not one of the basic pillars of development.

Conclusions

Two aspects are worth emphasizing from the conceptual framework of the early 1990s, given that it will affect the assessment of the current peacebuilding capacity of the organization. First, Boutros-Ghali's framework clearly contemplated peacebuilding as an activity that needed to take place for preventive purposes, during peacemaking and peacekeeping, and in the post-conflict context. In his framework, peacebuilding would only succeed if it could integrate the many political, security, and socio-economic factors necessary to ensure that conflict will not occur or recur.

Second, much blood and treasure could have been saved had national policymakers and foreign interveners applied Boutros-Ghali's dictum that peace will not be long lasting without effective "reconstruction and development;" that peacebuilding requires peace-related activities such as reintegration of former combatants and other such activities that makes it fundamentally different from development-as-usual; that humanitarian assistance should be accompanied from the very beginning with investment and capacity building to avoid long-term dependency; and that effective reintegration requires the creation of job opportunities and a level playing field for small enterprises and farmers.

With a single term in office, Boutros-Ghali failed to put his dictum into practice. Regrettably, the UN continues to lack the capacity to make his dictum operational. Building up such capacity must become a top priority of Secretary-General António Guterres if he is serious about improving the peacebuilding capacity – both preventive and post-conflict – of the organization.

Notes

1 Mats Berdal, *Building Peace After War* (London: Routledge, 2009), 11.
2 Álvaro de Soto, Foreword in Mats Berdal and Dominik Zaum, eds, *Political Economy of Statebuilding: Power After Peace* (London: Routledge, 2013), xvii–xx.
3 Boutros-Ghali, *An Agenda for Peace*, 11.
4 Ibid., 32.
5 De Soto, Foreword, xviii.
6 Boutros-Ghali, *An Agenda for Peace*, 32.
7 De Soto, Foreword, xvii–xviii.
8 Boutros-Ghali, *An Agenda for Peace*, 7–8.
9 Ibid., 8.
10 Ibid., 32.
11 De Soto and del Castillo, *Obstacles to Peacebuilding*, 70.
12 Boutros-Ghali, *Supplement*, 5.
13 Ibid., 10.
14 UN, *Report of the Panel on United Nations Peace Operations* (New York: United Nations, 2000), 3.
15 See *UN Peacebuilding: An Orientation* (New York: United Nations, 2010), 45.
16 Boutros-Ghali, *An Agenda for Peace*, 32.
17 Boutros-Ghali, *Supplement to An Agenda for Peace*, 10.
18 By mentioning both reconstruction and development, Boutros-Ghali clearly makes a distinction between the two that other people have ignored.
19 Boutros-Ghali, *An Agenda for Development*, 2.
20 The complex issues of disarming, demobilization, reintegration and demining, however, are only relevant to the post-conflict situations.
21 Boutros-Ghali, *Supplement*, 10.
22 My arguments at the time are discussed in del Castillo, *Rebuilding War-Torn States*, 38–39.
23 See Future UN Development System (FUNDS) web page.
24 Boutros-Ghali, *Supplement*, 16.
25 United Nations, Annual Report of the Secretary-General on the Work of the Organization (New York: General Assembly document A/47/1, 1992), 26–27.
26 Ibid.
27 De Soto and del Castillo, *Obstacles to Peacebuilding*, 79.
28 Del Castillo, *Rebuilding War-Torn States*, 2008, 127–28.
29 Boutros-Ghali, *An Agenda for Peace*, 11.
30 De Soto and del Castillo, *Obstacles to Peacebuilding*, 77.
31 Ibid., 71.
32 Boutros-Ghali, *Supplement*, 1995, 19.
33 Ibid.
34 Ibid.
35 Boutros-Ghali, *An Agenda for Peace*, 30.
36 De Soto and del Castillo, *Obstacles to Peacebuilding*, 77. For more on sovereign decisions and ownership, see del Castillo, *Rebuilding War-Torn States*, 230–231.
37 Boutros-Ghali, *Supplement*, 5.

38 Gerald Helman and Steven Ratner, "Saving Failed States," *Foreign Policy* 89 (1992–93), 3–20.
39 The earlier period in Iraq was often referred to as "US-led occupation."
40 See Carl J. Schramm, "Expeditionary Economics," *Foreign Affairs* 89 (March 2010). See also papers commissioned by the US Military Academy at West Point for a Conference on Expeditionary Economics: Towards a Doctrine for Enabling Stabilization and Growth (West Point, NY: February 15–17 and May 24–26, 2011).
41 Berdal, *Building Peace After War*, 18. Berdal provides an excellent *tour d'horizon* of peacebuilding issues, including political economy ones, in many UN operations. On this subject, see also Elizabeth M. Cousens, introduction in *Peacebuilding as Politics: Cultivating Peace in Fragile Societies*, Cousens and Chetan Kumar, eds. (Boulder, Colo., and London: Lynne Rienner Publishers, 2001), 5–10; Ho-Won Jeong, *Peacebuilding in Postconflict Societies: Strategy and Process* (Boulder, Colo: Lynne Rienner Publishers, 2005); Roland Paris, *At War's End: Building Peace After Civil Conflict* (New York: Cambridge University Press, 2005); Roland Paris, "Post-Conflict Peacebuilding," in *The Oxford Handbook on the United Nations* (Oxford: Oxford University Press, 2007); Michael Barnett et al., "Peacebuilding: What Is in a Name?" *Global Governance*, 13 (2007), Table 2, 46; Michael Pugh, Neil Cooper and Mandy Turner, "Introduction to Whose Peace?" in *Critical Perspectives on the Political Economy of Peacebuilding*, Pugh, Cooper, and Turner, eds. (London: Palgrave Macmillan, 2008); Charles T. Call and Elizabeth M. Cousens, "Ending Wars and Building Peace: International Responses to War-Torn Societies," *International Studies Perspectives*, 9 (2008); Robert Ricigliano, *Making Peace Last: A Toolbox for Sustainable Peacebuilding* (Boulder, Colo.: Paradigm Publishers, 2012); Rob Jenkins, "Post-Conflict Peacebuilding," in Thomas Weiss and R. Wilkinson, eds, *International Organizations and Global Governance* (London: Routledge, 2013); and Jenkins, *Peacebuilding*, 18–43.
42 United Nations, *Annual Report of the Secretary-General on the Work of the Organization* (New York: General Assembly document A/53/1, 1998, paragraph 61). Cited by Berdal, *Building Peace After War* (2009: 18).
43 Ibid.
44 Call and Cousens, "Ending Wars and Building Peace," 3.
45 Boutros-Ghali, *An Agenda for Development*, 2.

2   Economic reconstruction amid the multidisciplinary transition to peace

- **The security transition**
- **The political transition**
- **The social transition**
- **The economic transition**
- **Interrelations among the four distinct transitions**
- **Conclusions**

As civil wars or other internal chaos ended in the aftermath of the Cold War – either through peace negotiations, military interventions or national uprisings for regime change – and notwithstanding the distinctive characteristics of each particular case, countries, often cajoled by foreign interveners, entered into a path of peace, stability, and prosperity.

The key challenge of such transition is to prevent the recurrence of hostilities, that is, to make the transition irreversible. This entails the complex task of addressing the root causes and consequences of the conflict. All aspects of this transition are closely interrelated and reinforce each other:

> Failure in any one of these areas will put the others at risk. Planning, management, coordination, and financing of this multi-pronged transition are highly burdensome. Given the state of countries coming out of protracted conflicts, the international community [foreign interveners] will need to provide financial aid, technical assistance, and capacity building at every stage of the transition. ... Inadequate mandates, insufficient expertise, poor governance and lack of legitimacy have been present to different degrees in all recent experiences with post-conflict reconstruction.[1]

Academic and policy debate, the media, and the academic literature have largely focused on the security, political, and social transitions to the neglect of the economic one. This is despite the fact that the economic transition is fundamental for the others to succeed since peace has serious economic consequences, as Keynes posited in the aftermath of World War I.

Failure to create viable economies and give former combatants and other groups affected by the war a stake in the peace process has been a major reason for the disappointing record with peacebuilding in the aftermath of the Cold War. A "peace dividend" – including better living conditions, a rewarding job, and reconciliation with former enemies and neighbours – has proved necessary, if not sufficient, for peace to be long-lasting.

Although this book focuses on the economic transition itself, to understand the challenges and constraints under which such transition takes place, it is necessary to cursorily analyze the other simultaneous transitions to describe what each one entails and what the interactions among them may be. Many of the experts and decision makers dealing with the other transitions often make their recommendations without taking into account what such recommendations mean to the economic and financial situation of the country, or to the country's dependence on foreign aid.

More worrisome, despite the close interconnectedness, both analysis and policymaking largely proceeded with a "silo mentality"[2] – that is, with each transition discussed in isolation by their respective experts – rather than in an integrated manner, given that the issues are by no means independent of each other.

In fact, they do interrelate in complex and convoluted ways, as Diagram 2.1 shows in the section on "Interrelations." Despite it, diplomats, security, and human rights experts often roll their eyes at even the mention of economic issues. At the same time, economists are not generally interested in countries that have such little impact on the global economy and where the problems may be "too political" anyway.

But, as President Clinton famously noted at Sarajevo (Bosnia and Herzegovina, 30 July 1999), "It is not enough to end the war; we must build the peace" – and this cannot be done with a silo mentality. This chapter will discuss the complex, challenging, and multidisciplinary transition from war to peace (Table 2.1) and the various interrelations among the different aspects of it which require an integrated approach if peacebuilding efforts are to succeed. The economic transition will be discussed in more detail in Chapter 3.

The security transition

As Secretary-General Kofi Annan noted in 2004, "Unlike inter-states war, making peace in civil war requires overcoming daunting security

Table 2.1 Transition from war to peace

Transition	From	To
Security	Violence and insecurity	• Improving public security; • Creating or improving security institutions (civilian police + army).
Political	Lawlessness and political exclusion	• Developing a participatory, fair, and inclusive government; • Promoting respect for the rule of law and for human, property, and gender rights.
Social (national reconciliation)	Sectarian/ethnic, religious, ideological or class confrontation	• Promoting national reconciliation to reintegrate war-affected groups into society and rebuilding the social fabric of the communities after civil war or other chaos; • Developing an institutional framework to address differences through peaceful ways.
Economic (economic reconstruction, economics of peace, political economy of peace)	Ruined and underground war economies, state-controlled policies and large macroeconomic imbalances	• Establishing a basic macro/micro framework; • Rehabilitating infrastructure and services; • Creating a viable economic environment for rural development and entrepreneurship; • Eradicating illicit activities (drugs/corruption).

dilemmas. Spoilers, factions who see [peace] as inimical to their interest, power, or ideology, use violence to undermine or overthrow settlements."[3]

Ideally, violence must surrender and public security must improve before countries can fully engage in the reactivation of their economies. Different analysts have noted how security is the foundation on which progress in other areas rests;[4] that security must be put first, since all recovery will prove futile in a chronically insecure environment, and resources will be squandered and can even be hijacked by violent power-seekers;[5] and that efforts of donors and national actors (governments, the private sector, and communities) will not succeed otherwise since insecurity lowers the return on donors' projects and distorts domestic actors' incentives.[6]

UN peacekeeping operations, NATO, or occupying forces time and again provide basic support to enforce cease-fires, disarmament and demobilization of former combatants, as well as other confidence-building measures that are necessary to improve security in the short run. However, peacekeeping operations and foreign forces have often remained in the country for long periods at great cost for the international community, with Liberia and Afghanistan being infamous examples. Yet for stabilization to be lasting, indigenous actors must ultimately bear the responsibility for providing security.[7]

To establish minimum security requires tough legislation, a reformed military force under civilian control, an active and well-trained civilian police force, and an effective judiciary. Although such reforms usually take a long time, without a rapid move in this direction, addressing the problems of violence, impunity, and human rights violations will not be possible. The financial costs of these reforms are often large and hard to finance.

Despite such reforms, security conditions will not be optimal at all times. In fact, many peace transitions have taken place, or are currently taking place, under security conditions that are far from ideal, often with large parts of the territory outside the control of the authorities. This is true of the ongoing transitions in Afghanistan, Iraq, and the Democratic Republic of Congo (DRC). Nevertheless, efforts to improve security should always be at the top of the post-conflict policy agenda and be a priority for national leaders and foreign interveners alike.

In addition to the difficulties of reactivating the economy without minimum levels of security and the large cost of the security transition, there are other problems relating to this transition that need to be taken into consideration in any peace strategy. Failing to do so put the whole peace process in peril.

Perhaps the most important problem relates to the vicious circle created by delays in creating appropriate security forces, resulting in weak governance, lack of legal investment, drug production, insurgency and terrorism, and higher insecurity nationally, regionally, and even globally. This is why moving away from the economics of war to the economics of peace is critical to the transition (Chapter 3).

As the US Army and US Marine Corps *Counterinsurgency Field Manual* notes, in insecure areas of a country controlled by the insurgency, "considerable resources are needed to build and maintain a counter-state." Because of governance failures, the insurgency often provides basic services and infrastructure as well as means of livelihood to the population of those areas, which obviously has serious financial implications for them. As the *Manual* points out,

Sustainment requirements often drive insurgents into relationships with organized crime or into criminal activity themselves. Reaping windfall profits and avoiding the costs and difficulties involved in securing external support makes illegal activity attractive to insurgents. Taxing a mass base usually yields low returns. In contrast, kidnapping, extortion, bank robbery, and drug trafficking – four favorite insurgent activities – are very lucrative.[8]

Although the *Manual* uses the FARC (Spanish acronym for the Revolutionary Armed Forces of Colombia) as an example, it could have used the case of Afghanistan which provides a perfect illustration of this point. As foreign minister Abdullah wrote in the *Washington Post* in October 2002, almost a year after the Bonn Agreement, delays in creating a national army and police forces led to an incipient sprouting of the insurgency. By mid-2003, as security deteriorated further, it became obvious that the belief that the Taliban had vanished had been wishful thinking. Security experts have attributed Taliban early gains to the failure of the government to provide effective police protection. This in turn created major obstacles to economic reconstruction.[9]

At the same time, there is always some kind of economic activity that can prosper, even in unstable situations. People need to eat and trade (or barter) and hence some of these activities will have to take place in such areas. What kind of support they need, however, should be the focus of a debate, which so far has been missing. One thing is clear: what was labelled "expeditionary economics" – using foreign military forces for economic reconstruction and improved governance in insecure areas – has usually been expensive and futile in chronically insecure environments. Gaining "heart and minds" while bombing at the same time has not proved a good recipe.

Operating under the expeditionary economics mode, the US government created provincial reconstruction teams (PRTs) – consisting of a mixture of civilian experts and military officers – to provide humanitarian and reconstruction support in insecure areas in Iraq and Afghanistan. Military commanders had plenty of money to spend and, as one commander put it, "we thought that by throwing as much money as possible to the problem, we would get it solved." This created serious price distortions and promoted corruption. Moreover, it created the resentment of inhabitants of more secure areas which received much less support by behaving well.[10]

The US oversight bodies have collected plenty of evidence on the problems of the PRTs in countries such as Afghanistan and Iraq.[11] They have also collected extensive evidence that US investments – particularly in large infrastructure such as dams, power plants, and others – have gone to waste in insecure areas.[12]

The political transition

Whatever the political solution reached, the transition involves the passage from some kind of oppressive, autocratic and exclusionary regime to a more inclusive, pluralistic, and participatory system based on the rule of law; respect for human, property, and gender rights; transitional justice; and improved governance.

War-torn countries, as any other country, will choose their political leaders and develop their institutions, policies, and governance influenced by a number of historical, cultural, religious, ethnic, or other local idiosyncrasies. Contrary to countries unaffected by violent conflict, however, the political transition in war-torn countries will normally take place amid large foreign intervention and donor-imposed political and economic conditionalities. The latter is the consequence of the large dependence on foreign aid and peacekeeping forces or foreign troops that most of these countries have in the transition. It is in this way that issues of sovereignty and ownership frequently become blurred under such conditions.

Indeed,

> Peace agreements often dictated the terms for the interim and/or transitional arrangements. As the new authorities – be they interim, transitional, or elected – assumed power, they had to consolidate their legitimacy, something that proved extremely difficult in most cases. With whatever legitimacy they had and whatever territory they controlled at the time, governments needed to provide security, justice, human rights protection, and basic services and infrastructure to the population. They also had to carry out stabilization and reform for the reactivation of the economy and for the effective utilization of aid.[13]

Nobel Laureate Roger Myerson's work is pivotal to understand the challenges of the political and economic transitions in war-torn countries, as well as to design and carry out more effective foreign interventions going forward. Based on his theoretical work in game theory, which he has applied to such transitions, Myerson argues that foreign interveners should take account of the political nature of the state that is being built. Because the state is a political system that puts some people into positions of power and induces the rest of the nation to

accept their authority, the feasibility and financial cost of a stabilization mission will depend critically on the way that the state distributes
power (which in war-torn countries includes economic aid).[14]

In Myerson's view, "The interim leader's ability to build the first
national patronage network after the intervention can become a decisive advantage over all potential rivals. Thus, in handing 'interim' …
authority to one leader, the foreign interveners may be effectively
choosing the long-term leader of the nation."[15] This fits perfectly the
political transition in Afghanistan.

As Myerson points out, "when foreign forces help to defend the
authority of a state, its national leaders have more incentive to cen-
tralize political power narrowly around themselves. But such centralization can alienate key local leaders and so can substantially
increase the need for costly foreign efforts to maintain the states."[16]

Centralized regimes please donors that find it convenient to have one
strong national leader who is empowered to work with them in all the
countless complications related to their intervention. In Aghanistan,
for example, such a centralized system was alien to Afghans. In it,
provincial councils were not given any autonomous powers, which
alienated local leaders not aligned with the government and forced the
government in turn to rely more on the foreign interveners to keep the
country together.[17]

Myerson recognizes, however, that once a centralized government is
established with foreign intervention – as it was in Afghanistan and also
in Iraq – forces against decentralization are strong. Naturally, incumbent
presidents feel threatened by potential competition from elected local
leaders who could eventually build a good reputation by providing
public services and infrastructure to local citizens in an inclusive and
effective way. Since one of the problems with reconstruction has been
that most of it takes place in the larger cities, decentralization could
contribute to the gains from peace being more equitably shared across
the country.

At the same time, Myerson notes that in a centralized system the
president appoints the provincial/state governors. For this reason, close
supporters of the incumbent president also have a strong, vested interest in maintaining such centralization on the expectation of becoming
governors or mayors at some point.

Successful stabilization, as Myerson argues, depends on the new
regime developing a political network that could distribute power and
patronage throughout the nation. Although the word "patronage" is
often used disparagingly, Myerson uses it with a positive connotation:
to acquire and keep its legitimacy, the government needs to allocate its

scarce resources fairly across its population through the provision of services, infrastructure, and support of private sector activities. In aid-dependent, war-torn countries, this applies particularly to the distribution of aid. The government requires trusted local leaders to do such distribution effectively and fairly.[18]

Delays in setting up municipal and other local elections make things worse. Communities in which responsible leadership is lacking and governance is weak are the perfect breeding ground for insurgencies to take root and thrive. By delaying local elections and having fewer promising leaders competing for the presidency, democracy will not prosper. In Myerson's view, decentralization in the political and economic sense could broaden support for the regime, reduce its dependence on foreign interveners, and make reconstruction more effective in rural areas.[19]

In Afghanistan, the lack of local political leadership and insecurity in many provinces allowed warlords to continue collecting customs (a major source of tax revenue) and drug profits in areas under their control since *Operation Enduring Freedom* started in October 2001. Central government's domestic revenue averaged only 5 per cent of GDP in the first five years, a major obstacle to the implementation of critical peace-related projects and a key factor in the deterioration of security.[20]

Drawing on the experiences of the DRC and Afghanistan, Jean-Marie Guéhenno argued that the political dilemma was not so much about centralization versus decentralization as it was about how to connect the various levels of government in a cost-effective, transparent, and accountable way.[21] By supporting communities financially and technically, donor countries could contribute to improving governance at the local level and also to increase the capacity of the community-level institutions to improving lives and livelihoods in their areas. In his view, to be effective this needs to be done with the approval of the appropriate ministries.

From a macroeconomics point of view, I would argue that it would be difficult as well as ineffective and expensive to finance local governments outside the national government framework. This is because the Bretton Woods Institutions (BWIs) and other multilateral organizations only deal with national governments. Also channelling funding directly through NGOs, outside the national budget has proved expensive and ineffective. At the same time, governments cannot be expected to make good macro-management decisions without appropriate information with respect to the money that enters the country. At the same time, channelling aid outside the national budget does not contribute to capacity building in the public sector and often leads to a lack of policy ownership, which makes policies unsustainable in the long-run.

For investment and other economic purposes, it is particularly important that governments build up legitimacy, starting as soon as possible during the political transition. Political legitimacy at the national level affects economic policymaking options since uncertainty surrounding the sustainability of economic reform and property rights have been major deterrents to sustainable investment, as in Kosovo and Iraq (Chapter 7).

Political scientists have discussed the problems of having elections too soon. Myerson argues in favour of having local elections as soon as possible. This may help in building up the political credibility of local leaders, which is key for countries with large rural populations.[22] In terms of the war-to-peace transition as a whole, national elections in particular often deflect attention from the peace process and politicize it, as happened in El Salvador.[23]

The social transition

The social transition involves a process of national reconciliation in order to build social cohesion in societies divided by ethnic, religious, sectarian, political, ideological, and/or economic cleavages. After committing atrocious acts against each other, former adversaries are expected to return to the same communities and learn to live together in peace.

As de Soto has pointed out, the UN moved into a new uncharted direction in the post-Cold War era where,

> After internal conflict, fighting forces are doomed to coexist under the same roof, and it cannot be taken for granted that fraternal reconciliation will follow fratricidal confrontation. To avoid relapse of internal conflict, channels and institutions – to ensure that future such disputes can be peacefully resolved – must be put in place.[24]

The institutional framework often includes the creation of civil society organizations, national ombudsmen, and human rights prosecutors. In many cases, for example, El Salvador and Rwanda, "truth commissions" were established to examine the most notorious human rights violations, not only as a catharsis, but also to make recommendations aimed at preventing the recurrence of such abuses. As Helena Meyer-Knapp notes, finding an appropriate way to ease the suffering left behind by the war is a key ingredient of peacemaking and peacebuilding.[25]

In addition to building trust, improving cohesion, and reintegrating former combatants and other militia, as well as returnees, displaced populations, and other war-affected groups into society in general, these groups must also be reintegrated into productive activities so that they can have a dignified livelihood, a critical task of the economic transition.[26]

Reintegration – which points to the close interconnectedness of the social and economic transitions – is *sine qua non* for national and local reconciliation. Such a tremendous challenge requires the effective and inclusive reactivation of stagnant and mismanaged war economies and the prompt rehabilitation of basic services and infrastructure.

Furthermore, reintegration programs require advance planning, bold and innovative solutions, large financial resources, and staying the course with the right policies, frequently for many years. The contrasting experiences of El Salvador and Afghanistan provide stark evidence of things that work and those that are still missing in how the foreign interveners support reintegration.[27]

The economic transition

The economic transition involves the move away from war-ravaged, mismanaged, and largely illicit economies into stable and viable ones that enable former combatants and ordinary people to earn a decent, licit, and legitimate living.

The economic transition is the much-neglected aspect of the transition to peace. Such neglect is unwarranted and misguided since the economic transition is of fundamental importance in supporting the other aspects of the transition. It is also critical to avoid the aid dependency in which many countries indulge at this time.

That the economic transition takes place simultaneously with the others does not mean, however, that war-torn countries can afford to wait to have security, the elected authorities, the rule of law, the policies and the institutions, the good governance, and the human capacity in place before they engage in production, investment, and trade. Indeed, the economics transition needs to take place within whatever context is in place, and it cannot wait for the foreign interveners to get their act together, or for civil servants to be trained so that they can do it right. Thus, economic policies, institutions, and capabilities will need to adjust as other aspects of the transition improve.

The economic transition needs to begin as soon as possible, not only because this is essential to creating political and social stability, but also because donors are more willing to support peace transitions when countries do their part to ensure their success and sustainability (with the few exceptions often reflecting deep geopolitical interests). This transition is indeed most challenging in the midst of the political, social, and institutional vulnerabilities, the damage to human and physical infrastructure, and the macroeconomic imbalances that are the legacy of conflict.

The economic transition has unquestionably been the least talked-about aspect of war-to-peace transition in donors' policy circles, in public debate and in academic discourse as well as in the extensive and fast-growing literature on war-torn countries. Most analyses have focused primarily on issues such as creating security forces, establishing the rule of law, strengthening human and gender rights, improving the justice system, and promoting political reform and holding elections.

Interrelations among the four distinct transitions

Although security may well be a precondition for the success of the overall transition to peace, as many experts assert, political reform, national reconciliation efforts, and economic reconstruction will in turn affect the security conditions in the country. This is what – in the economic jargon – is called "reverse causality" and others call a "virtuous circle" or "two sides of the same coin."[28] These terms allude to the fact that the effect works both ways: political reform, national reconciliation, and economic reconstruction may prove futile without security, but security will not take root without progress in those three areas. Whatever one may call this two-way process, it has proved to be critical to a successful transition to peace, stability, and improved welfare.[29]

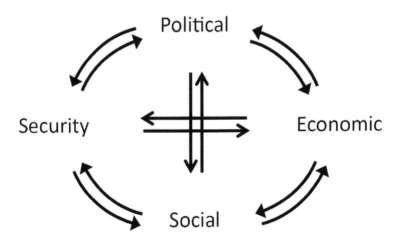

Figure 2.1

Given that policymakers in most countries in a transition to peace cannot rely on adequate and timely flows of aid, effective economic reconstruction is key for political transformation, security reform, and national reconciliation (the other aspects of the multidisciplinary transition) to succeed. Without effective economic reconstruction, peacebuilding efforts will remain elusive.

Indeed, economic policymaking is likely to enhance or go against efforts at national reconciliation. For this reason, every policy should be considered carefully since reconciliation between former enemies has proved *sine qua non* to preserving peace and stability and promoting prosperity. At the same time, reconciliation programs often have economic and financial consequences that governments and donors might consider a diversion from the overriding need for funding basic services and infrastructure and for creating economic opportunities.

This must not be the case. The rebuilding of a mosque might contribute to stability more as a confidence-building measure for the community than a productive investment may, if that is where the community has set its priority. This, of course, does not eliminate the need for productive investments, but the various needs must be weighed carefully, always taking into account local needs and priorities.

With a few exceptions, the UN has failed to denounce misguided economic policies and misplaced priorities in the transition to peace in countries such as Liberia and Afghanistan. Such policies have excluded the large majority from economic gains (in favour of small domestic elites) and hence are creating increased inequality and sowing the seeds for future conflict. Such policies have often led to rapid but unsustainable growth by failing to create a level playing field for the large majority of men and women, particularly in agriculture on which they largely depend.

By focusing on a misguided "peace through security" strategy in Afghanistan and Iraq, the US government has also ignored inter-relationships and reverse causalities. It has basically proceeded as if peace could be established by military means alone. Experience attests to how inefficiencies and lack of progress with respect to the three other areas led in turn to the deterioration of security in both Afghanistan and Iraq, with tragic human and financial consequences both to the countries and to foreign interveners.[30]

Conclusions

A successful multidisciplinary transition to peace, stability, and prosperity entails improving the well-being of different groups that need to feel part of the peace process and to have an economic and political stake in it. This requires improved security; a more participatory economic and political system; respect for human, gender, and property rights; reconciliation between former enemies; and the reactivation of the economy. The latter is critical to create the income-generating opportunities and improved living conditions necessary to reintegrate war-affected groups into society and productive activities on a long-term basis. Without it, security will not last, reconciliation will not take place, and peacebuilding may be ephemeral.

The UN has yet to recognize the importance of sustainable productive reintegration of former combatants and other war-affected groups as a critical component of peacebuilding. Going forward, the UN must support the creation of viable and inclusive economies in countries in which it has operations if it wants its peacebuilding record to improve.[31]

Notes

1 Del Castillo, *Rebuilding War-Torn States*, 15–16.
2 Del Castillo, *Guilty Party*, 167.
3 United Nations, *A More Secure World: Our Shared Responsibility* (New York: Report of the Secretary-General's High Level Panel on Threats, Challenges and Change, General Assembly document A/59/565), 2 December 2004, 70.
4 Scott Feil, "Laying the Foundations: Enhancing Security Capabilities," in *Winning the Peace: An American Strategy for Post-Conflict Reconstruction*, Robert C. Orr, ed. (Washington, DC: The CSIS Press, 2004), 40.
5 Barnett R. Rubin, Humayun Hamidzada, and Abby Stoddard, "Through the Fog of Peace Building: Evaluating the Reconstruction of Afghanistan" (New York: Center on International Cooperation, June 2003), 1.
6 Tony Addison and Mark McGillivray, "Aid to Conflict-Affected Countries: Lessons for Donors," *Conflict, Security and Development*, 4/3 (December 2004), 363.
7 See, for example, Feil, "Laying the Foundations: Enhancing Security Capabilities," 40.
8 David H. Petraeus and James F. Amos, *Counterinsurgency Field Manual* (Washington, DC: Department of the Army, 2006, Chapter 1), 11.
9 Abdullah Abdullah, "We Must Rebuild Afghanistan," *Washington Post* (October 29, 2002), and Seth Jones, "It Takes the Villages: Bringing Change from Below in Afghanistan," *Foreign* Policy (November/December 2010), cited in del Castillo, *Guilty Party*, 147.
10 For details, see del Castillo, *Guilty Party*, 220.
11 Operating with less military muscle and much less money, non-US PRTs had some limited success without creating the serious distortions that the US ones did.
12 SIGAR and SEGIR Quarterly Reports to Congress Quarterly Reports to Congress (Washington, DC: several years).
13 Del Castillo, "The Economics of Peace in War-Torn Countries: The Historical Record and the Path Forward," paper commissioned by UNU-WIDER

on the occasion of its celebration of 30 years in development research (Helsinki, 17–19 September 2015).

14 Roger Myerson, "Rethinking the Fundamentals of State-Building," *PRISM 2*, No. 2 (March 2011), 91. See also Myerson, "Decentralized Democracy in Political Reconstruction," presentation at the High Level Meeting of Experts on Global Issues and their Impact on the Future of Human Rights and International Criminal Justice at ISISC (Syracuse, Italy, September 2014).

15 Roger Myerson, "Standards for State-Building Interventions" (Chicago, Ill.: University of Chicago, mimeo, 2012), 7.

16 Myerson, "Rethinking the Fundamentals of State-Building," 91.

17 Ibid., 95–96.

18 Ibid., 92–93.

19 For more on decentralization, see Myerson, "Decentralized Democracy in Political Reconstruction."

20 Del Castillo, *Guilty Party*, 145–46, 197.

21 Guéhenno also warned that foreigners need to be aware that their promotion of decentralization in countries that are fragile can be misinterpreted as attempts to further weaken or even dismember the country (personal correspondence).

22 Myerson, "Standards for State-Building Interventions," 8.

23 De Soto and del Castillo, "Implementation of Comprehensive Peace Agreements," 189–204.

24 De Soto, Foreword in *Political Economy of Statebuilding*, xviii. De Soto also noted that helping to bring this about will increase the depth and duration of the UN's involvement. "This was a responsibility that could not be shirked by the Security Council."

25 Helena Meyer-Knapp, *Dangerous Peace-Making* (Olympia, Wash.: Peace-Maker Press, 2003), 192.

26 For issues related to productive reintegration, see del Castillo, *Rebuilding War-Torn States.*

27 For analysis and references, see del Castillo, *Rebuilding War-Torn States*, 255–272. For the specific problems in Afghanistan, see del Castillo, *Guilty Party*, 148–153, 192–198, and 243 and footnote 6 (for references).

28 Barnett R. Rubin, Humayun Hamidzada, and Abby Stoddard, "Through the Fog of Peace Building: Evaluating the Reconstruction of Afghanistan" (New York: Center on International Cooperation, June 2003), 18; Marvin G. Weinbaum, "Rebuilding Afghanistan: Impediments, Lessons, and Prospects," in Francis Fukuyama, ed., *Nation-Building: Beyond Afghanistan and Iraq* (Baltimore, Md.: The Johns Hopkins University Press, 206), 139; del Castillo, *Guilty Party*, 148.

29 Perhaps the most complete and interrelated analysis of the four areas of the transition can be found in Paul K. Davis, ed., *Dilemmas of Intervention: Social Science for Stabilization and Reconstruction* (Washington, DC: RAND, 2011).

30 Del Castillo, *Guilty Party*, 156–58.

31 Del Castillo, *Guilty Party*, 149, 243.

3 The economics of war, the economics of conflict resolution, the economics of peace, the economics of development

- Terminology, phases, sequence, challenges, and policies
- Economic reconstruction: the evolving context from the Marshall Plan to the post-Cold War period
- Post-conflict economic reconstruction vs. development
- Conclusions

One could have thought that with its renowned record of setting the stage for world peace, the Marshall Plan could have established the basis for the economic transition in the post-Cold War period. Although the Plan holds some far-reaching lessons, it took place in a radically different political, security, social, and economic context. For that reason, a new paradigm was required.[1]

Chapter 3 discusses first the terminology and sequence as well as the main challenges and overriding economic policymaking prescriptions for each stage in the path from war to peace. The chapter then analyzes the differences in the post-Cold War context as compared to the time of the Marshall Plan. Finally, the chapter discusses similarities between countries in post-conflict situations and other fragile countries undergoing development as usual and analyzes how such similarities often lead to their conflation in policymaking – with serious consequences for peacebuilding efforts.

Chapter 4 will then track the contrasting views with respect to many of these issues in the UN and the Bretton Woods Institutions (BWIs) since the early 1990s.

Terminology, phases, sequence, challenges, and policies

Interchangeable terminology, phases, sequence, and policy challenges

In the economics area, the long-term objective for war-torn countries embarking on the transition to peace, stability, and prosperity is to move out of the underground economy – of illicit, rent-seeking, and mostly unproductive activities that thrive during wars – back onto a path of "normal development."

As Diagram 3.1 shows, the term "normal development" is used interchangeably with "the economics of development," "development-as-usual" or "long-term development," as it is in the literature. These terms refer to the process that countries at low levels of development – unbounded by deadly conflict – need to embark on to satisfy their basic socioeconomic needs and other aspirations.

But this is a long-term proposition for war-torn countries. To get there, however, such countries need to make peace first and then go through an intermediate and distinct phase: the "economics of peace." As in the literature, the term "economics of peace" is used interchangeably with "the economic transition" (Chapter 2), "economic reconstruction," or "the political economy of peace," depending on where the focus wants to be.[2]

The four distinct economic phases – the economics of war, the economics of conflict resolution, the economics of peace, and the economics of development – are not necessarily sequential; they often overlap in various and complex ways in different places and at different times. Each has specific challenges and policymaking issues (Diagram 3.1).

Irrespective of the shape the economic transition takes, the overriding short-term objective of the economics of peace phase must be to reactivate investment, increase the provision of public goods, and create employment opportunities for the large majority while minimizing at the same time the high risk that these countries have of relapsing into conflict. This can only be achieved through conflict-sensitive and inclusive macro- and microeconomic policies, targeting the root causes and the consequences of conflict.

The short term objective of the economics of peace is thus fundamentally different from short term relief activities, often carried out for humanitarian purposes to bring minimum levels of consumption to vulnerable populations. There has been much conflation between short-term humanitarian relief and short-term reconstruction, and between the latter and long-term development. Many analysts have failed to distinguish between the strikingly different objectives as well as policymaking challenges and constraints between these phases.[3]

The economics of peace needs to succeed before development can take root. Doyle and Sambanis make it absolutely clear that peace-building is necessary to avoid relapsing into war on the path from peacekeeping to long-term development and that the economic aspects of it have been neglected. In relation to UN interventions they argue that,

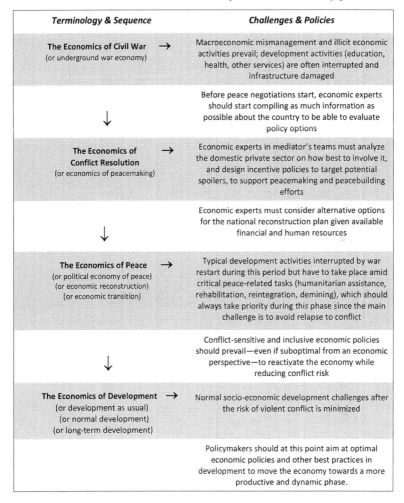

Terminology & Sequence	Challenges & Policies
The Economics of Civil War (or underground war economy) →	Macroeconomic mismanagement and illicit economic activities prevail; development activities (education, health, other services) are often interrupted and infrastructure damaged
↓	Before peace negotiations start, economic experts should start compiling as much information as possible about the country to be able to evaluate policy options
The Economics of Conflict Resolution (or economics of peacemaking) →	Economic experts in mediator's teams must analyze the domestic private sector on how best to involve it, and design incentive policies to target potential spoilers, to support peacemaking and peacebuilding efforts
↓	Economic experts must consider alternative options for the national reconstruction plan given available financial and human resources
The Economics of Peace (or political economy of peace) (or economic reconstruction) (or economic transition) →	Typical development activities interrupted by war restart during this period but have to take place amid critical peace-related tasks (humanitarian assistance, rehabilitation, reintegration, demining), which should always take priority during this phase since the main challenge is to avoid relapse to conflict
↓	Conflict-sensitive and inclusive economic policies should prevail—even if suboptimal from an economic perspective—to reactivate the economy while reducing conflict risk
The Economics of Development (or development as usual) (or normal development) (or long-term development) →	Normal socio-economic development challenges after the risk of violent conflict is minimized
	Policymakers should at this point aim at optimal economic policies and other best practices in development to move the economy towards a more productive and dynamic phase.

Diagram 3.1

Good as UN peacebuilding is in expanding political participation, it has not helped to jump-start self-sustaining economic growth. Economic growth is critical in supporting incentives for peace … and helps achieve war avoidance even in the absence of extensive international capacities. … Thus, narrowing the policy gap between peacekeeping, with its humanitarian assistance, and development assistance, with its emphasis on structural transformation, is a good peacebuilding strategy. UN peacebuilding would clearly benefit from an evolution that made economic reform the additional element that plugged this decisive gap.[4]

The effective use of economic policies in peacebuilding strategies and in the implementation of peace agreements in this area are often made difficult by the design of the agreements themselves, as Chapter 7 illustrates. That is why particular attention should be paid to the "economics of conflict resolution."

The fact that peace mediators in general lack economic and financial experts – despite having multidisciplinary teams consisting of mostly political, human rights, gender, justice, and security experts – is perhaps a major factor why peace agreements have been difficult to implement effectively. Particularly lacking in the peacemaking and post-conflict periods are experts on the intricacies of budgetary, fiscal, investment, employment, and financial policies, all of which are key to the effective, inclusive, dynamic, and sustainable economic reconstruction of the country.

A key contribution of an economic expert during peace negotiations would be to identify those that have benefited from the war economy and are potential spoilers so as to design incentive policies to lure them into supporting peacemaking and peacebuilding efforts.

It is indeed necessary to understand the economic factors that fuel the war, to design effective peace agreements and to be able to implement them. In 2000, Mats Berdal and David Malone noted

> comparatively little *systematic* attention has been given to the precise role of economically motivated actions and processes in generating and sustaining contemporary civil conflicts. ... There is now much evidence to suggest that the failure to account for the presence of economic agendas in conflict has, at times, seriously undermined international efforts to consolidate fragile peace agreements. ... In particular, the tendency ... to treat 'conflict' and 'postconflict' as separate categories and distinct phases in a quest for 'lasting peace' has carried with it the expectation (and planning assumption) that the formal end of armed hostilities also marks a definitive break with past patterns of violence. In fact ... even in the best circumstances this is rarely the case. Grievances and conflicts of interest usually persist after the end of hostilities and, in turn, affect the 'peace building' activities.[5]

Another contribution of an economic expert during peace negotiations would be to lead a working group with selected representatives of the two negotiating parties and of the private sector to think about how to reactivate the economy and create the sustainable job opportunities and support for startups that have proved essential to sustain the peace. Such a group would have to reach some consensus on the desirable macroeconomic and microeconomic policy framework, on employment, on other aspects of the productive and financial sectors, on institutions and the business climate, on essential services and infrastructure, and on trade and investment relations with the rest of the world. An action plan identifying priorities for the first 100 days and for the first year and how it could be financed would help mediators design more realistic, effective, and implementable agreements.

Most public and policy discussions on peace and the private sector focus on the business sector in donor countries to the neglect of the domestic private sector in war-torn countries and the specific situation of foreign investors in them.[6] Because it takes many different forms, talking about the "private sector" as a whole may not make much sense for policymaking purposes. Before involving the domestic private sector – as they should – mediators' teams must analyze carefully the specific situation on the ground.

The private sector is defined to include in general a variety of businesses willing to engage in risk taking and productive initiatives in formal and informal markets, where profit-making and competition drives production. For peacebuilding purposes in particular, the often large number of farmers in war-torn countries operating mostly at subsistence levels – which may not really fit the typical definition of private sector – should be included in any analysis of the sector.

There are basically four types of investors operating in the private sector: There are domestic investors producing for the internal market and those producing for the foreign market (exporters). There are also foreign direct investors producing for the domestic market and those producing for export.

Because war-torn countries are by no means homogeneous, the four types of investors may not only behave differently in each country, but also across countries. This is because they have different incentives, can benefit from different opportunities, and can create different risks to peace processes. That is why each case needs to be considered carefully. Failing to acknowledge the differences – as it is mostly done in peace processes – as if the private sector were homogeneous within and across countries has created false expectations, inappropriate policies, unimplementable peace agreements, and poor results.

Peace agreements and regime change following military intervention or political upheaval create great expectations. I said it already and it is worth repeating: A peace dividend in terms of better living conditions and rewarding jobs is necessary for peace to be long lasting. If governments fail to reactivate the economy in such a way as to allow for the viable and long-term reintegration into productive activities of former combatants and other conflict-affected groups, disgruntled members of these groups will probably take up arms again.

Without peace, development will not prosper. Thus, although development is the long-run objective, peacebuilding and peace consolidation must be the short-run and intermediate goals until the high risk of violent conflict can be managed.

That war-torn countries have to go through an intermediate phase – the economics of peace – does not mean, of course, that development activities interrupted during the war should not restart and be nurtured as soon as possible. But such development activities require investment, both human and financial, and will take time to have an impact. Education, good health, and improved roads will all be critical to the development of a country and will strengthen peace in the future. In the short run, however, such investments cannot be expected to have a major peacebuilding impact. Expecting that they do – without doing anything else – will likely bring the country back into conflict.

To avoid such a fate, war-torn countries will have to adopt emergency policies promptly and decisively in the early transition to deal with the aftermath of conflict, including the rehabilitation of basic services and infrastructure, demining, and the productive reintegration of former combatants and other conflict-affected groups. Such activities are *sine qua non* for effective peacebuilding.

Moving away from the economics of war has proved particularly challenging. This requires bringing under control as soon as feasible activities such as drug production and trafficking, smuggling, extortion, money laundering and capital flight, and illegal logging as well as exploitation of minerals and gemstones. Moreover, as Thomas Weiss and Peter Hoffman noted, unusual predatory economic opportunities abound in war-to-peace transitions, including the appropriation of aid for illegal purposes.[7]

There are many reasons for the urgency of moving away from the economics of war. Illicit, rent-seeking, and highly lucrative activities such as these are an ideal source of finance to insurgencies and terrorist groups, as they are to corrupt national politicians and businessmen. Thus, security stabilization and good governance will be elusive in their presence.

Another reason to move quickly away from the economics of war is to avoid having donors, avid to finance the private sector, end up supporting economic elites of warlords, corrupt officials, and others that accumulated capital illegally during the war and in its immediate aftermath. If this continued, it would entrench poor governance, corruption, and other illicit practices in the post-conflict period, as has happened in Haiti, Bosnia, Kosovo, Afghanistan, Iraq, and Liberia.

However, and despite the urgency, income-earning opportunities elsewhere have to be created before bringing drug production and other such illegal activities under control. This is because poor farmers and other vulnerable groups depend on such activities for food and other basic necessities.[8]

Unless the economics of peace succeed, war-affected countries will not be able to move into a development-as-usual phase. Moving from one phase to the other has been complex and problematic for various reasons that I will analyze and illustrate with regard to specific countries in Chapter 7.

Confusing terminology across organizations and in the academic literature

The terminology used by practitioners and academics alike has been a constant source of confusion. In general, the term "reconstruction" has been used as a synonym for the multidisciplinary war-to-peace transition as a whole, covering the four different areas. In the economics area, the term "economic reconstruction" means different things to different people and its connotation has even changed over time.[9]

The term "economic reconstruction" is used to cover war destruction, even though in countries coming out of war in the post-Cold War period much needs to be built rather than rebuilt. The term allows for the fact that countries should not try to recreate policies and institutions of the past that led to the conflict in the first place, although some do, with Liberia being a prime example (Chapter 7). Policies and the new or reformed institutions in the post-conflict period must take into account not only the root causes of the conflict but also the consequences of the war and how these have affected society in general and the economy in particular.

I argue that the terms "reconstruction" or "rebuilding" are preferable to "construction" or "building," terms that some experts have suggested as preferable.[10] The latter give the wrong impression that war-torn countries are *tabula rasa* and that post-conflict peacebuilding and statebuilding efforts can ignore past institutions and policies.

Moreover, there is a large number of cultural, historical, ethnic, or religious values that are important to the specific countries and their societies and therefore should be reflected in institutional building and policy decisions of both national leaders and foreign interveners. Iraq provides a useful illustration (Chapter 7).[11]

Different actors often use different terms with the same purpose. For example, the press and many analysts as well as some politicians in donor countries refer to "economic reconstruction" interchangeably with "nation-building" (the construction of a national identity) or "state-building" (the construction of a functioning state) or simply "development."[12] The US Department of State prefers the term "reconstruction and stabilization" (or vice versa), and so does the US Agency for International Development (USAID).

The World Bank Group uses the term "post-conflict reconstruction," and the International Monetary Fund (IMF) refers to the economic transition as "reconstruction and growth" or "recovery and reconstruction." The UN uses the encompassing term "peacebuilding." Although Boutros-Ghali referred to "reconstruction and development," reconstruction has become the aspect of peacebuilding to which the UN pays least heed to. UNDP uses the term "early recovery,"[13] often conflating humanitarian assistance with reconstruction. Unless it is set in the right context, the term "post-conflict stabilization" can also be confusing, although most of the time it refers to stabilization in the security sense (as used by the US Department of State and military), it can also refer to economic stabilization as used by the BWIs.

Using the terms "economic reconstruction" and "development" interchangeably – as many policymakers, analysts, and institutions often do – conflates the fundamentally different objectives of the two activities and denies the need for strikingly different policies and timeframes in each case. The two may start at the same time as the country moves out of war, but development activities will take time to have an impact, so they may not, by themselves, contribute to peacebuilding in the short term. Quick impact reconstruction policies, on the other hand, can be targeted toward the overriding goal of avoiding relapse.

The two terms also differ with respect to time and duration. While "economic reconstruction" may last ten years or more, it nevertheless encompasses a specific time period, a time period that can be delineated, although with little precision. It usually coincides with the finalization of peace-related programs (often specified in national reconstruction plans) or with the end of foreign combat forces in the countries and the assessment that the probability of relapse is relatively low. The "development" of the country, on the other hand, is a long-term and open-ended proposition.

Economic reconstruction: the evolving context from the Marshall Plan to the post-Cold War period

The definition of the term "economic reconstruction" had to evolve over time because of radically different conditions. Following World War II, reconstruction under the Marshall Plan took place in industrial countries with educated labour forces and with strong political and economic institutions and policy frameworks in place that could easily be adapted to post-conflict economic reconstruction. At the same time, there was no need for reconciliation since, following interstate wars, former combatants return to their countries and do not need to coexist in the same space. For this reason, the term "economic reconstruction" at the time referred mostly to the rehabilitation of basic services and infrastructure for the reactivation of world production and trade.[14]

By contrast, in the post-Cold War context, economic reconstruction took place in countries at low-levels of development, with young and fast growing populations, with weak policy and institutional frameworks, and with large macroeconomic imbalances. Under such conditions, economic reconstruction required a broader definition: it had to include not only the rehabilitation of basic services and infrastructure destroyed during the war but also the modernization or creation of a basic macro- and microeconomic institutional and policy framework necessary for effective policymaking, for the reactivation of the economy, and for the effective and transparent utilization of aid. Stabilization was necessary to address the large internal and external macroeconomic imbalances of the past and to reactivate the economy.

In the new context, the challenge became creating viable economies on the ashes of war. As wars ended, economies emerged with little income, production, and savings and therefore could not invest, relying mostly on foreign aid even for current expenditures. Because foreign aid[15] has been largely scarce, untimely, and/or poorly utilized, these countries found it difficult to create an adequate productive base, to promote reconciliation, and to reduce security instability at the same time, often reverting to conflict.

The problem has not only been underinvestment but also the type of investment. While investment often takes place to satisfy the needs of expatriates and small domestic elites early in the transition, economies will not be viable unless they can provide sustainable work opportunities for the large majority of men and women, particularly the large percentage of youth, typical of these economies, which is both a blessing but also a source of concern because of the demands it creates.[16]

It was thus that, in the new context, economic reconstruction had to acquire a holistic meaning. It involves activities ranging from the provision of basic health, education, water and sewerage and other basic needs for families and children to the economics of boosting agricultural yields and livestock productivity for small farmers and to the business of getting initial access to capital, technology, and infrastructure for the creation of small- and medium-size enterprises.

Additionally, reconstruction involves the design of policies and institutions targeted at the reactivation of investment, production, trade, and the management of aid. This, together with the need for national reconciliation following intrastate wars, has proved to be a most challenging and expensive proposition.

Contrary to these two experiences, the reconstruction of Korea and Vietnam[17] did not fit into either pattern and combined aspects of reconstruction following intra- and interstate wars. A cursory discussion of such experiences is useful to understand the challenges of the last quarter of a century. Both Korea and Vietnam, countries at low-levels of development at the time, did not attempt the political transition towards a more participatory government and remained a single-party system.

The situation with respect to aid was also different. Large US aid supported Korea's reconstruction. Due to the US embargo, which lasted until 1993, there was no involvement from the BWIs or the Asian Development Bank in Vietnam's reconstruction. Vietnam also saw a collapse in aid from and trade with the former Soviet Union at the time it renewed efforts at reconstruction by adopting "DoiMoi" (renovation) in the late 1980s.

By contrast, in the post-Cold War context, countries have relied on a large number of donors and other actors. This has created various problems, not only in terms of aid coordination, inefficiencies, and duplication but also as a result of the large distortions created by the unwieldy international presence in the respective countries, which has often been compounded by the large presence of UN peacekeepers or foreign forces.[18]

In Vietnam, despite the low levels of aid, the country had a major comparative advantage. Although it was a poor country, just as Mozambique, East Timor, Afghanistan, and Liberia, it was strikingly different in terms of education: a mixture of Confucian and Communist influences in Vietnam had resulted in a highly literate population with no gender gap.

Extensive untapped natural resources (oil and gas, coal, gold, gemstones and tungsten), in combination with a relatively educated and low-cost labour force, attracted foreign investment to these sectors. Although resource-rich countries like Liberia, the Democratic Republic of Congo (DRC), Angola, and Afghanistan always lure foreign investors, the potential benefits in terms of employment generation for the local population are limited as a result of poor education.

Post-conflict economic reconstruction vs. development

Although countries in post-conflict reconstruction share some common features, each one is distinctive, owing to the specific interplay of the many factors that influence the war-to-peace transition. Such factors include the circumstances in which war or conflict began (internal strife, regional conflict, ethnic or sectarian rivalries, or control of natural resources) and the ways in which countries have achieved peace (peace negotiations, military intervention or public upheaval for regime change).

Other factors include the level of development (differences in initial conditions, human capital and absorptive capacities) and the political support as well as the aid and technical assistance that the countries can expect to garner as a result of geopolitical factors. Countries also differ in whether they have a sovereign government and legislature in place, whether the UN (Kosovo, East Timor) has been mandated, or whether an occupying force (the United States in Iraq) has assumed executive and legislative powers.

Since the end of the Cold War, countries in post-conflict economic reconstruction – that is, undergoing the economics of peace – do indeed share a number of characteristics with other fragile countries in the normal process of development, unaffected by war. These are listed in Table 3.1. The similarities between countries in post-conflict reconstruction and others unaffected by violent conflict in the normal process of development have led to a conflation between "reconstruction" and "development." But there are a number of activities that are peculiar only to "reconstruction."[19]

A critical factor in making peace sustainable – as we have seen most tragically in Afghanistan in the early 2000s and even in Lebanon in the summer of 2006 – is the need to disarm, demobilize and reintegrate former combatants and other conflict-affected groups effectively and permanently into the productive life of the country. This entails a number of activities also detailed in Table 3.1 that make

Table 3.1 Characteristics and peculiarities

Fragile countries in normal development (development challenge)	Countries in post-conflict reconstruction (reconstruction challenge)
Human capital and infrastructure in shambles	The same but often worse
Macroeconomic mismanagement has led to fiscal and external imbalances that require tough stabilization and structural reform	The same but often worse
Lack of transparency; poor governance; corrupt legal, judicial, and police systems; inadequate protection of property rights; incompetent central banks; weak tax and customs administration; and noncredible public expenditure management	The same but often worse
Highly dependent on official aid flows, mostly in the form of grants	The same but often worse
Protracted arrears on payments on foreign debt; the provision of financial aid is constrained by the need to normalize relations with creditors; often require debt relief on unsustainable external aid burdens	The same but often worse
Need to develop a number of capabilities in various areas through training and institutional building	The same but often worse
	Special needs of post-conflict countries (development-plus challenge)
	Need to move away from the war economy
	Delivery of emergency aid to former conflict zones (some of which might not yet be under government control)
	Disarmament, demobilization, and reintegration of former combatants and other armed groups into society and productive activities
	Demining (mine clearance)
	Return of refugees and internally displaced groups, reintegrating them into productive activities

Fragile countries in normal development (development challenge)	Countries in post-conflict reconstruction (reconstruction challenge)
	Rehabilitation and reconstruction of productive assets destroyed because of the conflict
	Reform of the armed forces and the creation of a national civilian police.
Access to foreign aid	*Access to foreign aid*
Official Development Flows (ODA) amount on average to 1–10 percent of Gross National Income (GNI), with few exceptions (mostly islands or very small countries).	ODA can spike to 50–100 percent of GNI in the immediate transition from war and fall rapidly thereafter, with few exceptions.

post-conflict economic reconstruction a *development-PLUS* challenge: countries emerging from protracted civil wars have to confront the normal challenge of socio-economic development while accommodating, at the same time, the additional burden of reconstruction and peace consolidation.[20]

This *development-PLUS* challenge is particularly arduous since, after years of political polarization and ideological or ethnic confrontations, building consensus on macroeconomic policymaking is hard. At the same time, putting the economy back on a path of stabilization and inclusive and sustainable growth becomes imperative to create improved livelihoods and public goods for conflict-affected groups and the resident population in former zones of conflict.

Table 3.1 also shows a major difference in terms of the aid resources available to countries under normal development and those carrying out a development-plus challenge (see also Table 6.1).

Given the basically nonexistent capacity of war-torn countries to rely on domestic savings for investment in the early transition, the controversy over aid during the last few years has wrongly focused on whether aid should be increased or eliminated altogether rather than on how it can be made more effective and accountable.[21]

The debate has also failed to distinguish between "development aid" on the one hand, and "humanitarian" and "reconstruction aid" on the other. While countries in the normal process of development (with few exceptions) complement their own savings capacity – their main source of development finance – with low but stable levels of development aid, humanitarian and reconstruction aid in war-torn countries usually spikes after the crisis. The large volume of aid (and the concomitant large presence of the international community) not only creates all kinds of distortions in the national economies but also provides a serious challenge to its effective and noncorrupt utilization.

Thus, despite the similarities with other fragile countries pursuing normal development, countries in postconflict reconstruction are clearly distinct – have different needs, different objectives, different risks, and different amount of aid – from those pursuing normal development.

Because of the fundamentally different objectives, policymaking during the economics of peace and during the economics of development must also be fundamentally different, something that the BWIs have taken time to accept, as discussed in Chapter 4.

At the same time, these countries face the challenge of having to utilize large and quickly reversible volumes of aid and, as a result, to deal with the large political and military involvement of the international community. The key challenge in this regard is to ensure that economic policies to reactivate the economy and generate inclusive employment are conflict-sensitive, that is, tailored to do minimal harm to the fragile peace and to rein in spoilers.

Conclusions

Because economic policies are critical to effective peacebuilding, this chapter analyzes the four phases of the transition – the economics of war, the economics of conflict resolution, the economics of peace, and the economics of development – to help the debate of how each can contribute to or derail efforts of war-torn countries to move to a path of peace, stability, and prosperity.

The chapter also establishes the fundamental difference between postconflict economic reconstruction and normal development. The main objective of economic reconstruction – the economics of peace – should be to avoid the recurrence of conflict, which calls for conflict-sensitive policies and rules out optimal economic policies. This should be so even if the development objectives are delayed or even derailed. Insisting on optimal economic policies in the early transition – as the BWIs often preach – has often resulted in conflict recurrence (Chapter 7).

Notes

1 For a discussion of the Marshall Plan, see Dulles, *The Marshall Plan*. For a discussion of how the Marshall Plan differs from economic reconstruction

in the new context and the lessons for it, see del Castillo, *Rebuilding War-Torn States*, and *Guilty Party*.

2 I often use "the economics of peace" as a discipline, "economic reconstruction" to emphasize the broad economic tasks of rebuilding, "economic transition" to differentiate it from the other aspects of the simultaneous transition to peace, and "the political economy of peace" to emphasize political constraints.

3 Sultan Barakat and Margaret Chard point out that in post-conflict situations, foreign interventions are normally led by the short-term relief principle. See Barakat and Chard, "Building Post-War Capacity: Where to Start?" in *After the Conflict: Reconstruction and Development in the Aftermath of War* (London: I. B. Tauris & Co. Ltd., 2010), 173.

4 Michael W. Doyle, and Nicholas Sambanis, 2006, *Making War and Building Peace* (Princeton, N.J. and Oxford: Princeton University Press), 132.

5 Mats Berdal and David M. Malone, eds, *Greed and Grievance: Economic Agendas in Civil Wars* (Boulder, Colo.: Lynne Rienner Publishers, Inc., 2000), 1 and 9. For other seminal work in this area, see Karen Ballentine and Jake Sherman, *The Political Economy of Armed Conflict: Beyond Greed and Grievance* (Boulder, Colo.: Lynne Rienner Publishers, Inc., 2003).

6 This was the case, for example, with the Business and the Private Sector groups at the United States Institute of Peace, in which I participated.

7 Thomas G. Weiss and Peter J. Hoffman, "Making Humanitarianism Work," in S. Chesterman, M. Ignatieff, and R. Thakur, eds, *Making States Work: State Failure and the Crisis of Governance* (Tokyo: UN University Press, 2005), 299–300.

8 See, for example, various studies done by AREU in Afghanistan.

9 When the economic context is clear, "reconstruction" is used interchangeably with "economic reconstruction" to avoid repetition.

10 David Sedney, a former US deputy assistant secretary of defence, argued along these lines at an event at the USIP (Washington, DC: April 2016).

11 For an interesting analysis of how the United States rightly took into account past budgeting practices in Iraq, see James D. Savage, *Reconstructing Iraq's Budgetary Institutions: Coalition State Building After Saddam* (Cambridge: Cambridge University Press, 2013).

12 Even the use of these terms as synonyms is confusing since "statebuilding" and "nationbuilding" are concepts that mean different things to different people. See Carolyn Stephenson, "Nation Building," in *Beyond Intractability*, Guy Burgess and Heidi Burgess, eds. (Boulder, Colo.: Conflict Research Consortium, University of Colorado, 1 January 2005). Also, although these two concepts are distinct from peacebuilding, people often use them interchangeably. See Jenkins, *Peacebuilding*. For an analysis on differences between peacebuilding and statebuilding or nationbuilding, see Roland Paris and Timothy D. Sisk, eds, *The Dilemmas of State Building* (London: Routledge, 2009), 1–20; and Francis Fukuyama, *State-Building: Governance and World Order in the 21st Century* (Ithaca, NY: Cornell University Press, 2004).

13 For more details on the use of these terms by different organizations, see Jenkins, *Peacebuilding*, 32–33.

14 See Dulles (1993).

15 Unless specified otherwise, "aid" refers to OECD Official Development Data (ODA). See Table 6.1 for definition of what ODA includes.

16 Del Castillo, *Rebuilding War-Torn States*, 29–30, 22–25.
17 For more details, see del Castillo, "Economic Reconstruction of War-Torn Countries: The Role of the International Financial Institutions," *Seton Hall Law Review*, 38/4 (December 2008).
18 For a discussion of the distortions created by an extensive foreign presence in a country, see del Castillo, "The Economics of Peace: Five Rules for Effective Reconstruction," *Special Report 286* (Washington, DC: US Institute of Peace, September 2011), and *Guilty Party.*
19 Del Castillo, *Rebuilding War-Torn States*, 30–38
20 Graciana del Castillo, "Auferstehenaus Ruinen: Die Besonderen Bedingungen des Wirtschaftlichen Wiederaufbaus nach Konflikten," ["Post-Conflict Economic Reconstruction: A Development-PLUS Challenge"]. *Der Überblick* (Germany's *Foreign Affairs*) (4/2006, December). See also, del Castillo, "Post-Conflict Peace-Building: The Challenge to the UN," *CEPAL Review*, 55 (October 1995), 29.
21 Graciana del Castillo and Edmund S. Phelps, "Dead Wrong: If It Is to Become 'The Next Big Thing,' Africa Will Need Aid," *Argument, Foreign Policy* (6 July 2009).

4 Economic reconstruction vs. development

Evolving conceptual views

- **Contrasting views in the 1990s at the UN and the BWIs**
- **Evolving views in the 2000s: the World Bank and the IMF**
- **Conclusions**

Chapter 4 will discuss the evolving conceptual views with respect to economic reconstruction (the economics of peace) and normal development (the economics of development) developed at the UN and held at the Bretton Woods institutions (BWIs) in the 1990s. These institutions perform *sine qua non* functions in support of economic reconstruction since peacebuilding is not possible in stagnant, jobless economies.

The BWIs support countries in the transition to peace through many and interconnected channels, including policy advice, technical assistance and capacity building; financing through their own instruments, programs and trust funds; administering trust funds that donors set up for different countries; and catalyzing resources from other institutions and governments. Both institutions continuously carry out applied research to guide their respective interventions.

The chapter will track how these institutions' views and rhetoric changed in the 2000s, how academics and practitioners both contributed to shape such views, and how they have often been critical of these institutions' programs in war-torn countries.

In particular, the chapter will discuss how the International Monetary Fund (IMF) and the World Bank finally came to acknowledge that the economic reconstruction of countries ravaged by war is not development as usual – as some of us forcefully argued at the UN and in academic circles in the early 1990s. The chapter will also discuss how such belated recognition and the change in rhetoric, unfortunately, has not yet been translated into institutional and operational change so that economic policymaking could make a distinct difference in supporting peacebuilding efforts.

Nevertheless, the BWIs have come a long way since the early 1990s, when they argued that conflict had a political dimension well beyond their mandate and hence carried out their economic and development operations in war-torn countries with little consideration for politics. There has indeed been an important change in the way these institutions address their mandates and an increased acknowledgement of the interconnectedness of economic policies, political and security constraints, conflict and poverty alleviation. There has also been a positive move towards improving their terms of lending and towards making conditionality somewhat less harsh.[1]

As war ends, countries need to establish or reform as soon as possible the macroeconomic framework and its microeconomic foundations (including the institutional, legal, and regulatory systems). This framework is important since good economic management and stability are critical to the success of economic reconstruction.

Most parties involved would recognize the importance of good macroeconomic management and the need for solid microfoundations to support it and create an environment conducive to private investment and growth. The issue is whether the institutional framework and policies that post-conflict countries adopt, with the support of the BWIs, is adequate to allow them to play the active role governments need to play in reconstruction to ensure that the peace (political) objective of the transition prevail over the development (economic) one to make certain that conflict does not recur. In setting up this framework, the BWIs, particularly the IMF, have played a critical role since the early experience in El Salvador. In fact, as Kristen Boon argued, despite a lack of mandate, the BWIs have adopted quasi-legislative functions in many of these countries – including Afghanistan and Iraq – in establishing policies and institutions for economic reconstruction.[2]

Because the peace objective should prevail over the development one, the goals of international assistance to post-conflict countries should be determined at the highest political level – including the UN Security Council and the UN Secretariat – and not by the BWIs, or even UNDP.[3]

Contrasting views in the 1990s at the UN and the BWIs

Countries transitioning to peace in the aftermath of civil war or other intrastate conflict a quarter of a century ago were at low levels of development. Because of this, those of us at the office of the UN Secretary-General initially thought that the challenge was to resume development as usual as soon as possible with the support of UNDP and the World Bank. That is how these two development organizations assumed de facto leadership of the economics transition.

It took only a few months for some of us, working on countries such as El Salvador, Mozambique, and Cambodia, where the UN had established multidisciplinary operations in the early 1990s, to become fully aware of the serious mistake. We soon realized that economic reconstruction, the economics of peace, needed a new paradigm.

We also realized that, because of the explicit mandate of development organizations to collaborate with governments, UNDP and the World Bank lacked the impartiality, or at least the perception of it, to deal with unequal partners. Such partners included a sovereign government and one or more nonstate actors, such as the FMLN in El Salvador, which also happened to be signatories of the peace agreement. Under such conditions only the Secretary-General had the impartiality to deal with both partners on an equal basis. Development organizations had to play a critical technical role, but only the UN Secretariat could lead at the political level.[4]

From the early collision between the UN-brokered peace agreement and the IMF-sponsored economic program, we realized the quintessentially "political" nature of the transition underway. The Salvadoran experience provided the first glaring example, of many more to come, of the extent to which these transitions are not simply a matter of resuming development-as-usual, something that the IMF and the development organizations such as the World Bank and UNDP rejected outright at the time. Indeed, by taking place amid the complex multidisciplinary war-to-peace transition and by being constrained by it, economic reconstruction was fundamentally different from normal development.

Neither UNDP nor the World Bank agreed at the time, despite repeated requests from the Secretary-General, to support the arms-for-land program, the most important venue for productive reintegration in El Salvador. In late 1992, in a meeting at the Secretary-General's office where the intention was to get the World Bank involved with the program, the Bank's country team argued that there were about 300,000 peasant families without land and that preferences should not be given to a few. It was typical of the Bank at the time to stick to the equity principle – to attend to all those in need equally – rather than to the peacebuilding principle, where preferences are given to groups most affected by the crisis to ensure that they would give up arms, even if other groups in the country have comparable economic needs.[5]

This development-as-usual approach to peacebuilding led to mis-understandings and confrontations between the UN and the IMF from the beginning as the economic and peace processes moved forward separately. As mentioned in Chapter 1, Secretary-General Boutros-Ghali expressed strong concern in April 1993 that the Fund and the UN were not working on a fully coordinated and transparent basis toward the overriding goal of consolidating peace and human security in El Salvador. In his view, implementation of the agreements must not be conditional on the availability of foreign financing, as the IMF insisted. He argued that it was the government's responsibility to define fiscal policies and public expenditure priorities that would enable it to fulfill its commitments.[6]

Although the IMF Managing Director was unhappy at the time with the Secretary-General's public statement, the two organizations started working more closely on El Salvador, Angola, Rwanda, and Bosnia. At the request of the Secretary-General, and with my partici-pation, the IMF prepared a minimalist monetary and fiscal framework for policymaking in war-torn countries that could support the political process and would be simple enough so as not to put unnecessary pressure on the scarce technical, administrative, and managerial capa-city of those countries. These papers, however, were not published and have not been used. In fact, few people at the UN even seem to know of their existence.[7]

In 1995 the IMF acknowledged its development-as-usual approach in El Salvador. The Fund recognized that while cooperation between the UN, the Fund, and the Bank had been instrumental in planning technical assistance and a macroeconomic framework for Rwanda, such coordination had initially not occurred in the negotiation of El Salvador's National Reconstruction Plan. As a result, the fiscal impact of the Plan had not been fully assessed when the peace agreement was drawn up.[8]

The inability of the Salvadoran government to comply with the requirements of the Plan created tremendous challenges for the UN. Nevertheless, the issue of economic reconstruction nevertheless failed to spark a rigorous theoretical and practical debate among policymakers, practitioners, donors, academics, economists, and other stakeholders as it had done at the time of the Marshall Plan.

In the absence of this debate, few economists continued to argue that optimal or first-best economic policies are manifestly not the best recipe for dealing with the challenges of economic reconstruction. While still at the Secretary-General's office, I wrote an article published in April 1995 in the *CEPAL Review* entitled "Post-Conflict Peace-Building: A

Challenge for the United Nations." In it, recognizing that "stabilization and structural reform have proven to be a necessary condition for development, but not sufficient by themselves" and that "there cannot be sustained development without peace and no durable peace without development," I posited that,

> Policy choices … are more restricted in countries coming out of conflict, which must reconcile the often-conflicting demands of peace and development. [Among the] reasons why we would argue that these situations are different and therefore deserve special treatment from the international community [is that] countries coming out of armed conflict … face a *double challenge* [emphasis added]: on the one hand, they have to confront the normal challenge of socio-economic development … . On the other, they have to settle for less than optimal policies in their economic reform efforts so as to accommodate the additional financial burden of reconstruction and peace consolidation . … The imperative of peace consolidation competes with the conventional imperative of development, putting tremendous pressure on policy decisions, especially budgetary allocations.[9]

By the time I wrote this article, two things had become clear to us in the Secretary-General's office. The first was "[t]he need for the UN to become more immersed in the multidisciplinary aspects of post-conflict peace building requires major rethinking and an analytical and operational redefinition of relationships and comparative advantages." The second was that "[o]nly an integrated approach can avert the potential clashes of command and waste of resources… But in order to follow a truly integrated approach, it is essential first to build the necessary internal bridges between the political and economic sides of the United Nations Secretariat … ."[10] The first recommendation went largely unheeded and only tepid efforts were put into the other.

Perhaps due to the absence of a wide-ranging debate on the economic transition in the post-Cold War period, key actors in the development and peacebuilding fields have failed to accept the kernel notion that if the central purpose of peacebuilding is to avert relapse to conflict, a major component must be economic reconstruction, not development as usual.

Economic reconstruction requires the adoption of inclusive economic policies, even if at subsistence (low productivity) levels at an early stage, so as to ensure an immediate peace dividend for the large majority of the population. Such policies will not be optimal from an economic or development viewpoint, but higher productivity and optimal policies can and must follow as peace consolidates.[11]

Having missed that point, many of the actors have failed to accept the corollary that economic reconstruction requires impartial political leadership since the objective of peace, which is eminently political, should always prevail over the objective of development, which is eminently economic, because there cannot be sustained development without peace.

The passion with which some of us in the Secretary-General's office argued the point at the time was not echoed or matched by the leadership in general, particularly at UNDP and the BWIs.[12] Absent acceptance of this basic concept, economic reconstruction was approached – both by national governments and by foreign interveners – as if it were development as usual.[13]

The insistence that war-torn countries had to settle for second-best policies in the early transition was clearly not a prescription for bad economic policies. As James Boyce, an academic and distinguished economist who was leading a team of experts advising UNDP on El Salvador at the time, posited, "The special features of the [post-conflict] transition do not imply that sound economic policies are unnecessary, nor that they should be sacrificed to political expediency. But in the aftermath of civil war, the soundness of policies can be ascertained only in light of the political economy of the peace process."[14]

There was a clear difference of opinion at the time between the UN and the World Bank. At the Secretary-General's office we argued that war-torn countries have needs of a different nature which must lead to differences in policymaking. We also argued that, given the primacy of the political objective in economic reconstruction (to ensure non-relapse), a different yardstick should be used to measure success. Given that first-best economic policies were often neither possible nor desirable, it was not appropriate to measure success by purely economic or financial indicators.[15]

Thus, after 12 years of war, the main objective of the arms-for-land program in El Salvador was to give preference to former combatants and their supporters to ensure that they engaged in productive activities rather than being tempted to return to fighting in the absence of other means to support themselves. Elizabeth Wood rightly referred to "the transfer of private properties in the conflicted zones" as "one of the most politically sensitive parts of the agreement."[16]

In 1995, Boutros-Ghali attempted to increase the links between the UN political and economics departments as a first step to put his integrated approach to human security in practice. His first move was to ask the head of the Department of Economic and Social Affairs (hereafter economics department) to convene and chair an inter-departmental task force for drawing up an *Inventory of Post-Conflict Peacebuilding Activities*. The purpose was to identify actions and techniques relevant to post-conflict situations as well as the relevant UN agencies that could provide support in the different areas. The introduction argued that

> Post-conflict activities should be incorporated as soon as feasible into the development strategy of the country. However, during the immediate, fragile post-conflict phase, which is by nature transitory, such activities are quite distinct from normal development...[17]

This was because the political objective should prevail during this phase, an issue that de Soto and I had addressed in the 1994 *Foreign Policy* article and raised at the *International Colloquium on Post-Conflict Reconstruction Strategies* in Stadtschlaining, Austria, in June 1995.[18]

At the time, UNDP and some of the UN agencies disputed the specificity of economic reconstruction in the fragile transition phase and continued to argue for a "continuum from humanitarian relief to development," an operational concept that UNDP itself later acknowledged was not useful.[19]

Because of the political nature of peacebuilding activities, including economic reconstruction, we emphasized the leading role that the UN, through the Department of Political Affairs (hereafter political department), had to play vis-à-vis the agencies of the UN system and the BWIs, both strategically and operationally on the ground. Dame Margaret Joan Anstee, the chairperson of the colloquium and former Under-Secretary General and head of the UN operation in Angola, came to share our position fully, as reflected in her letter of 15 July 1995, to the Secretary-General to report on the colloquium as well as in the *Synopsis and Conclusions of the Colloquium*.[20]

In his reply to Anstee of 10 August 1995, the Secretary-General particularly noted "the finding of the Colloquium that the mission involved in post-conflict peacebuilding, while using a variety of tools, is essentially *political*, and is thus fundamentally different in nature from normal relief or development activities."[21]

In his letter, the Secretary-General also noted "the suggestion that appropriate systems and procedures need to be set up at Headquarters to ensure that these responsibilities are discharged on my behalf" and proposed that "a specific Department should act as a focal point, and marshal all the necessary staff and other elements needed on an *ad hoc* basis whenever circumstances demanded" and that this might be the political department.[22] Despite what seemed like a commitment on the part of the Secretary-General, this focal unit was never created, probably because Boutros-Ghali's mandate ended abruptly after one term in December 1996.

Evolving views in the 2000s: the World Bank and the IMF

The World Bank

It took over a decade for the World Bank to finally accept that post-conflict reconstruction is not development as usual. In a policy research report entitled *Breaking the Conflict Trap*, the Bank finally recognized the high risk that these countries face of relapsing into conflict and the need for a strategy different from development as usual. The World Bank explicitly acknowledged that

> development strategies should look different in countries facing a high risk of conflict, where the problems and priorities are distinctive. ... For [countries that are in the first decade of postconflict peace] the risks of further conflict are exceptionally high: approximately half will fall back into conflict within the decade. This is an area that probably has the most scope for effective international interventions to reduce the incidence of conflict.[23]

As Paul Collier, a former director of the World Bank development research group and lead author of the above-mentioned report, recognized in 2008,

> Indeed, until recently, the organizations dedicated to economic development did not systematically distinguish post-conflict settings as requiring a distinctive approach. Yet policy in the post-conflict phase needs to be distinctive, both that of the government and that of the donor agencies. It should not be simply development as usual.[24]

In a major speech on securing development the same year, Robert Zoellick, President of the World Bank at the time, reckoned that "too often, the development community has treated states affected by fragility and conflict simply as harder cases of development." Expressing concern about the poor record of war-torn countries, he finally accepted that "development projects may need to be suboptimal economically – good enough rather than first-best."[25] Since I had been arguing this since the early 1990s, I could not agree more with this belated recognition that optimal policies are not mostly attainable or even desirable in countries in the transition from war.

Zoellick also accepted that

> These are not quick-fix countries: Support needs to be for the long-haul…. Funding mechanisms need to ensure continuity and stability of resources over a decade or more…. But this work is not just a matter of money. Commitment to helping fragile states also means sustained attention to signs of fragility and conflict, and countering the myriad risks that threaten security, governance, development – and legitimacy.[26]

The Bank also started financing fragile and conflict-affected countries through the State and Peace-Building Fund to support national and local governance and peacebuilding. Changing the status quo, however, has never been easy, and these institutions have proved difficult to change.

In 2011, the *World Bank Development Report: Conflict, Security, and Development* (WDR), stressed the need to "accept the links between security and development outcomes." Interestingly, although Zoellick refers to his speech in the prologue, there is no mention of it, either in the 384-page report or in the bibliography.

In the report, the World Bank tardily acknowledges – without any reference to the extensive academic or institutional work, as if it were an innovative idea – that "institutional transformation and good governance, which are important in development generally, work differently in fragile situations" and that "reforms of institutions in fragile contexts need to be adapted to the *political context* [emphasis added] rather than be technically perfect [first best]."[27]

Although it does not explicitly advocate for second-best policies in cases where peace is at stake, the report recognizes "the extent to which countries that have become resilient to violence have often used unorthodox, "best-fit" reform approaches that allow for flexibility and innovation. In this regard, the report mentions public support for employment; nonelectoral consultative mechanisms; and combinations of state, private sector, faith-based, traditional, and community structures for service delivery" as examples.[28]

The report does not distinguish, however, between fragile low-income countries in general and war-torn countries, which, although mostly fragile, they need not be, as was the case with El Salvador, Guatemala, Bosnia, Kosovo, and now with Colombia.[29] Moreover, war-torn countries face a much higher conflict risk than other fragile states, hence policymaking in the two cases must not be conflated (Chapter 3).

By lumping together inter- and intrastate conflicts, all kinds of insecurity (political violence, insurgencies, gangs, common crime, terrorism, drug trafficking), and countries undergoing multidisciplinary transitions to peace with those that are not (India, Colombia), the policy prescriptions of the World Bank report are indeed weak and blurred.

Interestingly, as Gareth Jones and Dennis Rodgers from the London School of Economics observed, despite focusing mainly on "security, justice, and jobs," the report's bibliography has major omissions in these areas and "is revealing of a very partial reading of the relevant literature regarding conflict and violence."[30]

Indeed, the bibliography reflects the typical development-as-usual approach of the Bank and of academics consulting for them. As the Bank posted a concept note with the bibliography for the report online in the summer of 2010, I exchanged emails with Nigel Roberts, one of the directors, where I noted that

> Looking at the bibliography I was a bit concerned about the emphasis on econometric work which is pretty irrelevant as far as I am concerned in countries with such bad data. On Africa, the work of Tony Addison is very important and the same with Susan Woodward's on Bosnia and Kosovo. I was surprised not to see their work in the bibliography. It is definitely worth looking at it.[31]

This was to no avail. These and other literature omissions, many cited in this book, were particularly glaring since they were of clear relevance to understanding the serious obstacles to peacebuilding that the lack of sustainable employment opportunities was creating in these countries. Disappointingly, there was not much new in the World Bank report on job creation, an area in which many of us expected the World Bank to have a comparative advantage vis-à-vis the UN to make innovative proposals.

Indeed, as Jones and Rodgers rightly criticized,

> Even a cursory glance at the Report … makes clear that jobs are considered the least important of the oft-repeated trinity of 'security, justice, and jobs.' Not only substantially less space is devoted to job creation, but fewer of the empirical examples in the

Report concern this issue, certainly compared to security and justice. ... [T]he Report claims that 'the international community has not paid as much attention to labor-intensive private sector development as is warranted,' and suggests – unsurprisingly, perhaps – that job creation in conflict-affected areas must be market-led. ... The WDR does acknowledge that some 'simple', 'community-based' public works programmes that do not 'distort' private sector activities might also be implemented, but only if they can be 'well-administered' and are sustainable in the long run.[32]

In Jones' and Rodgers' view, the lack of intellectual honesty in the World Bank report extends beyond the bibliography,

> It mentions ... [employment programs in] Ethiopia ... or India ... both of which have been widely praised as innovative initiatives, including by the International Labour Organization (ILO) – which the WDR conspicuously fails to mention, except in two footnotes. ... Indeed, ... the WDR arguably ought to have paid more attention to [ILO 2010 review] if it had really wanted to go beyond simplistic market-based solutions.[33]

The authors point out that the problem is both "ideological and normative" and conclude that, in its area of competence, the World Bank approach is most conflict insensitive and development as usual. As they point out,

> The World Bank's international economic policy advisory services have generally focused on growth rather than jobs, seeing the latter firstly as epiphenomena of the former, and secondly labour as simply one of several economic variables that ought to be determined by competitive market forces. ... [C]ontrarily to most of the other policy recommendations made in the Report, the ones concerning job creation are not very context-sensitive, but actually smack very much of the 'blueprint' development prescriptions that the Report seeks to avoid.[34]

Although not exactly thrilled that the report failed to acknowledge our work of the past decades, many of us were nevertheless glad to see that, in many areas, the report and its directors took ownership of our own ideas and premises. As de Soto and I had argued in 1995, the purpose of the arms-for-land program was "to provide potential beneficiaries with a modest but tangible *stake* [emphasis added] in this densely populated country's natural wealth as well as a productive, life-sustaining [income-generating] activity." As I had also argued in 1997, "[t]he purpose of the land program was to provide demobilizing combatants with a viable livelihood and *a stake* [emphasis added], however tiny, in the country's wealth."[35]

Given how much the Bank had opposed the arms-for-land program in 1992 – precisely because we were giving former combatants an *economic stake* in the country's resources, while there were others with the same needs – it was comforting to read in *The Guardian* two decades later that one of the directors of the report, Sarah Cliffe, emphasized the need for "an economic stake in society for people."[36] In terms that were music to our ears, the World Bank report had finally recognized that

> To break cycles of insecurity and reduce the risk of their recurrence, national reformers and their international partners need to build the legitimate institutions that can provide a sustained level of citizen security, justice, and jobs – offering a *stake in society to groups* [emphasis added] that may otherwise receive more respect and recognition from engaging in armed violence than in lawful activities.[37]

Last but not least, the World Bank report also presented some strange examples and made uninformed statements with regard to Mozambique, for example. To show that war-torn countries are among the "fastest making progress on MDGs [Millennium Development Goals]," the report points out that "Mozambique more than tripled its primary completion rate in just eight years, from 14 percent in 1999 to 46 percent in 2007."[38] Mozambique is an odd example for the World Bank to use since – after a quarter of a century of peace and unusually high levels of aid – the country's position in the *Human Development Index* deteriorated (Chapter 6).

Rather than using Mozambique as an example of progress, the Bank should have used it as an example of flagrant development failure. At the same time, the report ignores key reconstruction lessons from Mozambique to avoid conflict recurrence, in which the country mostly succeeded. This was particularly true with their policies toward maintaining salaries and livelihoods of former combatants to facilitate reintegration. It incorrectly mentions "the absence of any fighting" after the signature of the peace agreement when in fact renewed fighting put peace at risk early on in the transition (Chapter 7).

Also, this and other reports of the World Bank (and the IMF for that matter) exaggerate the importance of high rates of growth in war-torn countries, particularly where production levels are extremely low and where large volumes of aid and the local presence of foreign interveners lead to spikes in demand. The report says that Mozambique grew at rates of close to 8 percent in the post-conflict period up to 2007, which the country did. What it does not say is that it grew from extremely low levels – with per capita income of only $140 in 1992 – and with high levels of official aid through the period – of 36 percent of GDP during the first decade and over 20 percent in the second one (Table 6.1). By 2016, per capita income amounting to $620 was only two and a half times larger in real terms.

President Obama's nomination of Jim Yong Kim for the presidency of the World Bank surprised many for various reasons. For the purpose of our analysis, the interesting thing is how critical of the Bank Kim had been in the past. Was his selection, a tacit acceptance by President Obama that the Bank was in clear need for major change?

The title of Kim's 2000 book, *Dying for Growth: Global Inequality and the Health of the Poor*, written with colleagues at Partners in Health, an NGO they co-founded, was quite graphic in describing how Bank policies to achieve high growth often resulted in growing inequality and a deterioration in social services. Attributing the Washington-consensus "ideology" to what the BWIs promoted since the late 1970s, the authors explain in a vivid and brutal way that

> Strong GDP growth is commonly taken as the primary vital sign of a healthy economy and the best proof that a society is 'developing.'... [P]olicy over the last several decades has been driven by the perceived imperative to achieve and sustain growth. The conviction that enhanced economic growth automatically brings with it increased prosperity and a better life for all – not the already affluent but, in the long run, the disadvantaged members of society as well – is widespread, and until recently, virtually unquestionable. ... The proponents of neoliberal principles argue that economic growth ... will eventually 'trickle down' to improve the lives of the poor. ... While most of the world's poor are dying – in the sense of *yearning* – to reap some of the benefits of this growth, others are dying from the austerity measures imposed to promote it.[39]

The impact of Kim's leadership since he became president of the World Bank in July 2012 is still too soon to tell. He made significant changes in personnel and has faced turmoil from the Bank staff's reluctance to change. Interestingly, the two coheads of the much criticized World

Bank 2011 report left the Bank but were rewarded with important jobs in peacebuilding at the UN.

At the World Bank, changes in rhetoric are clear. The issue is how much of it is going to translate into practical changes in the way policies and strategies are designed and implemented. While the Bretton Woods institutions only used "economic" or "rapid" to qualify "growth" for most of the last two decades, in the last five years they have adopted the use of "inclusive" to qualify both "growth" and "policies." So far, much ado about nothing.

The International Monetary Fund

After recognizing its development-as-usual approach on El Salvador[40] and improving its working relationship with the UN in Guatemala in particular, the IMF Managing Director, Michel Camdessus, used his "G-7 in 1996: What is at Stake" speech to recognize that "the volume of our technical assistance resources is insufficient and our methods especially, are ill-suited" to post-conflict countries where "it is necessary to effect rapidly a sort of blood transfusion between the government of yesterday and that of tomorrow ... This kind of assistance ... must be reinvented."[41] This was a clear call at the highest level of the organization to think and act outside the box.

Despite this early realization, the IMF took its time to accept the special nature of economic reconstruction and growth in war-torn countries and the need to allow for second-best policies in cases where peace is at stake. It was only in 2005 that Fund staff accepted that tax policy in post-conflict situations may require adopting policies that are not "first best" from an efficiency point of view, and executive directors at the Fund agreed, with the right caveat that policies which are not optimal should be phased out as soon as feasible.[42]

As the food crisis hit low-income countries in 2008, Managing Director Dominique Strauss-Kahn came to acknowledge the powerful link between economic policies, poverty, and social unrest that could lead to war: "The threat is not only economic," he said, adding, "There is a real risk that millions will be thrown back into poverty. ... This is not only about protecting economic growth and household incomes – it is also about containing the threat of civil unrest, perhaps even of war."[43]

In 2010, he noted that "[h]istory is replete with examples of how economic and financial insecurity stoke social tensions, which in turn can undermine political stability, and even result in war. Getting the economy right and addressing threats to its stability can play an essential role in fostering the conditions for peace."[44]

The IMF also recognized the importance of ownership in 2010 when, following a donors' meeting on Haiti, Strauss-Kahn noted that for reconstruction to work, "the Haitian authorities need to be on the driver's seat."[45] Whether the Bretton Woods institutions have imposed macroeconomic discipline and a market-based framework on war-torn countries, or whether there has been national ownership for such policies is a much debated issue.[46]

As Christine Lagarde was taking over the helm of the organization, a 2011 policy paper entitled "Macroeconomic and Operational Challenges in Countries in Fragile Situations" and the "Staff Guidance Note" that followed in 2012 provided new operational guidance for Fund's engagement with low- and middle-income countries in fragile situations. The Fund recognized the unique challenges that these countries faced and found that "the implementation of Fund-supported programs in fragile LICs [low-income countries] has been bumpy, possibly reflecting too bold reform agendas or too optimistic assessments of implementation abilities."[47]

Just as important is the Fund's recognition that the delivery of "quick wins" in countries in fragile situations – which have economic consequences – may have a dramatic impact on building internal public support for reform. The Fund also recognizes that explicit attention to inclusive growth, job creation, and basic social safety nets would likely be a central component of the strategy of the government and foreign interveners. It clearly acknowledges that "to enhance peace and security, providing employment opportunities for low-skilled, idle youth may be of utmost importance. ... The financial implications of these measures should be fully incorporated in the fiscal program."[48] I could not have put it better myself.

However, the Fund falls short of committing the organization to supporting such a strategy and does not explicitly say how much it is willing to make its programs more flexible to ensure financing for them. In 2013, Susan Woodward argued that the Bretton Woods institutions recognize the need for flexibility and adaptability but recur to the danger of moral hazard whenever they are requested or pressured to deviate from their script. As she stresses, "their policies are not designed for the particular needs and conditions of countries emerging from war."[49]

Nevertheless, the Fund, and the Bank, have changed the rhetoric in a notorious way, often overdoing it. Lagarde used the word "inclusive" or "inclusiveness" 11 times in a short speech to Rwanda's parliament in 2015.[50]

Interestingly, in a mea culpa entitled "Neoliberalism: oversold?" three IMF staff from the research department recognized that instead of delivering growth, some neoliberal policies have increased inequality, in turn jeopardizing durable expansion. Their assessment is confined to the effects of two policies: removing restrictions on the movement of capital ("capital account liberalization") and fiscal consolidation; that is, policies to reduce fiscal deficits and debt levels ("austerity").[51]

While the first policy does not affect war-torn countries since they have no access to international capital markets, they are hurt by import liberalization, which the BWIs recommend, and on which more research specific for these countries is needed. On the other hand, the issue of austerity needs to be analyzed in more detail on how it affects these countries in particular and how it can constraint the inclusive policies for which Lagarde has become a vociferous preacher.

One would think that the Fund's Independent Evaluation Office (IEO) is the perfect venue to assess whether the policy shifts expressed by management – as exposed in Lagarde's rhetoric and the Fund's documents – has been translated into the Fund's programming and what impact the changes are having, if any. However, reading the reports of the IEO one cannot but feel that their staff has made a concerted effort to avoid issues relating to conflict and fragility.[52]

Eurodad's (European Network on Debt and Development) *Conditionality Watch*, which monitors IMF programs, shows that the IMF continues to attach neoliberal policy conditions to its programs in war-torn countries, despite the findings of the research department. They show, for example, that the new program for Guinea demands the reduction of the public sector wage bill, that is, to shrink the state in a situation where such action could be explosive.[53]

Reading the latest 2016 Article IV (annual surveillance) report for Liberia, one cannot but wonder why the IMF does so little to translate its new rhetoric into concrete impact on the ground. The IMF clearly fails to strongly recommend more inclusive and human development focused policies that could help the country to avoid another ebola-type of crisis associated with the vulnerabilities of public services despite huge volumes of aid. More inclusive policies are a must in Liberia going forward, particularly as aid falls and security likely deteriorates when UN peacekeeping personnel finally leave after 13 years in the country.[54]

Conclusions

Over the years, theoretical thinking and practical work at the UN did eventually spill over to the work of the Bretton Woods institutions.

This is clearly the case with thinking about economic reconstruction of war-torn countries in the post-Cold War period, including mostly countries at low levels of development coming out of civil war or other internal chaos.[55]

The change in rhetoric and in recent publications of these institutions accepting the special needs of war-torn countries and recommending policies that lead to inclusion must be translated into specific action to ensure that this is generally the case. Indeed, the lack of broad-based, equitable, and sustainable growth has been one of the most serious obstacles to effective peacebuilding in the aftermath of the Cold War. That the BWIs continue to promote policies that have clearly not worked in the past, expecting that this time they will do better, should be a matter of concern.

As Nobel Laureate Edmund Phelps has noted in the foreword to *Rebuilding War-Torn States*, "the idea promoted by some multilateral and bilateral donors that the war-torn countries can afford to follow laissez-faire policies – that in these countries unfettered markets work best and only the advanced countries need the paraphernalia of subsidies, licenses, regulations, corrective taxes, and so forth – is a costly ideology.... There may be a need for ... well-designed departures from laissez-faire – just as the United States in the early years of the republic adopted some of the infant industry ideas of Alexander Hamilton. Prohibitions against any and all interventions in the market place in a country whose institutions and culture have been destabilized seems dogmatic and injudicious."[56]

Notes

1 Del Castillo, "Economic Reconstruction of War-Torn Countries: The Role of the International Financial Institutions," *Seton Hall Law Review*, 38/4 (December 2008), 1284–1287; del Castillo, "The Bretton Woods Institutions, Reconstruction and Peacebuilding," in *Ending Wars, Consolidating Peace: Economic Perspectives*, Mats Berdal and Achim Wennmann, eds. (London: Routledge for The International Institute for Strategic Studies, 2010), 82.

2 For a comprehensive analysis of the role that the UN Security Council gives the BWIs in peace and security, see Kristen E. Boon, "Coining a New Jurisdiction: The Security Council as Economic Peacekeeper," *Vanderbilt Journal of Transnational Law*, 41 (October 2008); and Boon, "Open for Business: International Financial Institutions, Post-Conflict Economic Reform and the Rule of Law," *New York University Journal of International Law and Politics*, 513 (2007), 513–581.

3 Del Castillo, "The Bretton Woods Institutions, Reconstruction and Peacebuilding," 82.

4 For a discussion of why development organizations should not lead economic reconstruction and why the UN Secretariat would need to lead it effectively, see del Castillo, *Rebuilding War-Torn States*: 45–47 and 51–66.
5 World Bank policy changed after James Wolfensohn took over in 1995 and the organization became more involved in war-torn countries' problems, including reintegration.
6 See Secretary-General Boutros-Ghali, press conference at the Economic Commission for Asia and the Pacific (ESCAP, Bangkok, Thailand, April 2003); and his report to the Security Council (New York: Security Council, UN/25812 (21 May 1993).
7 Del Castillo, *Rebuilding War-Torn States*, 280–289.
8 IMF, *Fund Involvement in Post-conflict Countries* (Washington, DC: EBS/95/141, 16 August 1995).
9 Del Castillo, "Post-Conflict Peace-Building," 29–30.
10 Ibid., 27.
11 For a discussion of sequencing in economic reform, see del Castillo, "Economic Reconstruction and Reforms in Post-Conflict Countries," in *Building Sustainable Peace: Timing and Sequencing of Post-Conflict Reconstruction and Peacebuilding*, Arnim Langer and Graham K. Brown, eds. (Oxford: Oxford University Press, 2016), 51–71.
12 Del Castillo, *Rebuilding War-Torn States*, 40–42.
13 Ibid., 25–26.
14 James K. Boyce, *Economic Policy for Building Peace: The Lessons of El Salvador* (Boulder, Colo.: Lynne Rienner, 1996), 4 [published earlier in *World Development*, 23 (December 1995)].
15 Del Castillo, *Rebuilding War-Torn States*, 43–45.
16 Elizabeth J. Wood, "The Peace Accords and Postwar Reconstruction," *Economic Policy for Building Peace*, 83.
17 UN, *An Inventory of Post-Conflict Peacebuilding Activities* (New York: Report of an Interdepartmental Task Force Established by the Secretary-General, 1996).
18 UN, *International Colloquium on Post-Conflict Reconstruction Strategies: The Chairman's Synopsis and Conclusions* (Stadtschlaining, Austria: Austrian Study Centre for Peace and Conflict Resolution, June 23–24, 1995); and United Nations, *Collection of Papers* for the colloquium.
19 UNDP, *Sharing New Ground in Post-Conflict Situations: The Role of UNDP in Support of Reintegration Programmes* (New York: Evaluation Office, DP/2000/14, January 2000), 13, 38.
20 For details, see del Castillo, *Rebuilding War-Torn States*, 30–33.
21 Ibid.
22 Ibid.
23 World Bank, *Breaking the Conflict Trap: Civil War and Development Policy* (Washington, DC: World Bank and Oxford University Press, 2003), 6–7. The report was prepared by Paul Collier, V.L. Elliot, Håvard Hegre, Anke Hoeffler, Marta Reynal-Querol, Nicholas Sambanis.
24 Paul Collier, "Postconflict Economic Policy," in Charles T. Call, *Building States to Build Peace* (Boulder, Colo.: Lynne Rienner Publishers, 2008), 103.
25 Robert B. Zoellick, "Securing Development" (Speech by the President of the World Bank to the International Institute for Strategic Studies, Geneva, Switzerland, 12 September 2008).

26 Ibid.
27 World Bank, *World Bank Development Report: Conflict, Security, and Development*, 104, 106–107. The lack of reference to previous work is also true when the report argues for "time and patience" and urges much longer-time frames both with regard to engagement with fragile states and to assessment of results; ibid., 193–194.
28 Ibid., 106–107.
29 The World Bank now accepts that fragility is not limited to low-income countries. The IMF uses the term "low- and middle-income countries in fragile situations," which I prefer to "fragile states."
30 Gareth A. Jones and Dennis Rodgers, "The World Bank's World Development Report 2011 on Conflict, Security and Development: A Critique Through Five Vignettes,"*Journal of International Development*, 23 (July 2011): 980–995 (p. 3 of electronic copy).
31 Personal exchange. Despite several attempts, Roberts could not see me or talk on the phone to discuss this and other issues.
32 Gareth Jones and Dennis Rodgers, "The World Bank's World Development Report 2011 on Conflict, Security and Development," 12.
33 Ibid. For citations from the World Bank, see *World Bank Development Report: Conflict, Security, and Development*, 200, 176.
34 Ibid.
35 De Soto and del Castillo, "Implementation of Comprehensive Peace Agreements," 195; del Castillo, "The Arms-for-Land Deal in El Salvador," 344.
36 Julian Borger, "World Bank Urges New Focus on Global Development in Fragile States," *The Guardian*, 11 April 2011.
37 World Bank, *World Bank Development Report*, 8 and 36.
38 Ibid., 6, 51.
39 Jim Yong Kim, Joyce V. Millen, Alex Irwin, and John Gershman, *Dying for Growth: Global Inequality and the Health of the Poor* (Monroe, Maine: Common Courage Press), 6–7.
40 IMF, *Fund Involvement in Post-Conflict Countries.*
41 Michel Camdessus, "The G-7 in 1996: What is at Stake," Address by the Managing Director of the IMF at the Colloquium 'Les Enjeux du G-7' (Lyons, France, June 1996).
42 For details, see del Castillo, *Rebuilding War-Torn States*, 280–81.
43 Cited by African Rising (2008).
44 See IMF, press release, "IMF Managing Director Dominique Strauss-Kahn Says Economic Recovery Linked to Global Stability and Peace," No. 10/22, 31 January 2010.
45 See *IMF Survey Online*, "IMF Chief Emphasizes Support for Haiti," 1 April 2010.
46 In some cases, the lack of national ownership is due to the fact that macroeconomic policies have been imposed by national leaders without public support. This was the case in Afghanistan in 2002. See del Castillo, *Rebuilding War-Torn* States, 170–171.
47 IMF, *Macroeconomic and Operational Challenges in Countries in Fragile Situations* (Washington, DC: 15 June 2011), 5; IMF, *Staff Guidance Note on the Fund's Engagement with Countries in Fragile Situations* (Washington, DC: 25 April 2012).
48 Ibid., 8.

49 Susan Woodward, "The IFIs and Post-Conflict Political Economy," in *Political Economy of Statebuilding*, 141–42.
50 IMF, "Rwanda – Taking on the Future, Staying Ahead of the Curve," speech by Christine Lagarde (Kigali, 27 January 2015).
51 Jonathan D. Ostry, Prakash Loungani, and Davide Furceri, "Neoliberalism: Oversold?" *Finance & Development*, 53 (June 2016).
52 See IEO webpage.
53 See Eurodad webpage.
54 IMF, *Liberia: Article IV Consultation and Staff Report* (Washington, DC: July 2016).
55 For other UN contributions, see Richard Jolly, Louis Emmerij, Dharam Ghai, and Frédéric Lapeyre, *UN Contributions to Development Thinking and Practice* (Bloomington: Indiana University Press, 2004).
56 Phelps, Foreword in *Rebuilding War-Torn States*, viii–ix.

5 Peacebuilding at the UN – from conceptualization to operationalization

- From Boutros-Ghali to Kofi Annan to Ban Ki-moon
- Peacebuilding architecture – world summit outcome (2005)
- The UN peacebuilding architecture 10-year record: an assessment
- It's the Economy, Stupid
- Conclusions

Chapter Five will discuss the tepid effort that Boutros-Ghali made to make his integrated approach to human security operational and argues that the progenitor of the concept of peacebuilding failed to take the small practical steps needed to put it into practice. It also argues that Kofi Annan did little better and that some of the reports during Annan's tenure had unintended consequences. The section explains the impact of these reports and describes the purpose and flaws of the Peacebuilding Architecture. The chapter concludes with a brief assessment of the latter, focusing on how it has affected economic reconstruction and therefore peacebuilding during the last decade.

From Boutros-Ghali to Kofi Annan to Ban Ki-moon

To paraphrase de Soto, "Far from midwifing cogent policy and strategy, *post conflict peacebuilding* was orphaned in infancy."[1] Boutros-Ghali's conceptualization of the need to integrate political, security, social, and economic issues in the post-conflict context notwithstanding, he was unable to make it fully operational at the UN Secretariat. As de Soto pointed out,

> With UN Headquarters speaking in dissonant voices, there was little hope of building a broader consensus within and beyond the UN. No wonder that some players took the conceptual fuzziness and sprawl as a license to go about their activities as before. Key

multilateral players swaddled themselves in the coat of many colours provided by *post-conflict peacebuilding*, making little or no effort to adjust their priorities or practices so as to synchronise them with the fundamentally political objective that it was meant to enshrine.[2]

At the same time, since 1995, the development institutions such as the UNDP, the World Bank, and bilateral agencies such as USAID created or expanded specialized departments to deal with post-conflict economic reconstruction and peacebuilding. This did not necessarily mean that peacebuilding structures were adequate for the challenge. In 2000, the Evaluation Office of UNDP found that, "In many cases, UNDP area-based economic and social recovery programmes amount to little more than a collection of loosely linked sub-activities rather than well-designed, coherent programme packages. In part this results from the pressures of post-conflict situations, but it is further exacerbated by a lack of experience, training and guidance."[3]

Most often, though, these institutions focused on the larger issue of "fragile states," including both conflict-affected and other poor and vulnerable states. As argued earlier, the latter unquestionably share many of the features of the former but lack the "high risk of conflict recurrence" that is unique to war-torn countries (Chapter 3). It is precisely such risk that distinguishes the two and makes return on investment in war-torn countries much higher. Likewise, such risk imposes constraints for policymaking in conflict situations different from those faced by other fragile states. It is precisely the inability to deal with such risk that has been at the heart of foreign interveners' critical failure to make peacebuilding more effective.

Kofi Annan, who took over as secretary-general in 1997, did little better than his predecessor to improve the operational capacity of the UN Secretariat to deal with war-torn countries. This was not for lack of expert opinions and commissioned reports. While the report *Renewing the United Nations: A Programme for Reform*[4] noted that "the SG [Secretary-General] has designated the Department of Political Affairs [the political department] as the United Nations focal point for post-conflict peacebuilding," Annan failed to take action, as Boutros-Ghali had earlier[5].

As the report envisaged, by becoming the leader in peacebuilding, the political department would provide "the mechanism for ensuring that the UN efforts in countries that are emerging from crisis are fully integrated and faithfully reflect the mission objectives specified by the Security Council and the Secretary General." This department would "carry out its functions in its capacity as convenor of the Executive Committee for Peace and Security." Despite the clear message, no operational steps were taken to ensure the department's ability to discharge this function, and an integrated approach under clear leadership remained elusive.[6]

Jean Arnault, who negotiated the peace in Guatemala in 1996 and was the special representative of the Secretary-General (SRSG) in several UN peace operations since then, argued that the 2000 *Report of the Panel on UN Peacekeeping*, known as the Brahimi Report, gave peacebuilding activities a much more critical role than previous reports.[7]

From an economics of peace point of view – which is what this book is all about – I will argue that the Brahimi Report rightly pointed out that the "peacebuilders' task [is] to support the political, *social and economic changes* [emphasis added] that create a secure environment that is self-sustaining." It also pointed out that "effective peace-building is, in effect, a hybrid of political and development activities targeted at the sources of conflict."[8] In this way, the Brahimi Report made a contribution, since many of the UN reports seemed to ignore such a need.

But, as I have argued elsewhere, the Brahimi Report had unintended and dire consequences by proposing that UNDP and the World Bank lead peacebuilding operations. In fact, such a recommendation was in direct contradiction to Boutros-Ghali's notion of "post-conflict peacebuilding," where such activities would be led at the "political" and "operational" level by the SRSG on the ground. By contrast, the Brahimi Report advocated a continuation of the failed development-as-usual approach to economic reconstruction and peacebuilding led by development institutions that had proven so ineffective in consolidating peace from the end of the Cold War to the turn of the millennium.[9]

Two elements of the Brahimi Report were striking. The report allocated responsibility for the formulation of peacebuilding strategies, including both preventive and post-conflict, to the Executive Committee, in which neither the economics department nor the IMF participated, although the World Bank was invited to join. Of 200 experts interviewed for the report, the Bank's staff was included, but no one from the IMF was. By doing so, the report essentially ignored critical economic reconstruction issues that haunted peace processes in the early 1990s and continued to do so – and confirmed the lack of communication between diplomats at the UN and economics officials at the IMF.

Did members of the panel consider that economic issues were not relevant to peacebuilding activities? How could financial requirements of peace-related programs be incorporated into the IMF-sponsored economic programs if peacebuilders at the UN and economic stabilization and reform gurus at the IMF who advised the government on these issues did not even talk to each other at a technical level? The otherwise positive decision of allocating responsibility to a committee chaired by the head of the political department was undone by this gaping omission.

The other striking feature is that the report concluded that, "operationally," that is, at the level of the implementation of post-conflict strategies on the ground, the UNDP had "untapped potential" and that, in cooperation with other UN agencies, funds, and programs including the World Bank, the UNDP was best placed to "lead peacebuilding activities." Thus, as Neclâ Tschirgi noted, peacebuilding found temporary and tenuous shelter under the roof of the development agencies.[10]

This was particularly puzzling since a UNDP evaluation of its work in conflict countries had recognized that "the normally close association of UNDP with governments seemed to leave it particularly ill-equipped to deal with new emergency situations."[11] As mentioned earlier, key nonstate actors do not generally perceive UNDP as an impartial player given its institutional partnership with governments. This was often a problem that we experienced while monitoring the peace agreement in El Salvador.[12]

After a decade of UN multidisciplinary operations, Susan Woodward warned in 2002 about the lack of any systematic analysis of the contribution of economic factors to peacebuilding.[13] Despite her seminal work in calling attention to this deficiency, academics and practitioners alike continued to largely neglect the economic aspects of peacebuilding. Such neglect was and continues to be glaring in comparison to the interest generated by other aspects of the transition, such as political and security reform, the rule of law, human rights and transitional justice. There have been, of course, important exceptions, many of which are listed in the bibliography.

Using the metaphor of a gaping hole in the UN institutional capacity, Annan recommended the so-called Peacebuilding Architecture. A matter of much debate is whether this architecture – adopted pursuant to the UN 60th anniversary World Summit Outcome in 2005 – improved the operational capacity of the organization in ensuring that peace is sustained in countries with multidisciplinary UN operations.[14]

As de Soto and I have posited in our 2016 *Obstacles to Peacebuilding Revisited*, on which this chapter relies heavily, the answer to this question seems to be unequivocal since, by design, the new architecture lacked an operational mandate. Has it had any other impact?

Or has it added to the confusion within the UN system and contributed to waste, cost-inefficiencies, and more suffering as peace, security, and prosperity continue to elude many of the countries under UN watch?

Peacebuilding architecture – world summit outcome (2005)

Identical resolutions of the General Assembly and the Security Council created the Peacebuilding Architecture in December 2005. This architecture has received much attention, particularly in relation to its tenth anniversary. A large number of studies, including two new books in this *Series on Global Institutions,* both by insiders and academics often working with them,[15] provide a comprehensive review of the justification for creating such structure and its achievements as well as its many flaws, from design to implementation.

It is not possible to delve here into the details of the origin, the shifting ideas and compromises in design along the way, the expectations of the new architecture, the evolving mandate and modes of operation, and the resources devoted to it, all of which have been analyzed at great length in the studies mentioned.[16]

My purpose here is to focus only on the elements that are necessary to analyze the impact that the architecture has had with regard to improving the capacity of the organization to deal with the economic and social aspects of peacebuilding. Has the architecture contributed to integrate the latter into the many other aspects (i.e., security, political, human rights, gender, and transitional justice) that affect a country's transition to peace, stability, and prosperity? I will also focus on points of disagreement with previous reviews or differences in emphasis as well as on specific issues that I find lacking from the discussion. Finally, I posit that the new fuss at the UN about "sustaining peace" looks like an effort to divert attention from the organization's continued lack of operational capacity to deal with peacebuilding, and I recommend that Secretary-General António Guterres address this issue head on upon assuming UN leadership in January 2017.

The final architecture was quite different from what the experts had recommended, reflecting political realities at the UN. It nevertheless contained the three institutions in the original design.[17] The Peacebuilding Commission (hereafter Commission), an intergovernmental advisory body to the Council and the Assembly and reporting to them, was composed of 31 member states elected on a rotating basis from various constituencies and making decisions by consensus, itself a recipe for paralysis and lowest common denominator decisions.[18]

The Commission's three main purposes are to advise countries on integrated strategies for peacebuilding and recovery; to marshal resources and ensure predictable and sustainable financing; and to improve coordination and coherence as well as to develop best practices and maintain support for these countries.[19]

The Commission organized itself into three distinct entities: the Organizational Committee, the Country-Specific Configurations (CSCs, the main instrument for promoting peacebuilding at the country level), and the Working Group on Lessons Learned. The three entities developed on separate tracks, and their performance depended greatly on their membership and leadership. According to Tschirgi and Richard Ponzio, "[r]umor had it that the host governments saw the PBC [Commission] as an 'ATM' at the UN and were reluctant to have non-donor countries (like El Salvador) chairing the CSCs."[20]

The resolutions also created the Peacebuilding Support Office (hereafter Support Office) to act as secretariat to the Commission; to coordinate peacebuilding efforts, including communication and information, within the UN and with outside actors; and to be the repository of best practices. This office was also assigned some analytical responsibilities for which it was not given adequate resources. As Carolyn McAskie, a former head of this office noted, its name "deliberately meant to underscore the non-operational nature" of the new entity.[21]

The resolutions further created the Peacebuilding Fund (hereafter PBFund),[22] with a mandate to provide quick impact and catalytic funding to fill critical gaps in countries at high risk of conflict relapse. With an initial target of $250 million and contributions surpassing that amount, decisions on lending are made at the Support Office, thus depriving the Commission of the power of the purse.[23]

However, donor support is not keeping up with targets. As Secretary-General Ban Ki-moon reported in 2015, "*My* [emphasis added] Peacebuilding Fund ... urgently needs additional resources to continue operations at the current level of $100 million per year."[24] By 2015, the PBFund was supporting around 20 countries, and over half of its resources were spent in the six members on the Commission's agenda, all of them in Africa.[25]

As another former head of the Support Office, Judy Cheng-Hopkins, rightly noted, the "gaping hole" metaphor which Kofi Annan used did not accurately depict the existing situation at the UN.[26] But his justification for the architecture – both the "devastating failures" in Angola and Srebrenica in the early 1990s – at the time Annan was in charge of peacekeeping operations and the bleak record that "roughly half of all countries that emerge from war lapsed back into violence within five years" were real indeed.[27]

There was then, and still remains, an archipelago of unconnected units in the UN system dealing with a variety of peacebuilding issues in a fragmented and inefficient way. As Rob Jenkins with good reason warned, "the *new* architecture did not supplant the *old* peacebuilding structures," including existing operational units in the political and peacekeeping departments. Instead, "the three new bodies were inserted on top of, adjacent to, and overlapping with pre-existing organization units engaged in peacebuilding work."[28]

With both the Commission and the Support Office lacking an operational mandate, the new architecture could not possibly solve the UN's own deficiencies to carry out effective peacebuilding. An improvement in the operational capacity of the organization could have been achieved by reforming, consolidating, and beefing up the existing operational capacity in the political and peacekeeping departments at headquarters and in UN operations on the ground.

In 2005 – and with a mandate from the Security Council – the political department had set up peacebuilding missions in the field in East Timor and Sierra Leone. In those operations, an executive representative of the secretary-general (ERSG) was appointed by the Council with an explicit peacebuilding mandate and other coordinating functions similar to those of the SRSGs that headed peacekeeping operations.[29]

Because of this, the new architecture clearly failed to overcome the potential clashes of competence, waste of resources, and bureaucratic hurdles that Boutros-Ghali argued was imperative to consolidate peace (which, for the record, he did not attempt to overcome himself). On the contrary, it clearly added to them in countries where such UN operations were in place.

While many praise the intergovernmental nature of the Commission as its most important feature,[30] Lise Howard specifically argues that the worst that could have happened to operational peacebuilding efforts on the ground is to be directed from New York, particularly when directives result from intergovernmental political bargaining or from a Support Office lacking appropriate analytical capabilities.[31] I could not agree more.

Recognizing that the mandates of the chairs of the Commission and the SRSG or the ERSGs in place in a country "could be seen as duplicative – advocating for the country, mobilizing resources, and bringing coherence amongst aid programs," Cheng-Hopkins nevertheless argues that

[t]he most successful chairs ... are those most conscious of their own comparative advantage – the ability to convene and speak frankly with other ambassadors in-country and thus gather valuable information; the ability to have a tête-à-tête with heads of state as government to government ... Chairs cannot be made *persona non grata* the way SRSGs can.[32]

Her justification for duplication and waste is odd in many ways. Government representatives – even those from P-5 (permanent five) countries in the Security Council can be made *persona non grata* and asked to leave host countries. This indeed happens from time to time. As Reuters reported, the president of Venezuela expelled three US diplomats, including the acting head of mission in October 2013.

The only reason to justify duplication, then, would be that the SRSG or the ERSGs cannot fulfil his or her position's mandate, in which case they must be replaced, rather than get somebody else to fulfil their mandate. To install yet another layer above or parallel to them not only complicates and confuses matters, it also leads to more inefficiency and waste. More worrisome, it imposes an unnecessary burden on weak and overstretched national governments by creating additional and often conflicting demands for their time, expertise, and other scarce resources.

In the 1990s, when I could observe it first hand, able SRSGs in Mozambique, Angola, and East Timor – Aldo Ajello, M.J. Anstee, and Sergio Vieira de Mello, respectively – were able to perform all of the tasks that Cheng-Hopkins mentioned without the need for anyone to cover for their professional or communication deficiencies. In the case of Mozambique (Chapter 7), for example, the fact that Ajello was speaking with one voice – that included the diplomatic community in Maputo with whom he consulted on a day-to-day basis – was a key factor in ensuring that the parties would view him

> not as the delegate of a remote bureaucracy in New York but as the representative of the international community. Each time the SRSG had to take a tough position against either party in order to keep the peace process on track, it was clear that he spoke on its behalf, a fact that was reinforced by strategically timed messages from the Security Council itself.[33]

In fact, Ajello also had the support of the Security Council that had appointed him. This has not been the case with the Commission's chairs since the Council has been rather dismissive of the Commission and has hardly consulted it.

As McAskie noted, soon after being admitted to the Commission's agenda, high-level delegations from Sierra Leone and Burundi arrived in New York in October 2006, with high expectations on how the Commission could facilitate putting "their development back on track." As she noted, with little funding for peacebuilding and an $8 billion peacekeeping budget it was difficult to change the "security trumps development" perception that many countries had. As she reckons,

> one of our most disappointing discoveries was the realization that many donor governments on the PBC [Commission] ... when asked what they were going to do concerning ...Burundi and Sierra Leone, ... politely explained that these countries were not on their lists of countries eligible for aid. ... Too many donors have confused 'funding for peacebuilding' with their generous contributions to the Peacebuilding Fund. The PBF [PBFund] ... [provided] quick-response funding for critical peacebuilding efforts. But it was never intended to substitute for long-term recovery, reconstruction, and sustainable development in post-conflict countries.[34]

It might have been a bit naive on her part to think that if the Security Council followed the practice of closing up operations as soon as the country's remaining needs were of a development nature (leaving the UN development group in charge to finance it through voluntary contributions), the Commission would come up with the necessary funding to cover such needs.

But it is precisely in those cases where the Commission could be most useful; that is, in countries exiting from the Security Council and requiring support for peacebuilding activities that would promote inclusive, dynamic, and sustainable growth that would allow them to sustain the peace and resume development as usual.

On a conceptual basis, Jenkins noted that the new architecture represented an attempt on the part of the UN to "rethink its doctrines and organizational structures" on how to promote peace and build states effectively.[35] Given the dismal record up to that time, this was long overdue.

By ignoring previous analytical and operational work at the UN since the early 1990s, however, new attempts often wasted a great deal of time and effort recreating ideas that already existed and trying to package them as if they were new. Issues such as the need for "redefinition of relationships and comparative advantages," the fundamentally "political" nature of peacebuilding, and the importance of "strong national ownership" of policies had been on the table for at least a decade. As they emerged in the new context, a sense of déjà vu and lack of progress was inevitable.[36]

McAskie argues that with a change in leadership at the UN in January 2007, the history of why and how the architecture came about was lost – "from the Brahimi Report, which gave birth to a more integrated approach to peace operations through the work of the High-Level Panel which proposed the PBA [Peacebuilding Architecture] in 2004, to the secretary-general's response in 2005 and the resolution which came out of the Millennium Plus 5 Summit in 2005." Tschirgi and Ponzio also note the loss of leadership at a critical time.[37]

But in fact the same thing had happened when Annan took over from Boutros-Ghali and many of the premises developed in the immediate post-Cold War period were lost in transition. That was particularly puzzling given that Annan had been an insider. Yet, it was not surprising given the lack of institutional memory at the UN that leads its member states and staff members to be constantly trying to reinvent the wheel when in fact they are mostly pedalling on a stationary bike.[38]

The UN peacebuilding architecture 10-year record: an assessment

There seems to be a broad consensus among academics and practitioners, in the review processes at the UN as well as in recipient countries, that the Commission and Support Office have not made a significant difference let alone improved matters in any important way. In 2014 Berdal, for example, noted that the 2005 Peacebuilding Architecture, specifically intended to coordinate the actions of peacebuilding actors, "has not managed to overcome the structural and political obstacles to effective coordination and delivery."[39]

Most other reviews have also been far from flattering and mention, among others, the "deep disappointment," "negligible relevance," "meagre net value-added," and "mixed" impact of the architecture. They also mention the "zombie nature of organizations that exist but do not have a life and have become symbols of "UN inaction."[40]

The 2010 intergovernmental review of the Peacebuilding Architecture acknowledged the unfulfilled expectations of the Commission, the lack of impact on the ground, and the weak relationship with the Security Council as well as the scarce weight that the Support Office had within the Secretariat. The review concluded that the UN was still not rising to the peacebuilding challenges.[41]

In its response to the review, the political department produced a 10-page memorandum, circulated to the Senior Peacebuilding Group, chaired by the Support Office, arguing that the 2005 architecture had fragmented rather than consolidated UN efforts to create stability and build peace, an evaluation that I share. The department's view was that the Commission should not be focusing on developing peacebuilding strategies but on marshalling resources for what had already been agreed.[42]

Mariska van Beijnum argued recently that the Commission is still confronted with considerable scepticism and criticism. The Commission "has not managed to reform itself in light of the criticisms expressed in the 2010 review, with major questions remaining about what [it] is able to offer in the face of new threats and challenges to peace, security, and development." Experts continue to mention as some of the more worrisome factors that no new country has been included on the Commission's agenda since 2011, its inability to prevent conflict escalation in countries under its watch, and its powerlessness to keep the Security Council informed on major violent conflicts in countries on its agenda.[43]

In 2015, as part of the 10-year intergovernmental review process of the architecture, the secretary-general appointed an advisory group of experts and had it chaired by a former vice-president of the Commission. In July 2015, the group released a report entitled *The Challenge of Sustaining Peace* (hereafter 2015 Report).[44]

The report rightly points out that the Commission has yet to fully deliver and acknowledge that peacebuilding at the UN is "an afterthought," that the organization continues to work in "silos" and that the different bodies dealing with peacebuilding still fail to work together.[45] The Commission and Support Office added to those other silos already existing in 2005 rather than consolidating them.

The report calls for a "comprehensive approach to sustaining peace" not unlike Boutros-Ghali's call for an "integrated approach to human security" (Chapter 1), but it also fails to propose a feasible strategy to make such an approach operational and viable in terms of human and financial resources.

The report fails to present any new idea, insight, innovation, or interesting empirical finding on the issue of "peacebuilding" itself or on the particular role of the Commission and Support Office. The case studies are most disappointing since they hardly add any new insights on the impact that the architecture is having in promoting peacebuilding – or failing to do so. Like the 2011 *World Development Report*, the 2015 Report is based on a partial bibliography and ignores key work in the area of peacebuilding.

Without any doubt, the 2015 Report contributes to the sense of *déjà vu* mentioned earlier by rehashing old arguments, often framed with new terminology to misguide newcomers to the field to think that they are new. For example, the report posits that "peacebuilding must be understood as an inherently political process" and calls for "inclusive national ownership" and "realistic timelines for UN operations." With a very restricted bibliography, the report does not even acknowledge extensive previous work on all these issues.

Some have even argued that the concept of "sustained peace" is a major contribution of the 2015 Report because it gives the sense of a continuous state of affairs where peacebuilding takes place for preventive purposes as well as for post-conflict ones. I would argue that this is yet another instance of disregarding the past.[46]

As I explained in Chapter 1, the conception of peacebuilding as both preventive and post-conflict activities dates back to the 1990s. Indeed, Boutros-Ghali explicitly made this clear in his *Supplement* by referring to "peace-building, whether preventive or post-conflict."[47] The reason he made a clear distinction in his *Agenda* between the preventive and post-conflict case is that the Security Council had asked him to recommend how to strengthen the capacity of the UN for preventive diplomacy, peacemaking and peacekeeping, so he only needed to add peacebuilding in the post-conflict context, a new activity at the UN for which he also wanted to make recommendations.

Soon after assuming leadership of the organization, Secretary-General Ban Ki-moon maintained such conception of peacebuilding for both preventive and post-conflict situations and also emphasized the issue of ownership. However, he improved the concept by explicitly noting that it needs to be "carefully prioritized," something that had been lacking in the past. In a memo to all his senior staff of 22 May 2007, Ban communicated his decision:

> In order to better develop an overarching strategy to inform peacebuilding efforts and ensure coherent and coordinated approaches across all UN agencies and with non-UN partners, the following is endorsed as the conceptual basis for peacebuilding:
>
> *Peacebuilding involves a range of measures targeted to reduce the risk of lapsing or relapsing into conflict by strengthening national capacities at all levels for conflict management, and to lay the foundations for sustainable peace and development. Peacebuilding strategies must be coherent and tailored to the specific needs of the country concerned, based on national ownership, and should*

comprise a carefully prioritized, sequenced, and therefore relatively narrow set of activities aimed at achieving the above objectives.[48]

Thus, the statement of Mr. Olof Skoog, permanent representative of Sweden and former Chair of the Peacebuilding Commission, that the 2015 Report "reminds us of the *conceptual shift in our thinking* [emphasis added] on peacebuilding, acknowledged by both the Council and the General Assembly. Peacebuilding can no longer be confined to post-conflict recovery. Sustaining peace encompasses activities aimed at preventing the outburst, resurgence and continuation of conflict," is unwarranted. It is made by someone clearly unfamiliar with the quarter of a century history of peacebuilding as a concept at the UN (Chapter 1).[49]

That Skoog thinks that that is the "single most important outcome of the peacebuilding review" is also quite telling. The membership cannot agree on how the Commission can perform its post-conflict peacebuilding activities more cost effectively, but it seems willing to let the Commission assume peacebuilding responsibilities also in conflict prevention.[50]

Neither the term nor the concept of "sustained peace, which has now become the new buzzword at the UN, is new. Ten years earlier, the term was used by James Dobbins and his colleagues at RAND in *The UN's Role in Nation-Building*, where one of the sections is entitled "Sustained Peace."[51] Several organizations have used the exact term in some of their events and programs.

Moreover, the terms "sustained peace," "sustainable peace," "durable peace," "peace sustainability," "making peace sustainable," and the "preservation of peace" have been used interchangeably since the 1990s, and all relate to the concept of preserving peace where it exists and making it long lasting after it is restored.[52]

At the same time, it is rather surprising that, without rigorously analyzing whether the UN record has changed in any significant and positive way since 2005, and without making any cost-effectiveness analysis of the use of resources to date, the report calls for more resources for peacebuilding.[53] Would increasing the capacity of the Support Office that the report recommends be more cost effective than increasing operational capacity at the peacekeeping and political departments, particularly the operational capacity of UN operations on the ground? One could be forgiven for wondering whether the report's recommendation might lead to throwing more good money after bad. That is my distinct impression.

A few months earlier, the Future United Nations Development System (FUNDS) project put together a group of experts and practitioners to analyze whether the system is equipped for twenty-first century peacebuilding. The report entitled *Peacebuilding Challenges for the UN Development System* states that "radical changes are needed if the UN and its development system are not to become even further marginalized." The report also notes that despite its decade of existence, the Commission has failed "to establish itself as a relevant and impactful institution." In fact, almost 40 percent of respondents to a FUNDS survey found that the Commission had proved to be "inefficient or very inefficient."[54]

As the FUNDS project recommends, a re-examination is long overdue of the UN field presence in conflict-prone states, including the nature and composition of a more unified country presence, its leadership, the selection and training of suitable staff, the provision of resources, and the clear and unified delegation of authority from headquarters in New York and Geneva. This is essential to better prioritize activities based on comparative advantages. Indeed, the report strongly calls for fixing what does not work rather than calling for new layers.[55]

It's the Economy, Stupid

If I were to coin a term for Secretary-General António Guterres on what is really missing from the UN peacebuilding agenda that could help countries overcome the high risk of conflict, I would paraphrase James Carville: "It's the economy, stupid."[56]

By rehashing old arguments, the 2015 Report detracted from its own conclusion that, ten years after the creation of the peacebuilding architecture, there was a need to take a "fresh look" at the "whole approach" to peacebuilding – not at the concept itself.[57] This is something that Secretary-General Guterres must seriously consider as soon as feasible.

By arguing that "[o]vercoming socio-economic grievances, offering populations the means to earn livelihoods and creating the foundations for inclusive, broad-based economic growth ... integral to any transition from conflict to normalcy," the 2015 Report has touched on a particularly important point.[58]

As Tony Addison warned in 2003, "well-designed economic reforms raise the chances that recovery will be broad-based, instead of narrow, in its benefits" but "badly designed policy change can be an impediment to the implementation of the peace process."[59] Over a decade later, the UN in general, and the Commission in particular, continues to ignore such an important paradigm.

Indeed, the Commission and Support Office have flagrantly ignored the need for inclusive economic and social policies as a key ingredient of peacebuilding. Lack of inclusion not only contributes to the high risk of conflict but creates a breeding ground for pandemics such as Ebola, which has affected three of the six countries on the Commission's agenda.

In these countries, failure to utilize aid effectively and inclusively has led to decrepit infrastructure and poor health systems that breed both disease and discontent among the large majority of the population. Instead of acting preventively in advocating improvement in basic conditions in countries under its watch, the Commission reactively put his efforts into fighting Ebola after it had hit three countries on its agenda by marshalling financing for it.

The issue that the UN membership and other foreign interveners should be debating is precisely this: how to support policies that can help overcome some of the major obstacles to peacebuilding which have been impairing the UN record over the last quarter of a century. Most importantly, the debate should focus on how to discourage current policies that lack inclusion and interfere with UN peacebuilding efforts at all levels.[60]

Criticisms of the lack of country diversity on the Commission's agenda (all six countries are from Africa) and the fact that no new country was selected in the past four years should not be disparaged.[61] However, a more critical question is why the Commission has failed to attract countries (on the Security Council agenda or not) at an early stage of the transition to peace or at a later stage in countries about to exit from the Council, where it is clearly where it can have an impact.

In countries exiting the Council, the transition from reconstruction to normal development has proved particularly difficult because of the ineffective and fragmented support that these countries get from the UN development system. This is a phase in which countries need support to sustain the progress they have painfully achieved – or such gains are likely to be reversed (Chapter 7).

Given the mandate of the Commission to marshal resources and ensure predictable and sustainable financing, it could also play an important role in supporting peacebuilding efforts in the so-called "aid orphans." The inclusion of Liberia in 2010 – hailed by the former head of the Support Office Cheng-Hopkins as one of the main achievements of her early mandate – was a flagrant mistake. The latter was probably explained by the fact that she went "mindlessly and desperately, to get two new countries to overcome the criticism that only four countries were in the Commission's agenda."[62]

Clearly unnoticed by the Support Office was the fact that Liberia was one of the two largest recipients of economic aid, which amounted to a staggering 55 percent of GDP a year on average during the first decade. At the time of its inclusion on the Commission's agenda in 2010, and still six years later, Liberia had a large peacekeeping operation in place (Tables 6.1, 6.2). By 2007, after five years in the country, the cost of the UN operation to keep the peace was still over 70 percent of Liberia's GDP.[63]

The conclusion of the 2015 Report that "despite a decade of focus, financing for sustaining peace remains scarce, inconsistent and unpredictable,"[64] seems also to ignore the situation of Liberia that received unprecedented levels of aid and peacekeeping support. At the same time, the travesty of including it in the Commissions agenda deprived aid orphans of much-needed funding.

As the report notes, the existing architecture pays insufficient attention to supporting inclusive development processes that can sustain peace. This has been particularly true in the case of Liberia where a continuation of "growth without development" policies of the past have left 75–80 percent of the population living at subsistence levels and excluded from any peace dividend in terms of better livelihoods or services.[65]

Surprisingly, it was Karin Landgren, the SRSG and head of the peacekeeping operation in Monrovia, who bluntly told the Commission in unambiguous terms in May 2015 that the main sources of potential instability were "structural factors including Liberia's economic model (based on the export of unprocessed resources)." In her view, the "growth without development" model, which has not changed for over a hundred years, provides "limited benefits to citizens" and has "limitations for the development of human capacity." This, together with "social exclusion, including as a result of patronage networks" which are dominant in the economic and political life of the country, "leave[s] potential for popular resentment and vulnerability to future shocks."[66]

This is but one indication that, after six years of having Liberia on its agenda, the Commission and Support Office have disregarded problems related to the inadequacy of economic and social policies in countries on their agenda. In fact, Landgren herself felt that many members of the Commission were rolling their eyes as she brought up the issue of the inappropriateness of the economic model and how, in her view, this was a major potential source of instability as the UN peacekeeping operation withdraws from Liberia after more than 13 years in the country.[67]

Last but not least, there also seems to be a wide consensus that the Commission has not been able to integrate its work with that of other actors or improve its leverage within the system in any significant way. Except in very isolated episodes, the Security Council has not requested its advice. The Support Office has failed to fulfil its mandate to improve communication and understanding among stakeholders. In fact, it has made little effort to articulate the pros and cons of different strategies or programs, or to develop best policy options, practices, and sequences for different situations, most probably as a result of its lack of analytical capacity.

Conclusions

In a recent briefing to the General Assembly, Secretary-General Ban remarked that "[t]his Assembly and the Security Council have adopted truly historic resolutions that recognize the inclusive nature of sustaining peace. They also underscore that sustaining peace is a core United Nations responsibility."[68] Since these concepts – integration/inclusiveness, sustainability, and peacebuilding as a core UN activity – have been in the UN debate since Boutros-Ghali's *An Agenda for Peace* in 1992, the new buzz about "sustaining peace" seems to be an effort by the membership and the Secretary-General to divert attention from the organization's continued lack of operational capacity to have a real impact on conflict-prone countries.

It is certainly easier to wrap up an old problem in a new package that trying to solve it. Secretary-General António Guterres must take the challenge. After more than ten years of Annan's Peacebuilding Architecture, there are few indications of much improvement, as evidence will be provided in the next two chapters. On the contrary, the architecture seems to have added confusion at the UN headquarters and particularly on the ground. It would be a missed opportunity if Secretary-General Guterres does not take a fresh look at peacebuilding, both in the postconflict context and as "the front line of preventive action" as soon as he can.[69]

Notes

1 De Soto, Prologue in *Political Economy of Statebuilding*, xix.
2 Ibid.
3 UNDP, *Sharing New Ground in Post-Conflict Situations: The Role of UNDP in Support of Reintegration Programmes* (New York: United Nations, UNDP Evaluation Office, DP/2000/14), February 2000, 22.
4 UN, *Renewing the United Nations: A Programme for Reform* (New York: General Assembly document A/51/950), 14 July 1997.
5 Jenkins, *Peacebuilding*, 53.

6 Upon taking over in 1997, Kofi Annan had created a senior management group and four executive committees in the areas of peace and security, economic and social affairs, development cooperation, and humanitarian affairs. These high-level bodies focused on interagency and interdepartmental coordination.
 7 Jean Arnault, "A Background to the Report of the High Level Panel on Peace Operations" (New York: mimeo, 2015).
 8 UN, *Report of the Panel on United Nations Peace Operations* (New York: General Assembly/Security Council documents A/55/305 and S/2000/809), August 2000 [known as the Brahimi Report], 18 and 21.
 9 This was institutionalized by having the head of UNDP as deputy to the SRSG in charge of humanitarian and development activities, supposedly encompassing economic reconstruction. See del Castillo, *Rebuilding War-Torn States*, 56–58.
10 International Peace Academy, "Post-Conflict Peacebuilding Revisited: Achievements, Limitations, Challenges" (New York: IPA, prepared by Neclâ Tschirgi, 2004), 5.
11 UNDP, *Sharing New Ground in Post-Conflict Situations: The Role of UNDP in Support of Reintegration Programmes* (New York: Evaluation Office, DP/2000/14, January 2000), 13.
12 This is precisely why development organizations should not lead economic reconstruction. See del Castillo, *Rebuilding War-Torn States*: 45–47.
13 Susan L. Woodward, "Economic Priorities for Successful Peace Implementation," in *Ending Civil Wars: The Implementation of Peace Agreements*, Stephen John Stedman, Donald Rothchild, and Elizabeth M. Cousens, eds. (Boulder, Colo. and London: Lynne Rienner, 2002), 183–214.
14 The process leading to the resolutions started in May 2004 with the secretary-general's appointment of a high-level panel and the report *A More Secure World: Our Shared Responsibility* (New York: Report of the Secretary-General's High Level Panel on Threats, Challenges and Change, General Assembly document A/59/565), 2 December 2004. It was followed by the report, *In Larger Freedom: Towards Development, Security and Human Rights for All* (New York: Report of the Secretary-General, General Assembly document A/59/2005), 21 March 2005. It continued in the September 2005 World Summit of heads of state and government, from which emerged the Word Summit Outcome (General Assembly resolution 60/1 of 24 October 2005) endorsing the creation of the commission and the passage of identical resolutions (General Assembly resolution 60/180 and Security Council resolution 1645, 30 December 2005).
15 For an insider's views see E. Eloho Otobo, *Consolidating Peace in Africa: The Role of the United Nations Peacebuilding Commission* (Princeton, NJ: AMV Publishing Services, 2015) and various articles in Cedric de Coning and Eli Stamnes, eds, *UN Peacebuilding Architecture* (London: Routledge, 2016). For others, see *Mats Berdal*, "The UN Peacebuilding Commission: The Rise and Fall of a Good idea," in *Whose Peace?*; del Castillo, *Rebuilding War-Torn States*, 58–66; Jenkins, *Peacebuilding*; Daisaku Higashi, *Challenges of Constructing Legitimacy in Peacebuilding* (London: Routledge, 2015).
16 See in particular Jenkins, *Peacebuilding;* and Otobo, *Consolidating Peace in Africa*.

17 Abiodun Williams and Mark Bailey, "The Vision and Thinking Behind the UN Peacebuilding Architecture," in *UN Peacebuilding Architecture*, 82–83.

18 Del Castillo, *Rebuilding War-Torn States*, 58–62.

19 See descriptions of the three new entities in Jenkins, *Peacebuilding*, 46–51; Otobo, *Consolidating Peace in Africa*, 9–20 and 183–184.

20 Neclâ Tschirgi and Richard Ponzio, "The Dynamics that Shaped the Establishment of the Peacebuilding Architecture in the Early Years," in *UN Peacebuilding Architecture*, 45–46.

21 Carolyn McAskie, "Foreword: Reflections on the Birth of the UN Peacebuilding Architecture," in *UN Peacebuilding Architecture*, xxvii.

22 This nomination is to distinguish it from "the Fund," which is frequently used in this book to refer to the IMF.

23 Del Castillo, *Rebuilding War-Torn States*, 58–62; Jenkins, *Peacebuilding*, 48–49; Otobo, *Consolidating Peace in Africa*, 183.

24 UN, *Report of the Secretary-General on the World of the Organization* (New York: General Assembly and Security Council document A/70/357-S/2015/682), 2 September 2015, 16.

25 Jups Kluyskens, "The Peacebuilding Fund: From Uncertainty to Promise," in *UN Peacebuilding Architecture*, 61.

26 Cheng-Hopkins, "Epilogue: The UN Peacebuilding Architecture – Good Intentions, Confused Expectations, Faulty Assumptions," in *UN Peacebuilding Architecture*, 239.

27 UN, *In Larger Freedom*, 31.

28 Jenkins, *Peacebuilding*, 12.

29 Del Castillo, *Rebuilding War-Torn States*, 60–61; Cheng-Hopkins, Epilogue, 239.

30 Many of the functions that the Commission has with regard to advocacy, financing, and other matters were performed in the past by "Groups of Friends." For an excellent analysis of such groups, see Teresa Whitfield, *The United Nations, Groups of Friends, and the Resolution of Conflict* (Washington, DC: USIP, 2007).

31 Lise M Howard, *UN Peacekeeping in Civil Wars* (Cambridge: Cambridge University Press, 2008), cited by Jenkins, *Peacebuilding*, 39.

32 Cheng-Hopkins, Epilogue, 245.

33 Aldo Ajello and Patrick Wittmann, "Mozambique," in David M. Malone, ed., *The UN Security Council: From the Cold War to the 21st Century* (Boulder, Colo.: Lynne Rienner, 2004), 442. As a senior officer in the Office of the Secretary-General at the time, I had responsibilities over the Security Council and observed their consultations. The effectiveness of Ajello's methods was as clear for everyone to see as was the ineffectiveness of some others.

34 McAskie, Foreword, xxviii, xxxii, and xxxiv.

35 Jenkins, *Peacebuilding*, 4.

36 In *UN Peacebuilding Architecture*, some of the authors refer to those ideas by making reference to recent studies as if they related to the 2005 Architecture. For example, Cheng-Hopkins argues that what is different about peacebuilding (as compared to humanitarian and development) is that it is essentially a political activity. This is exactly what Boutros-Ghali wrote to Anstee in 1995, after the colloquium in which the UN system as a whole debated peacebuilding issues (Chapter 4). But rather than quoting the

Secretary-General (after all, she was in his office), she quotes from an article published 16 years later that argues that in creating the Commission there was implicit recognition of the importance of political factors in peacebuilding.

37 McAskie, foreword, xxxii; Tschirgi and Ponzi, "The Dynamics that Shaped the Establishment of the Peacebuilding Architecture in the Early Years," 44.

38 In the peacekeeping department there is at least a unit for lessons learnt.

39 Mats Berdal, "Peacebuilding and Development," in B. Currie-Alder, R. Kanbur, D. M. Malone, and R. Medhora, eds, *International Development* (Oxford: Oxford University Press, 2014), 368.

40 See Jenkins, *Peacebuilding*, 75–77, 108–109, for a review.

41 UN, "Review of the United Nations Peacebuilding Architecture" (General Assembly and Security Council document A/64/868-S/2010/393), 21 July 2010.

42 Cited by Jenkins, *Peacebuilding*, 67–68 and 140–142.

43 Mariska van Beijnum, "Achievements of the UN Peacebuilding Commission and Challenges Ahead," in *UN Peacebuilding Architecture*, 57 and 155–156.

44 UN, *The Challenge of Sustaining Peace* (Report of the Advisory Group of Experts, 29 June 2015).

45 Ibid., 7 and 26.

46 Cedric de Coning argued along these lines at the presentation of *UN Peacebuilding Architecture* (New York: Mission of Sweden to the United Nations, 31 May 2016).

47 Boutros-Ghali, *Supplement to An Agenda for Peace*, 10.

48 See Decisions of the Secretary-General, 22 May 2007 Policy Committee Meeting (Decision No. 2007/28 – Peacebuilding Support Office).

49 To be fair to *The Challenge of Sustaining Peace*, it points out only that the UN system needs "to place much greater emphasis" on prevention, not a major shift in thinking. Even the 2015 Report mentions Boutros-Ghali's definition in the *Supplement*, which leaves no doubt that his conception of the term "peacebuilding" also applied pre-emptively.

50 Security Council Meeting on Post-Conflict Peacebuilding: Review of the Peacebuilding Architecture (New York, S/PV.7629), 23 February 2016.

51 James Dobbins et al., *The UN's Role in Nation Building: From the Congo to Iraq* (Washington, DC: Rand, 2005), xxv.

52 These terms have been used interchangeably by UN secretaries-general, in UN discussions and in the literature since the early 1990s. See Tables 6.3 and 6.4.

53 UN, *The Challenge of Sustaining Peace*, 51.

54 Stephen Browne and Thomas G. Weiss, eds, *Peacebuilding Challenges for the UN Development System* (New York: Future United Nations System, 2015), 1 and 17.

55 Ibid., 2.

56 Carville was the campaign strategist to Bill Clinton's successful 1992 presidential campaign.

57 UN, *The Challenge of Sustaining Peace*, 8, 11 and 13.

58 Ibid., 20.

59 Tony Addison, ed., *From Conflict to Recovery in Africa* (Oxford: Oxford University Press, 2003), 9–10.

60 Academic work on issues as well as empirical evidence that need to be debated are included in Tables 6.3 and 6.4.
61 Otobo, *Consolidating Peace in Africa*, 202–203.
62 Cheng-Hopkins, Epilogue, 246.
63 Calculated by the author. The operation cost $688 million (Security Council data), and GDP was $942 million (IMF data). This share decreased thereafter but still averages about 17 percent of GDP after 13 years in place.
64 UN, *The Challenge of Sustaining Peace*, 9 and 42.
65 For a detailed analysis, see Graciana del Castillo, "Aid and Employment Generation in Conflict-Affected Countries: Policy Recommendations for Liberia," *Working Paper No. 2012/47* (Helsinki: UN/WIDER, 2012).
66 PBC Liberia Configuration Meeting with Ms. Karin Landgren, UN Special Representative of the Secretary General to Liberia, Chair's Summary, 5 May 2015, 2.
67 Comments at "Liberia in Transition – A Special Representatives of the Secretary-General Event Featuring Karin Landgren of UNMIL" (New York: International Peace Institute, 7 July 2015).
68 See Security Council resolution 2282, 27 April 2016; UN News Center, Informal Briefing to the General Assembly by the Secretary-General, 9 June 2016.
69 Doyle and Sambanis, *Making War and Building Peace*, 23.

6 The peacebuilding record, lessons, and challenges

- **The UN fails to keep the record**
- **A bleak 25-year peacebuilding record**
- **What do global indices show?**
- **Case studies on UN multidisciplinary operations**
- **Conclusions**

One would have thought that the UN itself – or still better, some independent evaluation office within the organization – would be best suited to assess the record of its multidisciplinary operations in making peace sustainable. However, the UN has not even attempted to establish such a record.

This chapter will present evidence to show that the record of UN multidisciplinary operations, in the aftermath of the Cold War, in assisting countries at low level of development to move from civil war or other inter-state conflict into a path of peace, stability, and prosperity, is indeed bleak. As part of the analysis, the chapter presents aid data to indicate the degree of aid dependency of many of these countries and presents the rankings of countries in a series of global indices to show the poor state of affairs.

The chapter also presents two tables, each identifying books that include case studies on the 21 UN operations in our sample and listing such case studies by country. While case studies included in Table 6.3 focus mostly on the political, security, and/or social aspects of the transition, those included in Table 6.4 also address the economic aspects that have affected peacebuilding efforts in those countries.

The UN fails to keep the record

In Larger Freedom (2005), Kofi Annan states,

> Our record of success in mediating and implementing peace agreements is sadly blemished by some devastating failures.

Indeed, several of the most violent and tragic episodes of the 1990s occurred after the negotiations of peace agreements – for instance in Angola in 1993 and Rwanda in 1994. Roughly half of all countries that emerge from war lapse back into violence *within five years* [emphasis added].[1]

Because the source is not footnoted, most readers would trust that the percentage came from the UN itself. In fact, most people would think that it is the type of data that the UN should collect. However, in my many interviews with officials over the years, I have found that the UN does not perform this task despite the fact that such data are basic for any analysis of this important matter. Moreover, there seems to be no agreement among high UN officials from where the information that "roughly half ... lapse back into violence within five years" was taken (plagiarized perhaps?). Despite it, this statistic has been quoted by many analysts over the years.

Some observers believe that the information came from *A More Secure World*, the 2004 report of the high-level panel that Annan appointed to make recommendations on improving peacebuilding. It would then be less of a sin to forget referencing it. This report, however, notes only that "[s]tates that have experienced civil war face a high risk of recurrence"[2] without specifying any percentage and attributing the findings to the World Bank's report prepared by Paul Collier and colleagues (Chapter 4). But the World Bank's report says that, in the first decade of postconflict peace, "the risks of further conflict are exceptionally high: approximately half will fall back into conflict *within the decade* [emphasis added]."[3] The risk of falling into conflict within five or within ten years is quite different.

This raises a number of troubling issues. First and foremost, how is it possible that the UN, as the global organization responsible for the maintenance of peace and security, uses conflict data from a development organization such as the World Bank? Moreover, in their report, *The Challenge of Sustaining Peace*, the group of experts appointed by Secretary-General Ban to advise for the review of the peacebuilding architecture (Chapter 5), used data from the World Bank 2011 *World Development* Report (criticized in Chapter 4).[4]

Second, and just as important, the data is presented without any information about the sample, which tends to vary greatly among different studies. We discussed earlier with regard to the 2011 World Bank report the problems of mixing different types of conflict for analytical and policymaking purposes. Is Annan's percentage referring to UN operations or to any conflict? In the aftermath of the Cold War or since the end of the Second World War? It is anybody's guess. Not surprising, there is such a confusion even among serious researchers.

For purposes of establishing the UN record, our sample is restricted to countries at low levels of development coming out of civil war or other intrastate conflict since the end of the Cold War and embarking in a political, security, and socioeconomic transition to peace with the support of UN multidisciplinary operations,[5] often in collaboration with the United States, Australia, the United Kingdom, France, or other donors that have a specific interest in the country. That we analyze what happened in these countries during the first decade in transition does not necessarily mean that a UN operation was in place throughout the decade. In fact, many were quite short lived, which was often the problem. But long-term operations also presented their own problems, particularly in terms of distortions created by their presence.

Table 6.1 lists the 21 countries in our sample. To establish relapse, we used the UCDP-PRIO data on conflict, supplemented by information on the UN operation itself. Given the parameters established for the sample, Namibia, for example, is not included since it was not coming out of civil war and the UN peacebuilding support was restricted to organizing elections. By restricting the sample to multidisciplinary operations, where the UN may get involved in supporting productive reintegration of former combatants and other conflict-affected groups, we can expect a higher risk of failure. As argued in this book, the UN is least prepared to deal with the socioeconomic aspects of peacebuilding. The UN has indeed found it easier to support elections than to implement the complex, expensive, and long-term aspect of productive reintegration, which requires the reactivation of the domestic economy without which sustainable employment will not be possible. Table 6.2 shows the disappointing record, despite the large amount of aid that many of these countries received in the transition to peace.

Because in some of these countries some donors have played a critical role and have affected the transition both positively and negatively, and the same is true of the Bretton Woods institutions and other foreign interveners, it would be unfair to blame only the UN if these countries revert to war.

In addition to the involvement of many foreign interveners in the country itself, another aspect that needs to be taken into consideration when analyzing the UN record in these countries is that, while they have experienced intrastate conflict of some sort, many of them have been affected by neighbouring countries in positive and negative ways, both during and after the conflicts, and in turn have had contagion effects of various kinds on them.

Table 6.1 Performance of war-torn countries with foreign interventions

War-torn countries[1]	PA/MI[2]	REL[3]	FSI[4]	GPI[5]	CPI[6]	AMLI[7]	AG[8]	HDI[9]
Afghanistan: 2002–2011	MI**	Yes	9	4	3	2	8.8	19
Angola: 1991–2000	PA	Yes	37	64	6	37	1.8	39
B&H[10]: 1995–2004	MI*/PA	No	88	102	93	94	7.9	102
Burundi: 2005–2014	PA	Yes	15	25	19	NA	4.5	8
Cambodia: 1992–2001	PA	Yes	46	59	18	6	7.1	51
CAR[10]: 2000–09	PA	Yes	3	7	24	NA	1.0	3
Côte d'Ivoire: 2002–2011	PA	Yes	21	45	60	53	0.7	17
DRC[10]: 1999–2008	PA	Yes	8	12	21	NA	2.5	2
El Salvador: 1992–2001	PA	No	96	51	97	124	4.4	115
Guatemala: 1997–2006	PA	No	61	46	45	66	3.5	63
Guinea-Bissau: 1999–2008	PA	No	17	47	10	5	3.3	11
Haiti: 1994–2003	PA	No	10	73	11	19	1.0	20
Iraq: 2003–2012	MI**	Yes	11	3	8	6	18.4	68
Kosovo: 1999–2008	MI*	No	NA	2	64	114	4.0	NI
Liberia: 2003–2012	PA	No	27	89	83	15	3.5	13
Mozambique: 1992–2001	PA	No	42	94	54	7	8.4	10
Rwanda: 1993–2002	MI*	Yes	32	35	125	38	5.3	37
Sierra Leone: 2001–2010	PA	No	34	119	47	24	11.0	5
Somalia: 1992–2001	MI*	Yes	1	5	1	NA	NA	NI
South Sudan: 2011–2015	REF	Yes	2	2	5	NA	NA	NI
Timor-Leste: 1999–2008	MI*	Yes	35	106	40	72	5.2	60

War-torn countries[1]	PA/MI[2]	REL[3]	FSI[4]	GPI[5]	CPI[6]	AMLI[7]	AG[8]	HDI[9]
Number of countries	21	21	20	21	21	16	19	18
Countries in Index			178	162	167	149		187
Relapse (%)		57						
AG higher than 7%							6	
AG of 3–7%							8	
Among the 25 worst			10	7	11	8		11
At the bottom 25%			16	9	12	9		13

Sources: Calculated by author using IMF World Economic Outlook Database (April 2016); and latest indices (2015–16).

Notes:
1. Countries with UN operations following peace agreements or military intervention coming out of civil war or other internal conflict (often with regional implications) that embarked in the transition to peace with UN support up to 201. Dates in brackets indicate first decade of the transition. All indices have been updated to end of August 2016.
2. Peace agreement (PA) or military intervention (MI). MI* indicates MI for humanitarian purposes and MI** for regime change.
3. Yes indicates that the country relapsed into some kind of generalized conflict that required intervention, led to large number of refugees, or collapsed the economy. The country may have had some localized conflict from the beginning of the operation. Information on the particular UN operation was used to determine relapse and was checked against UCDP-PRIO data on conflict.
4. FSI is the Failed States Index compiled by the Fund for Peace.
5. GPI is the Global Peace Index compiled by the Institute of Economics & Peace.
6. CPI is the Corruption Perception Index compiled by Transparency International.
7. AMLI is the Anti-Money Laundering Index, a measure of money laundering and terrorist financing, compiled by the Basel Institute of Governance.
8. AG is the average growth rate of the country during the first decade of the transition to peace calculated by the author using GDP growth from the IMF WEO April 2016 databank.
9. HDI is the Human Development Index compiled by the UNDP.
10. B&H stand for Bosnia & Herzegovina; CAR for Central African Republic; and DRC for Democratic Republic of Congo.

Table 6.2 Aid comparison across war-torn countries[1]

ODA disbursements[2]	t_0	t_1	t_2	t_3	t_4	t_5	t_6	t_7	t_8	t_9	t_0-t_2	t_0-t_4	t_0-t_9
As % of GDP													
Afghanistan: 2002–2011[3]	30	35	45	46	43	109	90	52	42	38	37	40	53
Angola: 1991–2000	3	4	5	10	8	7	5	5	6	3	4	6	6
B&H: 1995–2004[4]	NA	24	19	17	22	13	11	8	6	7	21	16	13
Burundi: 2005–2014	33	34	35	32	32	31	26	22	22	17	34	33	28
Cambodia: 1992–2001	8	12	11	16	12	10	11	8	11	11	11	12	11
CAR: 2000–2009[4]	9	9	6	5	9	7	9	10	13	12	8	7	9
Côte d'Ivoire: 2002–2011	9	2	1	1	1	1	3	10	3	6	4	3	4
DRC: 1999–2008[4]	1	1	3	13	60	19	16	15	8	9	2	16	15
El Salvador: 1992–2001	7	6	4	3	3	3	2	1	1	2	5	4	3
Guatemala: 1997–2006	2	1	2	2	1	1	1	1	1	2	2	2	1
Guinea-Bissau: 1999–2008	13	22	15	14	32	14	11	15	18	15	17	19	17
Haiti: 1994–2003	34	26	13	10	11	6	5	5	4	7	24	19	12
Iraq: 2003–2012	14	13	44	14	10	8	2	2	1	1	24	19	11
Kosovo: 1999–2008[5]	NA	NA	NA	NA	NA	NA	NA	NA	NA	NA	NA	NA	NA
Liberia: 2003–2012	21	36	33	34	74	115	45	109	49	32	30	40	55

ODA disbursements[2]	t_0	t_1	t_2	t_3	t_4	t_5	t_6	t_7	t_8	t_9	t_0-t_2	t_0-t_4	t_0-t_9
Mozambique: 1992–2001	67	52	49	42	26	23	22	16	19	21	56	47	34
Rwanda: 1993–2002	19	60	56	35	13	18	21	19	18	22	45	36	28
Sierra Leone: 2002–2011	31	24	26	21	20	25	15	18	18	14	27	24	21
Somalia: 1992–2001[5]	NA	NA	NA	NA	NA	NA	NA	NA	NA	NA	NA	NA	NA
South Sudan: 2011–2013	3	11	9	14	NA	NA	NA	NA	NA	NA	7	NA	NA
Timor-Leste: 1999–2008	NA	52	39	45	35	15	10	8	10	6	45	34	22

Source: Calculated by author using data from World Economic Outlook Database (April 2016); OECD total aid based on official development assistance (ODA) (August 2016)

Notes:
1. ODA (Official Development Assistance) disbursements during the first decade of the transition to peace; it also reports the average aid flows during the first 3 years (t0-t2), 5 years (t0-t4), and 10 years (t0-t9).
2. ODA includes grants, loans and debt relief from all donors to developing countries and territories and to multilateral agencies which are: (a) undertaken by the official sector; (b) with promotion of economic development and welfare as the main objective; (c) at concessional financial terms (if a loan, having a grant element of at least 25 per cent). In addition to financial flows, technical co-operation is included in aid. Grants, loans and credits for military purposes are excluded. Transfer payments to private individuals (e.g. pensions, reparations or insurance payouts) are in general not counted.
3. Data for Afghanistan was adjusted in 2008-09 to account for $8.8 billion debt relief from Russia which does not report data to the OECD.
4. B&H stand for Bosnia CAR for Central African Republic; and DRC for Democratic Republic of Congo.
5. OECD only reports ODA data on Kosovo since 2009; IMF WEO does not report data on Somalia.

So, as with any other evaluation or statistical analysis, many factors affecting the different countries in the transition to peace, stability, and prosperity need to be considered carefully and rigorously before any conclusions can be drawn.

A bleak 25-year peacebuilding record[6]

In an effort to build societies in the image of those of advanced countries, foreign interveners have tried to convert – practically overnight – insecure and destitute societies into liberal democracies with free-market economies, predominant private sectors, and independent central banks. Imposing such an unrealistic agenda on poor, polarized, mismanaged, and war-ravaged countries could reflect the ideological belief that only societies based on principles of democracy and free markets are capable of achieving and preserving peace and stability and of generating increased prosperity. It most probably represents efforts – particularly in countries rich in natural resources – to create adequate conditions where companies, contractors, and experts from donor countries can flourish.

The recipe has invariably been a combination of centralized government with early and relatively free national elections together with peacekeeping or counter-insurgency operations to keep the peace, humanitarian assistance to save lives and provide minimum levels of consumption, and a few large and relatively productive investment projects requiring new and expensive infrastructure that takes time to build. This recipe has benefitted mostly foreign investors and a few domestic elites, leading to increasing income inequality and little gains in poverty alleviation. Generally lacking a peace dividend for the large majority of the population – that is, a significant improvement in their lives and livelihoods – the recipe has simply not worked and continues to haunt peacebuilding efforts.

As they say, the proof of the pudding is in the eating, and the UN peacebuilding record of the last quarter of a century speaks for itself. Of the 21 countries in Table 6.1 in which the UN set up the type of operations described earlier, 12 have clearly relapsed into conflict (57 per cent) during the first decade of the transition.[7] Some of the countries that did not relapse during the first decade, such as Guinea-Bissau, went through more than a decade of recurrent episodes of political instability, including coups d'états and increased drug trafficking.

Some of these countries would have probably relapsed had it not been for costly and long-lasting peacekeeping operations or foreign troops in place to keep the peace. The record would be even worse if we had followed Doyle and Sambanis, who rightly code operations as "peacebuilding success" only if peacekeepers and military forces (which were keeping the peace) have left for at least two years.[8] Thus, Liberia would not be a success in keeping the peace since peacekeepers still linger in the country after more than a dozen years. It is yet to be seen what will happen when peacekeepers finally exit (Chapter 5).

Both Cambodia and Timor-Leste relapsed after the UN had filed them away as peacebuilding successes. In the case of Cambodia, the 1997 coup "raised questions about the merits of a nearly two billion dollar peace implementation operation that, just four years earlier, had congratulated itself for helping to resolve the country's internal divisions democratically."[9] Despite being included among those that did not relapse into conflict during the first decade, Haiti relapsed in the eleventh year.

Of those that managed to keep an unsettled peace, the large majority have ended up unable to stand on their own feet and have fallen into an aid trap. As an illustration, after more than two decades of peace and large volumes of aid, Mozambique is ranked among the lowest five percent of all countries included in the 2015 *Human Development Index (HDI)*. This is particularly appalling since it was better ranked – among the bottom 10 percent – in 1992, the year in which the peace agreement was signed.

Afghanistan has the ominous record of having both returned to conflict and fallen into an aid dependency from which it will take decades to detox. The latter is also true of Liberia, where the UN has kept the peace. In these two most aid-dependent countries, aid flows increased over the decade rather than decreasing, as it should have.

As Table 6.2 indicates, the level of aid that these countries received over the first decade in the transition varied greatly depending on the geopolitical interest of donors (Afghanistan, Iraq, Haiti), on historical ties (Liberia), on whether they had access to concessional financing from the international financial institutions or not (as El Salvador or Guatemala), on their own resources (Angola), or whether they were outside the radar of donors (the so-called aid orphans). Even those such as El Salvador that managed to avoid relapsing into war and becoming aid dependent have not made any socioeconomic improvement, with the country still ranked at the bottom 40 percent in the *HDI*, as it was in 1992.

Table 6.1 shows that many of the countries in the sample grew fast during the first decade in transition, although from low levels. In fact, five of them grew at average rates of 7 to 18 percent throughout the decade. The problem is that growth in most countries was neither inclusive nor sustainable and created all kinds of distortions to relative prices and resources in general that would continue to affect the countries' growth and development for years to come. Chapter 7 will provide country evidence.

What do global indices show?

If we look at how the countries in our sample perform over time in the different global indices, it is not a pretty picture (Table 6.1). Different global indices illustrate the seriousness with which corruption, illicit activities, conflict, lack of governance, and lack of inclusive socio-economic opportunities have affected current conditions in many of these countries in interrelated and convoluted ways. These factors also affect a country's chances of ever becoming stable, peaceful, and prosperous.[10]

The three most aid-dependent countries – Afghanistan, Liberia, and Mozambique – together with seven more in which the UN has provided long and expensive support over long periods of time are among the 25 worst performers in the *HDI*. As we mentioned above, the *HDI* shows that some are relatively worse off that they were at the time they started the transition.

As Transparency International notes, five of the 10 most corrupt countries in the world also rank among the 10 least peaceful places. Lack of peace in turn affects prosperity and development. Although on their own the different indices may be difficult to interpret, taken together they tend to give a rather realistic picture of what is going on in these countries.

Indeed, the most recent indices available in July 2016 are revealing.[11] The *Peace Index* includes five countries in our sample among its seven worst.[12] The *Failed States Index* includes 11 of these countries among its 25 worst performers, many of which are still at war; the *Terrorism Index* includes six of them among the 20 worst. Not surprisingly, many of these countries are or have been at the top of the foreign policy agenda of the United States and other major countries. The *Corruption Perception Index* includes nine of these countries, and the Basel *AML Index*[13] includes seven of them among the 25 worst ranked.

The ineffective way in which peacebuilding is addressed both by the UN and the United States is perhaps best illustrated in the case of Afghanistan, where both have been critically involved.[14] In the last two indices just mentioned on corruption and money laundering, Afghanistan is ranked second worst in corruption, surpassed only by North Korea and Somalia (which share the worst place), and only by Iran for money laundering.

The *Failed States Index* ranked Afghanistan in the eighth worst place, only slightly better than Syria and Yemen, both at war. The *Peace Index* ranked Afghanistan in the fourth worst place, after South Sudan, Syria and Iraq, also at war.

In the *Terrorism Index*, Afghanistan came second worst, after Iraq. These two countries, together with Nigeria, Pakistan and Syria, accounted for roughly 80 per cent of all deaths and 60 per cent of all terrorist attacks, and many of the immigrants flooding the Middle East and Europe.

The *Iceland Social Progress Index*, which measures the multiple dimensions of social progress, benchmarking success, and catalyzing human wellbeing, places Afghanistan at third worst among 133 countries for which this index is calculated. Only Chad and the Central African Republic are ranked worse.

Despite the huge amount of aid that the country has received over the last 13 years, Afghanistan has not been able to improve relative to other countries that have received little aid. Both the *HDI* and the World Bank *Doing Business Index 2016* continue to rank Afghanistan in the bottom 10 per cent of all countries.

Case studies on UN multidisciplinary operations

A number of books and edited volumes have presented case studies on the political, security, and/or social aspects of the transition to peace in the 21 countries in the sample, shown in Table 6.3. Table 6.4 shows those case studies that focus on or at least touch upon the much neglected economic aspect of such transition. Some of the latter, however, mostly treat economic reconstruction as if it were development as usual, or simply address a few specific issues (mostly on infrastructure and services rehabilitation or DDR programs).

These case studies are recommended for anyone interested in understanding the challenges, the policy constraints, and the lack of operational capacity at the UN to deal with the multidisciplinary aspects of peacebuilding. They will help the reader to understand why major changes are necessary if the UN record is to improve.

Conclusions

It is unfortunate that the UN does not keep a record of its multidisciplinary operations and their cost-effectiveness in supporting countries in their transition to peace, stability, and prosperity. The record we have compiled in this chapter will hopefully provide Secretary-General Guterres with evidence that the operational capacity of the organization needs to

Table 6.3 Case studies covering security, political, and/or social transitions in war-torn countries

Country/Operation	1	2	3	4	5	6	7	8	9	10	11	12	13	14	15
Afghanistan: 2002–2011	✓			✓		✓		✓		✓		✓	✓	✓	
Angola: 1991–2000	✓	✓					✓	✓	✓	✓	✓				
B&H: 1995–2004	✓	✓	✓		✓		✓	✓	✓	✓	✓	✓	✓	✓	
Burundi: 2005–2014	✓		✓	✓					✓						✓
Cambodia: 1992–2001		✓	✓				✓								
CAR: 2000–2009															
Côte d'Ivoire: 2002–2011														✓	
DRC: 1999–2008								✓						✓	
El Salvador: 1992–2001	✓	✓	✓		✓		✓		✓		✓	✓			
Guatemala: 1997–2006			✓				✓				✓				
Guinea-Bissau: 1999–2008															✓
Haiti: 1994–2003	✓	✓			✓				✓		✓		✓		
Iraq: 2003–2012						✓			✓				✓	✓	
Kosovo: 1999–2008			✓		✓	✓		✓		✓	✓		✓	✓	
Liberia: 2003–2012							✓				✓				✓
Mozambique: 1992–2001	✓				✓		✓		✓		✓	✓			
Rwanda: 1994–2003			✓		✓		✓		✓		✓				
Sierra Leone: 2001–2010					✓	✓	✓	✓	✓		✓	✓			✓

Country/Operation	1	2	3	4	5	6	7	8	9	10	11	12	.3	14	15
Somalia: 1992–2001		✓							✓	✓				✓	
South Sudan: 2011–2013					✓	✓			✓			✓	✓	✓	
Timor-Leste: 1999–2008				✓	✓	✓		✓	✓	✓			✓		

Sources:
1. Crocker, Chester A., Fen O. Hampson, and Pamela Aall (eds), *Herding cats: Multiparty Mediation in a Complex World* (Washington, DC: United States Institute for Peace Press.1999).
2. Cousens, E.M. and Chetan K. (eds), *Peacebuilding as Politics: Cultivating Peace in Fragile Societies* (Boulder, Colo.: Lynne Rienner Publishers, 2001).
3. Stephen J. Stedman, Donald Rothchild, and Elizabeth M. Cousens, *Ending Civil Wars: The Implementation of Peace Agreements* (Boulder, Colo.: Lynne Rienner, 2002).
4. Jennifer Milliken, *State Failure, Collapse and Reconstruction* (Malden, Mass.: Blackwell Publishing Ltd., 2003).
5. David M. Malone, *The UN Security Council: From the Cold War to the 21st Century* (Boulder, Colo.: Lynne Rienner, 2004).
6. Orr, Robert C. (ed.), *Winning the Peace: An American Strategy for Post-Conflict Reconstruction* (Washington, DC: The CSIS Press, Center for Strategic and International Studies, 2004).
7. Roland Paris, *At War's End: Building Peace After Civil Conflict* (Cambridge : Cambridge University Press, 2004).
8. William J. Durch (ed.), *Twenty-First-Century Peace Operations* (Washington, DC: United States Institute of Peace, 2006).
9. Mats Berdal and Spyros Economides, *United Nations Interventionism: 1991–2004* (Cambridge: Cambridge University Press, 2007).
10. Charles T. Call (ed.), *Building States to Build Peace* (Boulder, Colo.: Lynne Rienner Publishers, 2008).
11. Michael Pugh, Neil Cooper and Mandy Turner *Whose Peace? Critical Perspectives on the Political Economy of Peacebuilding* (New York: Palgrave Macmillan, 2008).
12. Jeroen de Zeeuw (ed.), *From Soldiers to Politicians: Transforming Rebel Movements After Civil War* (Boulder, Colo: Lynne Rienner Publishers, 2008).
13. Mats Berdal and Dominik Zaum (eds) *Political Economy of Statebuilding: Power After Peace* (Abingdon: Routledge, 2013).
14. von Einsiedel, Sebastian, David M. Malone, and Bruno Stagno Ugarte, *The UN Security Council in the 21st Century* (New York: International Peace Institute, 2015).
15. Cedric de Coning and Eli Stamnes, eds, *UN Peacebuilding Architecture* (London: Routledge, 2016).

Table 6.4 Case Studies Covering Security, Political, Social and/or Economic Transitions in War-Torn Countries

Country/Operation	1	2	3	4	5	6	7
Afghanistan: 2002–2011			✓		✓	✓	
Angola: 1991–2000		✓					
B&H: 1995–2004	✓		✓				
Burundi: 2005–2014							✓
Cambodia: 1992–2001	✓			✓	✓		
CAR: 2000–2009							
Côte d'Ivoire: 2002–2011							✓
DRC: 1999–2008	✓			✓		✓	
El Salvador: 1992–2001	✓				✓		
Guatemala: 1997–2006					✓		
Guinea-Bissau: 1999–2008		✓					
Haiti: 1994–2003			✓	✓		✓	
Iraq: 2003–2012			✓			✓	
Kosovo: 1999–2008							
Liberia: 2003–2012							
Mozambique: 1992–2001		✓		✓			
Rwanda: 1994–2003	✓						
Sierra Leone: 2001–2010				✓			

Country/Operation	1	2	3	4	5	6	7
Somalia: 1992–2001			✔				
South Sudan: 2011–2013							✔
Timor-Leste: 1999–2008				✔	✔		

Sources:
1. Michael W. Doyle, Ian Johnstone, and Robert C. Orr (eds), *Keeping the Peace: Multidimensional UN Operations in Cambodia and El Salvador* (Cambridge: Cambridge University Press, 1997).
2. Tony Addison (eds.) *From Conflict to Recovery in Africa* (Oxford: Oxford University Press, 2003).
3. James Dobbins et al., *America's Role in Nation Building: From Germany to Iraq* (Washington, DC: Rand, 2003).
4. James Dobbins, et al. *UN's Role in Nation Building: From the Congo to Iraq* (Washington, DC: Rand, 2005).
5. James K. Boyce and Madalene O'Donnell (eds), *Peace and the Public Purse: Economic Policies for Postwar State-Building* (Boulder, Colo.: Lynne Rienner Publishers, 2007).
6. Graciana del Castillo, *Rebuilding War-Torn States: The Challenge of Post-Conflict Reconstruction* (Oxford: Oxford University Press, 2008).
7. Arnim Langer and Graham K. Brown, eds. *Building Sustainable Peace: Timing and Sequencing of Post-Conflict Reconstruction and Peacebuilding* (Oxford: Oxford University Press, 2016).

change in fundamental ways if he wants to improve UN peacebuilding capacity, both pre-emptively and post-conflict.

Two other points are worth mentioning. In analyzing the record, one should remember that countries in which the UN sets up peacekeeping and peacebuilding operations are generally countries in crisis, just as when countries request a program from the IMF. So blaming the institutions for the crises is not the issue. The issue is whether these institutions can and have indeed helped the countries to come out of the crisis in a cost-effective way or not.

The second issue is that some countries in particular, notably the United States, just like the UN, have neglected economic reconstruction, the economics of peace, as a key ingredient and determinant of a successful transition to peace, stability, and prosperity. The silo approach to issues of security and development which was followed by both the UN and the United States does not help the transition, as the case of Afghanistan well illustrates.

Chapter 7 will focus on some of the economic problems that have affected the record of the past quarter of a century and that need to be addressed if the UN record with peacebuilding and development is to improve going forward.

Notes

1 UN, *In Larger Freedom*, 31.
2 UN, *A More Secure World*, 70.
3 World Bank, *Breaking the Conflict Trap*, 7. Collier has revised this figure in later publications.
4 Email exchanges with Henk-Jan Brinkman of the Support Office and Gert Rosenthal, who chaired the group of experts. The group of experts used data from the World Bank.
5 Most were peacekeeping operations but some were not. Some also transformed from peacekeeping into peacebuilding or integrated operations.
6 This section relies on statistical work done for the United Nations University, WIDER which has been updated for this book. See del Castillo, "The Economics of Peace in War-Torn Countries."
7 Both UCDP-PRIO data and UN information from the operations were used to determine whether countries relapsed into conflict (the former does not include Timor Leste or Kosovo). This figure may seem outrageously high. It is interesting to note that, with a totally different set of countries and timeframe, Doyle and Sambanis found that from 124 peacebuilding initiatives from 1945 to 1997, 57 percent of the initiatives failed since they could not find a minimum (or negative) measure of peace (absence of violence). If they applied a stricter version of peace which also required a minimum standard of democratization, then the failure rate increased to 65 percent. See Doyle and Sambanis, "International Peacebuilding: A

Theoretical and Quantitative Analysis," *American Political Science Review,* 94/4 (2000): 779-801.

8 Doyle and Sambanis, *Making War and Building Peace,* 91.
9 Cousens, introduction, 23.
10 The different indices can be found online by name.
11 Some but not all could be included in Table 6.1.
12 The five worst are (in order) South Sudan, Iraq, Afghanistan, Somalia, and the Central African Republic. The other two are Syria and Yemen.
13 It assesses country risk regarding money laundering and financing of terrorism, taking into account financial and public sector transparency and judicial strength.
14 Del Castillo, *Guilty Party,* 397–400.

7 Specific economic issues affecting peacebuilding in selected countries

- Peacebuilding following peace agreements in the 1990s
- Peacebuilding following military intervention at the turn of the millennium
- Peacebuilding in countries on the agenda of the Peacebuilding Commission
- Conclusions

In previous chapters we have analyzed how failure at economic reconstruction – the economics of peace – has often become a key obstacle to peacebuilding. The purpose here is not to present detailed case studies on the different countries and on the UN peacekeeping and peacebuilding operations in them (see Tables 6.3 and 6.4 for a list of such studies) but to illustrate specific issues that support peacebuilding or become obstacles to it.

All multidisciplinary studies are relevant to the discussion in this book. As I have argued in *Guilty Party: The International Community in Afghanistan*, the UN is still ill prepared to deal with issues of human security in an integrated, effective, and consistent way. This is due mainly to the fact that the UN departments, programs, and agencies, including the Bretton Woods Institutions (BWIs), operate (borrowing the term from Gillian Tett of the *Financial Times*) as a "plethora of silos,"[1] each functioning within its own expertise and with a one-track mind rather than with a multidisciplinary vision and purpose.

The practice of ignoring interrelations and "reverse causalities" among the four aspects of the transition, discussed in Chapter 2, deserves much of the blame. The tendency of diplomats and security experts to roll their eyes when economic issues are brought into the discussion – particularly those of a technical nature or those which are likely to cause denial of financing for their pet projects – has also been a problem. Likewise, the reluctance of serious economists to get involved in countries which have such little impact on the global economy and where the issues are "too political" has also been a problem.

This chapter will discuss economic issues that, over the last quarter of a century, have proved key to peacebuilding or have acted as major obstacles to it. Countries will be divided into three groups, depending on whether the UN operation took place following peace agreements in the 1990s; on whether they followed military intervention and/or took place during transitional administrations in the new millennium; or on whether the countries are on the agenda of the Peacebuilding Commission since 2006. As discussed in Chapter 6, these countries relied on reconstruction aid to very different degrees (see Table 6.2).

The analysis is somewhat imbalanced in terms of space between the three sections. This is due to various reasons. First, because in the first group many of the economic issues that affect post-conflict peacebuilding are determined during peace negotiations, issues relating to the economics of conflict resolution are also analyzed. Second, because of the time frame, since the first group also allows us to analyze some of the problems related to the transition from the economics of peace to the economics of development, once the risk of conflict relapse recedes. Third, many of the problems faced by countries in this group have been repeated in later experiences, most notably the constraints imposed by International Monetary Fund (IMF) sponsored economic programs on the implementation of UN-sponsored peacebuilding. Hence, there is no need for repetition.

Fourth, the second group illustrates best the difficulty of moving away from the economics of war. Finally, the third group in turn illustrates how some of the lessons learnt at the UN from previous operations, seem to have gone into oblivion in the context of countries on the agenda of the Peacebuilding Commission since 2006. In particular, we will argue that the Commission has missed the opportunity to advocate for more inclusive economic and social policies in these countries, all of which, except Rwanda, are at the bottom 10 percent of the *Human Development Index*.

Peacebuilding following peace agreements in the 1990s

Despite the fact that El Salvador, Mozambique, Cambodia, and Rwanda belonged to a new breed of UN operations that were multi-disciplinary in nature and sought to address the root causes and consequences of the conflict, they were quite different in a number of ways. Both El Salvador and Rwanda had strong, noncorrupt, and visionary leaders that often sought economic solutions outside the aid system.

President Cristiani gave up benefits under US Government PL480 because he rightly decided that the long-term benefit of basic grain production was more important for the country than the short-term assistance in kind. President Kagame managed to decrease the dependence on aid through foreign investment.

In several countries in this group, the issue of property rights was "backward looking." The government had to re-establish land titles and update registries to resolve title claims as soon as possible. However, once they were established and registries were updated, property rights would not create a serious impediment to investment. The challenge was completely different in the second group of countries, where the issue was "forward looking" as a result of lack of legitimate authorities.

The gender issue was also different. Women participated as combatants but they were not always included in reintegration efforts. In El Salvador, the reintegration programs, particularly the arms-for-land program, did not discriminate against women despite the fact that the agreement did not make any specific provision on gender. By contrast, women complained of being discriminated against once they were demobilized in Mozambique.[2] In Guatemala, the agreements explicitly had specific gender provisions, but since their implementation was patchy, former women combatants were probably worse off than in El Salvador. Rwanda has followed a much more consistent policy of gender empowerment than any of the other countries.

Both El Salvador and Mozambique lacked appropriate support in their transition to normal development, and both countries have failed to create dynamic and inclusive economies. Unlike El Salvador, Mozambique became a highly aid dependent country. In both cases, the transition to prosperity and improved human development that started enthusiastically after the signing of peace agreements 25 years ago has remained an elusive dream.

El Salvador[3]

Obstacles to peacebuilding created by IMF-sponsored economic programs

Many analysts agree that El Salvador's implementation of the UN-brokered peace agreement was among the most successful in the post-Cold War period, owing mainly to its emphasis on efforts to reintegrate former combatants, their supporters, and other war-affected people into productive activities.[4]

As discussed in the introduction, the inability to finance critical programs in the UN-brokered peace agreement because of constraints imposed in the IMF-sponsored economic program came close to derailing the peace process as the government was unable to comply with its commitments and the FMLN stopped demobilization.[5]

A combination of factors was involved. Donors were more willing to finance infrastructure projects than peace-related ones, and some even had specific restrictions on financing the land program requiring purchases. At the same time, monetary and fiscal targets in the IMF-sponsored economic program restricted the amount of deficit financing through domestic money creation.

This challenge made the UN more aware of the key importance of reactivating the postconflict economy in a broad-based and inclusive way for addressing the large economic consequences of peace, for creating employment, and for implementing specific programs that donors were reluctant to finance. Without an institutional memory at the UN, the Peacebuilding Commission seems unaware of such a key lesson.

"Economic and social questions" (Chapultepec Peace Agreement, Chapter V)[6]

Another lesson from El Salvador was that the design of the peace agreement on economic matters was key in facilitating or obstructing its implementation. As mediator, Álvaro de Soto reminisced,

> [t]he FMLN's handling of the economic and social question as the last substantive issue was particularly revealing, given the root cause of much of the unrest that had led to the insurgency was grinding poverty and marginalization ... the FMLN, whether because of factional divergences, lack of expertise, or a sober appraisal of political realities, left the examination of these root causes for a late stage ... studiously refraining from any revolutionary proposal. It did not try to tamper with the economic model that Cristiani's administration was promoting. ... Many combatants demobilized in bitter disappointment that their leaders had settled for much less than the revolutionary goals.[7]

In March 1995, Rubén Zamora, who played an important role on the side of the FMLN during the peace process (and is now permanent representative to the UN), argued that the positions of the two sides on the lack of "economic and social inclusion" were so far apart that putting them on the table could have endangered reaching a final peace agreement.[8]

Two additional factors are worth mentioning in this regard. While the FMLN lacked the economic expertise to negotiate better on these issues, so did de Soto's team at the UN. He recognized the deficiencies in the reintegration programs,

> for which the FMLN may share some of the blame, but for which I admit responsibility as the mediator. ... [W]e could have done a better job of marshalling expertise to ensure that the agreement reached was not seriously flawed – so much so that it had to be renegotiated and expanded on in a supplementary agreement in October 1992. ... A better-forged agreement on reintegration questions ... might well have lessened the postwar crime wave that bedevils El Salvador to this day.[9]

With appropriate economic expertise, the mediator's team could perhaps have had a closer relationship with the IMF throughout the negotiations to ensure that the 1992 budget contemplated basic financing to start this program (as subsequent budgets for 1993 and 1994 did). In those later years, the Salvadoran government achieved fiscal and monetary targets with a margin.[10]

The second problem with regard to the lack of economic expertise is that many of the socioeconomic questions in Chapter V of the agreement were not well designed and hence not implementable. David Holiday and David Stanley, identified the "specificity – or lack thereof of agreed upon reforms," as a main reason why "some aspects of UN peace-building remain fraught with pitfalls."[11] Some of the provisions of the arms-for-land program were excessively precise ("market-prices," land offered "voluntarily" by owners for sale), creating serious constraints to its implementation. At the same time, crucial parameters were completely lacking (number of beneficiaries, size of plots, amount of credit). No wonder the land program had to be renegotiated![12]

The role of the private sector in peacemaking and peacebuilding

The economic framework, adopted by the Cristiani government with the support of the IMF while war was still raging in 1989, relied on macroeconomic stability and market-based reforms, with the government providing the legal and regulatory framework.[13] Despite the role that the private sector was expected to play during the postconflict economics of peace phase – providing tax and tariff revenue, creating investment and employment, contributing to foreign exchange inflows through exports and investment, building infrastructure and providing basic services – the private sector was not involved at all in the economics of conflict resolution during peace negotiations.[14]

Zamora noted that although society as a whole benefited from the peace agreement, the private sector was one of the two "super beneficiaries" (the other being the political parties). This is because the agreement legitimized the private sector at the national level: all political forces agreed that the private sector was going to be the guiding force in the economy.

In his view, the private sector failed to realize the importance of the agreement to themselves. Since it had not participated, the sector lacked any sense of commitment with the Economic Forum (*Foro de Concertación Económico y Social*) in which the government, labour, and the business community would participate "on an equal footing for the purpose of working out a set of broad agreements on the economic and social development of the country."[15]

A greater engagement of the private sector in the conflict resolution stage would have been particularly desirable since the agreement stated that "[t]he [National Reconstruction] Plan shall pay special attention to the need to promote job creation on a massive scale and to increase the production of basic foodstuffs, which shall be a priority of the State."[16]

The need for the private sector to play a large role in conflict resolution and peacebuilding is increasingly noted in the literature and in different fora.[17] However, to engage this sector productively, and through conflict-sensitive policies to ensure that their involvement does not become a new source of conflict, will require economic expertise in the mediators' team. It is particularly important to ensure that private sector involvement will contribute to peacebuilding rather than being an obstacle to it.

In the case of El Salvador, raising expectations of "job creation on a massive scale" was illusory given the situation of the country at the time, its lack of access to concessional borrowing from the financial institutions, the large shock to coffee prices and other such factors. This was an important lesson from El Salvador: "Peace agreements should not build up expectations about what peace will bring which are unrealistic and difficult to satisfy. Unfulfilled expectations of disgruntled groups can seriously endanger an entire peace process" and lead to subsequent common crime and instability.[18] This is another reason why economic expertise to determine what is feasible or not is critical during peace negotiations.

"Exit" from the economics of peace to the economics of development

As the report of the High-Level Panel on Threats, Challenges and Change noted in 2004, "when peacekeepers leave a country, it falls off the radar screen of the Security Council."[19] The early exit of ONUSAL (United Nations Observer Mission in El Salvador) in 1995, even before its monitoring mandate was completed, highlights the problems that can afflict peacebuilding efforts in such context.

To get out of the country in a speedy fashion, the Security Council neglected unfinished business and the sustainability concerning the arms-for-land and other reintegration programs. The inadequate resources of MINUSAL (the successor UN peacebuilding operation) and, most importantly, the development-as-usual attitude of the UNDP and the World Bank, together with reduced involvement by critical donors, contributed to the difficulties of transitioning from the economics of peace to the economics of development.

Premature exit from the radar of the Security Council was clearly problematic. The UN gave UNDP, as coordinator of the UN development system, leadership over "unfinished business." Under UNDP, many of the gains were lost and the peace process withered. Lack of financial and technical support for the beneficiaries of the land and other reintegration programs forced many to abandon their newly acquired stake in the Salvadoran economy, with tragic consequences for security and licit livelihoods.[20]

At the same time, the support of some of the main donors waned. This is best documented in a 2004 report by Agneta Gunnarsson and other colleagues evaluating the role of the Swedish International Development Cooperation Agency (SIDA) in support of peace in El Salvador.[21] Sweden had channelled about 80 percent of its aid since 1992 through the UNDP. The report documents how UNDP selection procedures had miserably failed to recruit the right person to lead in a critical phase of the implementation of the agreement to ensure completion and sustainability. The UNDP stopped acting in support of the peace process. When Sweden's efforts to avoid this shift failed, SIDA stopped financing the UNDP.

This is the kind of situation where the Peacebuilding Architecture created in 2005 could have played an important role in cajoling the government, donors, UN agencies, and other stakeholders to continue supporting social and economic programs in the Chapultepec agreement that were left to wither as soon as the country lost the Security Council clout.[22]

Political and economic decentralization

El Salvador provides an example of how decentralization in the political and economic sense, as proposed by Myerson (Chapter 2), could strengthen democracy by avoiding the perpetuation of a single party in power and by being more responsive to the economic and social needs of the local population. In the case of El Salvador, decentralization meant that there was a process through which leaders and the party were building up experience at the local level for the national elections, and this eventually helped them gain the presidency.

Although elections in 1994 put another president from the government party in power, the FMLN opposition in the 2000 elections won 31 of 84 seats in the unicameral legislative assembly. This was a remarkable achievement for the FMLN, barely eight years after becoming a political party, allowing it to block bills requiring a two-thirds majority. This moved the country further ahead of the political transition. In the municipal elections of 1997, the opposition had won about 80 percent of the largest cities, probably due to building up credibility in the provision of economic services and political governance. As Myerson notes, the process was not a "winner takes all" game, as later on in Afghanistan, and the ability of both sides to win shares of local power through political and economic programs must have been helpful in sustaining the peace process, despite the delays and pitfalls in the productive reintegration process and in other socioeconomic programs.[23]

Other countries (Cambodia, Mozambique, Guatemala, Rwanda)

The early grim experience in El Salvador between the UN and BWIs ultimately convinced these organizations to start working more closely together in matters of human security in subsequent operations. Specific economic features of the transitions to peace, stability, and prosperity of Cambodia, Mozambique, Guatemala, and Rwanda are worth mentioning.

Cambodia

A notable aspect of the Paris Agreement of 1991 was the unprecedented civilian role mandated to the UN in the agreement.[24] The Security Council established UNTAC (United Nations Transitional Authority in Cambodia) in March 1992 with a mandate of only 18 months, and the operation withdrew on time, leaving behind various UN development agencies to help consolidate the fragile peace.

As Doyle and his colleagues remarked, the agreement enshrined the sovereignty of Cambodia but "charged the UN – for the first time in its history – with the political and economic restructuring of a member state. In addition to the repatriation of refugees, the disarmament and demobilization of local forces, the mandate included civilian duties such as controlling and supervising civil administration and facilitating economic rehabilitation.[25]

Brian Williams labelled the repatriation of Cambodian refugees a "qualified success." The UN moved 360,000 refugees, distributed a reintegration package, and initiated a number of rehabilitation projects. However, although the UN "promised two hectares of land to each returning family, in the end only 3 percent of the returning families received land." This illustrates once again the lack of adequate economic expertise at the UN that leads the organization to build up expectations that clearly cannot be satisfied from an economic point of view.

Demobilization of combatants, on the other hand, was an unqualified failure. Due to the Khmer Rouge's continued violence and noncompliance with the Paris Agreement, the disarmament and demobilization of other factions was judged imprudent and suspended in 1992. Disarming the Khmer Rouge would have required a much larger force than UNTAC had and a much longer time frame than the Security Council provided.[26]

The Cambodia case also illustrates the problems with the economics of war running amok. Unofficial support for the Khmer Rouge from various Thai generals on the western border undermined the peace process. The Khmer Rouge's easy access to logs, gems, arms, and ammunition, in violation of UN embargoes, was more enticing to them than the international aid or the prospect of an end to the embargoes in exchange for support to the peace process.[27]

Mozambique

In the case of Mozambique, the UN was not involved in the negotiation of the peace agreement but it oversaw its implementation through the establishment of UNOMUZ (United Nations Operation in Mozambique) in December 1992.[28] Mozambique illustrates two important points with regard to postconflict reconstruction. The first point is that peace agreements as well as mandates from the Security Council do not always reflect reality, making thinking outside the box essential to solve constraints throughout the peace process. This requires that UN operations be led by able, pragmatic, and innovative special representatives of the Secretary-General (SRSGs) with good credentials that can maintain a fluid and productive relationship with the government, with the diplomatic community in the country and in New York, with high-level officials of the Bretton Woods Institutions (BWIs) and with other stakeholders as needs may arise.

The second point is that finance is often a constraint not only to economic reconstruction itself but often to political and security reform. In this case, the SRSG will also need to create the appropriate mechanisms to ensure that lack of finance does not become an insurmountable obstacle to peacebuilding, as it almost became in El Salvador and in Mozambique.

Aldo Ajello was the kind of leader that UNOMUZ required. He built close relationships with the diplomatic community in Maputo, with Security Council members, with the agencies, and with other stakeholders that allowed him to speak with one voice. This gave him strong leverage with both parties, including at difficult times.

Ajello used sticks as well as carrots effectively. Under Ajello's leadership and with strong support from the local diplomatic community, two funds were created that had a significant peacebuilding impact.[29] A UN trust fund was created to provide RENAMO (the Mozambican National Resistance) with the resources it needed to transform itself into a political party. Almost $18 million were raised and demobilization started.

As Collier has pointed out, while diamonds in Angola made UNITA so rich – by reputedly accumulating over $4 billion in financial assets during the first war and using it in the second one – that nothing donors could offer mattered, donors in Mozambique were able to offer a package to RENAMO which "made peaceful political contest an attractive option."[30]

The second trust fund was created to support reintegration in a more effective and sustainable way. Indeed, the peace agreement contemplated that the government would provide former combatants with six-months' salary, which was obviously inadequate for full reintegration. To reduce the "real risk of violence, banditry, and major disruption during the election campaign to come," ONUMOZ put together a new reintegration scheme providing for an additional eighteen months' salary to each demobilized soldier, and 80,000 accepted the package. Both trust funds were guided by an important lesson learned from Angola that demilitarization was imperative before elections.[31]

Guatemala

El Salvador, Cambodia, Mozambique, and Rwanda had Security Council mandated operations to support the transition to peace. Guatemala, on the other hand, was not under the magnifying glass of the Council, which clearly diminished the UN's leverage vis-à-vis those involved in the implementation of the peace agreements. This was partly because of the fact that military issues – the ambit of the Security Council – were by then less important. But it was also because the agreements contemplated wide-ranging development goals that the Council considered well beyond its mandate.[32]

The UN-brokered peace agreement between the government and the URNG (Guatemalan National Revolutionary Unity) signed in December 1996 envisaged important political, social, and economic changes, including substantial increases in tax collection that would support higher public spending in the social sectors. Optimistically, the agreement contemplated an increase in tax revenue from 8.5 percent of GDP in 1996 to 12 percent by the year 2000 (later extended to 2002).

Relations between the UN and the IMF had changed in a major way since the two organizations were at odds in El Salvador in 1992. In Guatemala, the IMF was involved in the peace process from the very beginning, with its staff maintaining a relationship with the secretary-general's envoy, Jean Arnault, the UN Secretariat, and the UNDP in the field leading to the signing of the peace agreement in 1996.

Out of the ordinary, it was the UN-mediated agreement that was imposing economic conditionality and the IMF who was trying to support the peace process by insisting that the fiscal targets imposed by the agreement should be reached, what James Boyce labelled "political conditionality."[33] Not surprisingly, given its ambitious level and the past record in this area, the government failed to achieve the fiscal target, despite efforts by the Fund.

As a result, relations between the government and the IMF were strained in subsequent years, and an agreement on an IMF-sponsored program was not concluded until 2002. Without it, donors reduced commitments and financing became totally inadequate for the breadth of the agreement's coverage and the high expectations that it had created. Domestic financing was also inadequate, with tax revenue remaining below 10.5 percent of GDP even 10 years into the peace process.

Just as stringent economic conditionality imposed by the IMF-sponsored economic program in El Salvador in 1992 endangered the peace process, economic conditionality imposed by the UN-mediated peace agreement in Guatemala endangered its implementation by precluding an IMF-sponsored economic program, a condition for other financial support. As a result, aid peaked at only 3 percent of GDP in 2000 (Table 6.2).[34]

Public insecurity and human rights violations continued largely due to the failure to disarm and reintegrate former combatants productively into society. Stanley and Holiday argue that the UN's inability to verify compliance with the accords reflected the absence of Security Council clout, while other international actors like the United States, which had played a critical role in El Salvador, lacked leverage because of Guatemala's limited wartime dependence on its assistance.[35]

The UN envoy's team in peace negotiations could have also benefitted greatly from the right economic expertise. The impossibility of financing what was being negotiated was clear to many of the economists involved at the IMF and even at the UN.[36]

Rwanda

The Hutu-led government of Rwanda and the Tutsi-led RPF (Rwandan Patriotic Front) signed the Arusha Agreement in August 1993, brokered by Tanzania under a broad mandate from the Organization of African States. As described by Gilbert Khadiagala,

> Efforts to implement the agreement, however, faltered from the start and finally collapsed in April 1994 when the death of [the president] was followed by the massacre of more than 1 million Tutsi and moderate Hutu in a three-month rampage. ... The Rwanda genocide resulted in part from the weakness of the Arusha Agreement and the paltry efforts to implement it.[37]

Rwanda's economy had faced harsh times before and during the civil war, even before the devastation of the genocide. A severe famine hit the country at the end of the 1980s due to a prolonged drought and the collapse in coffee prices. Economic and social conditions were aggravated by strong demographic pressures and high population density, with GDP per capita plunging between 1989 and 1994. As the perception of paralysis engulfed the government, the RPF took the opportunity to strike from Uganda in October 1990. Despite the political crisis,

> [t]hree weeks after the invasion, the government announced austerity measures mandated by the World Bank and the International Monetary Fund (IMF) structural adjustment program. These policies entailed devaluation of the currency and more cutbacks in government spending on education, healthcare, and the civil service. Structural adjustment measures plunged the majority of Rwandans into the insecurity of unemployment and landlessness, alienating a population considerably weakened by the economic shocks of the late 1980s. The conditions further deteriorated in the course of the civil war, as meaningful economic activity ground to a halt and thousands of people lost their lives or were internally displaced.[38]

Paul Kagame, who had led the RPF and became vice-president in 1994 and president in 2000, assumed leadership of post-conflict economic reconstruction from the very beginning. Strong efforts at unification and reconciliation following the 1994 genocide were rightly accompanied by robust government use of aid to support subsistence agriculture that provided livelihoods to 80 per cent of the population.

Because economics policies focused on having a broad impact on the population at large, rather than privileging elites, poverty reduction is a good indicator of the peace dividend enjoyed by Rwandans. The IMF notes that poverty fell from about 57 to 39 percent, with inequality, indicated by the Gini coefficient, falling from 0.52 to 0.45 over the last decade. As they should in the postconflict period, "the poorest have benefited the most from growth. Inclusive growth was led by policies geared towards agriculture through investments in fertilizers, improved seeds, electrification, irrigation, and rural roads, and towards improving the provision of social services, especially to the rural poor. Access of the poor to financial services also improved."[39]

Strong government leadership, a reasonable strategy, and lack of widespread corruption made a big difference in terms of facilitating and making policymaking more effective. There was no attempt to transform Rwanda overnight into the perfect market economy in which the government gave up its prerogative of supporting small and vulnerable producers. Neither was there an attempt to go into high productivity sectors immediately, which requires infrastructure that takes time to build. By contrast, the government's first priority was to ensure that the large majority of the population had enough to eat and could cover other basic necessities with regard to health, education, etc.

Later, with support from donors, the government moved to promote value chain production in the coffee sector to improve productivity by mechanizing depulping and other processes with modern equipment. Between 2000 and 2006, production increased from 18 tons of fully washed coffee to 940 tons. The World Bank noted that greater economic security among participants in the coffee value chain lowered distrust toward ethnic groups and improved efforts towards reconciliation.[40]

Despite the government's frequent defiance of donors, they did support Rwanda's reconstruction. Notwithstanding the difficulties of escaping the legacy of the genocide, the government has not become aid dependent and in fact has managed to decrease its dependence gradually by seeking solutions outside the aid system (see Table 6.1).[41]

Rwanda's longer-term goal all along has been to become a regional hub for communications, computing and logistics. The country caught world attention as enthusiastic reports appeared in the *Financial Times* and elsewhere discussing plans to transform the country into a knowledge-based economy by modernizing its main sectors using information and communications technology. To achieve this, fibre-optic cable was being laid throughout the country so that it would have the most advanced broadband wireless Internet network on the continent.[42]

Rwanda's strategy was quite different from the classic neoliberal agenda followed by Liberia and Afghanistan not only to please donors but mostly resulting from the dogmatism of their own leaders, some of them former officials of the World Bank. Contrary to these two countries that likewise have about 80 percent of their population dependent on rural livelihoods, Rwanda focused on subsistence agriculture before adding value and avoided dependence on food imports, which the other two countries did not.

While human-rights experts complain about the lack of freedom of the press and other of liberties and the uncertainty about the political transition that Rwanda may face in the future, the economic transition is moving ahead better than expected.[43] Kagame's authoritarian leadership, and the wider options he has managed to open up for his country in terms of investment opportunities, has allowed him to stand up to the advice of the development agencies when he does not think it is good for his people. This has ensured national ownership of Rwanda's economic policies, which is important to make them sustainable.

Rwanda's leader wants to remain in power in his own country, while those responsible for the economic reforms in Liberia and Afghanistan were particularly avid to please donors and achieve international recognition since they had aspirations to greater jobs in the international community.

Conflicts between the political and economic transitions matter, and they should be debated in a multidisciplinary context. But if foreign interveners really want to have an impact on war-torn countries, they might need to debate whether to set strict rules for limits (on term periods, nepotism, and corruption) and for appointments at the UN and the BWIs for national leaders, who often seem more interested in pleasing these institutions than in improving the welfare of their citizens.

Peacebuilding following military intervention at the turn of the millennium

This group includes countries that embarked on the multidisciplinary war-to-peace transition under very different circumstances. Contrary to Afghanistan, where a sovereign government was making all executive decisions, Kosovo, East-Timor, and Iraq started their war-to-peace transitions as UN- or US-led transitional administrations where foreign interveners temporarily made all executive and legislative decisions.

Countries in this group can be used to illustrate the issue of sequence in economic reconstruction and peacebuilding.[44] Although many activities can and must be carried out with whatever framework is in place at the time, and must be adjusted as the framework changes over time, there are certain activities that entail a specific sequence, and it is not possible to carry them out unless others take place before them. For example, even if policymakers wanted to start providing credit for microenterprises immediately, this will not be possible until the monetary authorities and the basic legal framework are in place. In Kosovo, for example, the first challenge we faced at the UN was to restore the payments system and adopt the deutsche mark as the currency since Kosovo was a province and as such it did not have its own currency. Without doing that, all other policies would have been ineffective. In countries like Afghanistan and Kosovo, reactivating agriculture in many areas was not possible without first removing land mines and unexploded ordnance devices.[45]

Currency exchange was necessary in Iraq to eliminate Saddam Hussein's portrait from the banknotes; in Afghanistan, it was necessary because of the existence of several currencies and the large degree of counterfeiting. Against all expectations, the currency exchange proceeded smoothly and on time in both countries. In Kosovo, Afghanistan, and Iraq, lack of effective reintegration haunted peacebuilding efforts and contributed to the insecurity that afflicted these countries.[46]

Afghanistan[47]

After more than two decades of continuous conflict, US-led military intervention led to the rout of the Taliban in November 2001. The political framework for the post-9/11 reconstruction in Afghanistan was established at Bonn and signed on December 2001. As Ahmed Rashid noted in his bestselling book *The Taliban*, "[t]he Bonn agreement was not a peace treaty: the vanquished were not represented."[48]

Moreover, the agreement called for a "broad-based, gender-sensitive, multiethnic, and fully representative government." This foreign-conceived political model resounded as wishful thinking at the time rather than a realistic prospect for a country with such a culture, religion, history, economy, and illiteracy rate.

Marina Ottaway and Anatol Lieven of the Carnegie Endowment for International Peace warned from the very beginning about the fantasy of the Bonn Agreement to create a modern state in Afghanistan and the lack of capacity of the international community to support it. People basically needed to restore some kind of normal life and

economic activities in the absence of armed conflict and ethnic har-
assment, "even if it is not life in a modern state. ... More ambitious
state-building plans must be left for another generation, and to the
Afghan themselves."[49]

Barnett Rubin and colleagues at the Council on Foreign Relations in
New York also warned that vast sums of money should not be thrown
at Afghans. Assistance should start slowly and carefully, with the bulk
of the assistance focused on rural areas, where 80 percent of Afghans
lived. Afghans needed to feel that recovery was changing their lives.[50]

The advice of these two teams went unheeded – as did the good and
bad lessons from a decade of economic reconstruction elsewhere – and
the United States and allies moved with a big bang into Afghanistan.
In March 2002, the UN established UNAMA (United Nations Assistance Mission in Afghanistan), and Lakhdar Brahimi was appointed
SRSG. He envisaged a "light footprint" for the UN in Afghanistan,
limited to facilitating the political process established at Bonn (in contrast to previous operations in Kosovo and East Timor). Not surprisingly, he left the UN agencies to lead reconstruction, the perfect recipe
for the development-as-usual approach that the Brahimi report had
recommended in 2000 (Chapter 5).

Warlords – many of whom had fought the Soviets in the 1980s,
among themselves in the civil war (early 1990s), with the Taliban while
they held de facto control (late 1990s), and with the Taliban with US
support (after 9/11) – continued to control areas outside Kabul while
maintaining their armed militias. This gave them control over border
customs, crippling a main source of government revenue and creating a
major problem for effective economic policymaking since there was little
production and income to tax in the early period, and import tariffs
were the only source of revenue. At the same time, donors channelled
from 80 to 85 percent of their aid outside the national budget.

Contrary to Kosovo and East Timor, Afghanistan was a sovereign
country at the time of the transition and thus had to be in charge of its
own destiny. However, as a very poor society destroyed over the years
by foreign forces (rather than by civil conflict alone) and with a history
of humanitarian intervention, Afghanistan had to fight to chart its
reconstruction path and formulate its own economic policies.

The Bonn process appointed Hamid Karzai as transitional leader.
As could have been predicted by Myerson's premises, after heading the
interim and transitional authorities, Karzai became the first democratically elected president of Afghanistan in October 2004. Because there
was no legislative body until after the parliamentary elections in September 2005, he had to adopt laws and regulations to establish the

macroeconomic framework by executive decree, not always a simple proposition for a transitional government.

Three specific factors perhaps had the largest weight in derailing Afghanistan's path towards peace, stability, and prosperity.

Economic policymaking and the macroeconomic framework

In Afghanistan, Minister of Finance Ashraf Ghani (now president) opted in 2002 to replace the existing currency with new afghani bills issued by the central bank rather than to adopt the dollar as the IMF recommended. War-torn countries often try to build up credibility by adopting a foreign currency. This had been the practice in Kosovo and East Timor at the turn of the 1990s. Both the policy of maintaining the national currency and the currency exchange itself worked well in Afghanistan.

On monetary and fiscal grounds, on the other hand, the macroeconomic framework was totally inadequate for a war-torn country. The complex and inflexible framework – including total independence on the central bank (with the government losing control on monetary policy) and with a strict no-overdraft rule to avoid deficit financing – created serious problems for economic reconstruction and peacebuilding. Such a constraining framework did not exist in other war-torn countries, including El Salvador.

Ghani's grandiose scheme, for which he had little support even within the cabinet, to move Afghanistan into the twenty-first century overnight was a complete failure from which the country never recovered. The lack of civil service capacity to deal with complexities required lots of training and the hiring of foreign experts at tremendous cost to the state. According to the World Bank, one-quarter of Afghanistan aid went into technical assistance and capacity-building,[51] mostly to pay the high salaries of foreign consultants. Efforts to create macroeconomic stability acted against security stabilization and peacebuilding, and the experience of Afghanistan illustrates how much easier it is to achieve the former than the latter.

Delays in starting economic reconstruction – waiting to have the macroeconomic framework, other institutions, experts, and infrastructure in place – deprived Afghans of an early peace dividend in terms of improved services and better livelihoods.

A combination of lack of flexibility and dogmatism deprived the government of the ability to support pro-poor policies in the rural sector, despite the rhetoric in many government and donors' reports. It precluded the government from adopting active policies to support the sector, including subsidies and price-support mechanisms, and was an obstacle to moving away from the underground economy, particularly poppy production and the opium trade, which is known to undermine peace, governance, and the rule of law.

Likewise, such combination impeded the reactivation of employment and economic activity in other sectors, even if initially at low productivity levels or even operating in the red. For example, the Spinzar Cotton Company could have targeted the 5,000 jobs it had in the 1930s, but because it had become a state-own enterprise during communist times, it was instead put up for privatization. Employment creation in this company could have kept armed militias and others occupied.

Not surprisingly, the country gradually fell back into conflict starting in 2003. Delays also led to unnecessarily high levels of humanitarian assistance – to achieve minimum levels of consumption for the population rather than investment to create jobs and inclusive growth – and from there to aid dependence.

An strategy along the one that experts recommended could have saved lots of blood and treasure. By contrast, the misguided policies and misplaced priorities of a development-as-usual strategy – as if the high risk of relapse could be ignored – were a major factor behind Afghanistan's ominous record: The country both returned to conflict and will not be able to stand on its own feet for years to come.

Wrong policy sequence

As I argued elsewhere,[52] in addition to the specific sequence of some economic activities, the path and timing of economic policies and structural reform are key to effective post-conflict reconstruction. Afghanistan focused on adopting the perfect framework and first-best economic policies rather than engaging in the economics of peace, where the overriding objective should have been avoiding conflict relapse, not creating a productive economy.

Secondly, initial efforts to move the economy directly into higher productivity through commercial agriculture were misguided since building the necessary infrastructure takes time and production was delayed. While high productivity growth must be the longer-term objective, during the initial phase Afghanistan should have supported subsistence agriculture and other low-productivity production to keep people fed and occupied.

Finally, and after 13 years in transition, Afghanistan has failed to replace aid with foreign direct investment and net exports. In fact, despite the great potential in mining, foreign direct investment has collapsed since 2005 and it is almost nil at the present time. As a result, Afghanistan has fallen into an aid trap.

Missed opportunities and the drug sector

Following the 2000 Taliban ban, opium poppy production in Afghanistan was practically eliminated, falling from over 4,500 metric tons in 1999 (the peak level during Taliban rule) to 200 metric tons in 2001 – about the same level existing just before the Soviet invasion at the end of 1979. This provided a historic opportunity to cripple the drug sector going forward and improve security by depriving the insurgency and terrorist groups of funding.

By contrast, the delays in the creation of security forces and the lack of early support for subsistence agriculture to improve its returns – in part for ideological reasons but in part also for lack of domestic financing – allowed farmers to increasingly turn to growing poppies, with support from traders who provided credit and technical advice, bought the opium in situ, and shared the risks while the government remained passive.

Drug production often took the best available land, replacing food crops and making large imports necessary. At the same time, drug production and trafficking financed the insurgency, created insecurity, and promoted corruption among government officials and others involved, making good governance impossible to achieve.

Misguided policies and misplaced priorities resulted in the absurd situation that annual poppy production averaged 5,200 metric tons during foreign intervention (2002–15), more than twice what it was produced during the Taliban rule (1996–2001).[53]

Aid channeled outside the government budget

In Afghanistan, aid channeled outside the government budget created all kinds of problems.[54] As Herman Schaper, a former Dutch Ambassador to the UN and NATO rightly put it, "The best way to build capacity is not to deal with dozens of different programs devised by individual donors, but to have donors fund programs that are well-coordinated on the basis of Afghan priorities and with an Afghan lead." At the time, the Netherlands was the only country that fully channeled aid to Afghanistan through the budget. Parallel aid systems that lead to separate strategies are not only ineffective but also expensive and need to be eliminated as soon as feasible.[55]

Alastair McKechnie, a former director of the World Bank, argued that channeling aid through the Afghan budget using the reconstruction trust fund administered by the Bank was more cost effective. A basic package of health services contracted outside government channels was about 50 percent more expensive. As he pointed out, channeling aid through the budget had the additional advantage of allowing the government to build up its capacity and legitimacy with the electorate, the parliament, and donors by demonstrating its ability to oversee services and become accountable.[56]

The target of bringing at least 50 per cent of donors' assistance on-budget was only reached in 2014.[57] By channeling aid off-budget for so many years, donors contributed to a fragmented, cost-ineffective, and unsustainable economic reconstruction strategy. A piecemeal approach of having a donor build a school here, another one a road there, and still a third one a dam elsewhere, which is what happened in Afghanistan, led to schools without teachers; to clinics without health providers, equipment, or drugs; and to roads used for drug trafficking.

"Expeditionary economics" utilized mostly by the US military to restart economic activity in insecure areas in Afghanistan and Iraq and their policy of spending as much as possible in many projects, hoping that some would stick, was also ineffective, distortive, and wasteful, as is well-documented by US oversight bodies.

Long-term dependency

Despite rapid growth of about 8 percent on average from 2002 to 2015, accumulated GDP during this period was only $170 billion. With an economy of that size, foreign interveners were irresponsible in creating institutions – most notably the security forces – that the country will not be able to finance for years to come. Some figures are illustrative of the huge fiscal problem that the country faces, for which the United States is much to blame. Of the roughly $100 billion that the US Congress appropriated for reconstruction in 2002–15, about 60 percent of the total was used to create and maintain the security forces. This amount was equivalent to about 40 percent of accumulated GDP.

Since operational (current) expenditure to pay the wages and pensions of the military and police forces constitute a large part of security costs, it will have to be financed through aid for at least a decade longer, and most probably more. In 2015, with fiscal revenue at 10 percent of GDP covering only roughly one-third of the national budget, grants still covered the other two-thirds. Most notorious is the fact that grants still financed over 60 per cent of operational expenditure (which includes wages and salaries of the security forces). After 13 years of intervention, this is indeed striking since donors are normally reluctant to finance this type of expenditure except in the very short run.

This is not only "fiscal folly," as I called it earlier, but diverting such a large amount of aid to the security forces has deprived the large majority of Afghans from the benefits of economic aid.[58]

Kosovo, Timor-Leste, Iraq[59]

At the time that the Security Council put the UN transitionally in charge of Kosovo and East Timor, the two were provinces rather than independent countries, and the UN played an intrusive role by performing civil administration functions that are normally the sole prerogative of sovereign governments. In both cases, the Council mandated the SRSG to exercise all executive and legislative power through the issuance of regulations. As a result, the UN, supported by other bilateral and multilateral organizations, performed, for the first time, macroeconomic management, civil administration, and economic reconstruction functions which it had never performed before – except in a very restricted way in Cambodia – and for which it was not prepared.

These two UN transitional administrations,[60] however, had different destinies which affected policymaking. While the path to independence was clear from the beginning in the case of East Timor, this was not the case in Kosovo, which could only declare its independence unilaterally in 2008, restricting its policymaking options. The same was true of Iraq during the administration of the Coalition Transitional Authority (CPA).

In the multidisciplinary transition to peace, countries need to address the issue of property rights head-on since it is a precondition for current and future investment. Because of the transitional nature of the authorities in charge and the uncertainty going forward in Kosovo and Iraq, these countries faced "forward-looking" property rights issues – rather than the "backward-looking" ones discussed earlier which affected East Timor as well. The difference was that in Kosovo and Iraq investors did not know what would happen when legitimate authorities assumed power, and this obviously discouraged investment. These issues are more difficult to resolve.[61]

Early proposals to privatize the Trepca mining complex in Kosovo, the oil sector and/or other public companies in Iraq were naïve and obviously unsuccessful. Nevertheless, they had a negative impact on the prospects for national reconciliation. With less dogmatism and more realism, the policy of operating the Trepca mines as a public enterprise could have succeeded in keeping Kosovar Albanians and Serbs working together in the mines as a peacebuilding project, even if the mines could not be expected to be profitable in economic terms.

Kosovo also illustrates the need to adopt emergency policies during economic reconstruction, knowing well it would create longer-term distortions. In anticipation of a harsh winter, short-term programs to winterize destroyed houses in the mountains, after inhabitants refused to move to shelters in Mitrovica, were a waste of money in terms of the future housing development of the province. However, these programs were essential to save lives and had to be done promptly. A more effective solution had been found but had to be ruled out due to the EU's long bidding processes and restrictions on involving companies from nonmember countries.

Other distortions created during Kosovo's reconstruction were also typical. Because the international presence was large in Pristina, the UN often employed engineers and doctors as drivers and translators. This not only resulted in a shortage of professionals for the civil service but affected the future capacity of the country since these people would lose their skills over the years.

In contrast to Afghanistan's complex economic framework which was inadequate for the available human resources, a simple, transparent, flexible, and realistic framework for commercial policy and customs in Kosovo designed by the EU in 1999 had very good results in collecting fiscal revenue for the national budget.[62]

Timor-Leste provides an example of how security problems can derail the transition to peace, stability, and prosperity – at the time many considered it a success story.[63] As the country fell into renewed violence, the Security Council had to establish a new operation in mid-2006. The main challenge in 1999, when the UN assumed transitional administration, had been to improve social and economic conditions in the country.

Rather than utilizing a large portion of the increasing oil and gas revenue for such purpose, Timor Leste, with IMF support, created a Norwegian-style petroleum fund. According to the IMF, "the key element [of this fund] is a saving rule under which only interest income will be used" for development purposes. This policy was strongly supported by the World Bank, as Ramos-Horta, then Foreign Minister, noted in a speech to the 60th General Assembly.[64]

Although it is best practice to save for a rainy day, in war-torn countries it pours every day, and what is best practice under normal development may be a wasted opportunity during the post-conflict transition. There has never been a serious debate among policymakers whether resource-related income should be saved for future generations in a fund for a financial return or if it should be invested in human and physical infrastructure to improve the productive capacity of future generations as well as that of the present generation. The latter, if effectively and transparently invested, would probably produce a higher rate of return than the former. Most importantly, as East Timor well illustrates, without immediate gains, the country is likely to relapse into conflict.[65]

What policymakers should not even consider is to replicate institutional arrangements that originate in a completely different environment. What may be best practice for a developed country such as Norway, with an aging population and at the top of the *Human Development Index* (*HDI*), will certainly not be best practice for a developing country like Timor-Leste, which had one of the fastest growing populations in the world with a large proportion of it younger than 15 years old, one of the lowest per capita income levels, seriously damaged infrastructure, and which was at the bottom of the *HDI*. A different institutional arrangement for its oil and gas revenue could have likely accelerated economic reconstruction and prevented the renewed violence that broke out in 2006. Indeed, the petroleum fund, in conjunction with a policy of zero domestic or foreign borrowing, was too restrictive for a country with such characteristics and such needs.

In Iraq, the currency exchange presented different challenges from Afghanistan given that it took place while "360 tons of cash" were flown into the country from funds that the international banks had frozen abroad owing to sanctions.[66] No other war-torn country has ever had access to such large domestic funding.

Iraq provides the perfect example of things to avoid in the early transition. Perhaps the CPA's major mistake was to fire all Baath Party officials from positions of responsibility and to disband the Iraqi army without a program to disarm, demobilize, and reintegrate them. These two measures left 400,000 to 500,000 armed people unemployed and deprived the civil service of critical technical expertise. The foolishness and short-sightedness of this policy at a time when unemployment could have verged on 60 percent cannot be justified on any grounds. The CPA partly reversed the ban in the following weeks, but considerable damage had already been done.[67]

Iraq is also a good example of how resource-rich countries need a fair allocation of resources. A legal framework that contemplates such allocation can support economic reconstruction, while an unfair one is likely to become a major obstacle to reconstruction and peacebuilding. In Iraq, this remains an unresolved issue. As the secretary-general pointed out in 2015, his SRSG "continued his efforts to mediate between key Iraqi stakeholders, including by facilitating an important agreement on revenue-sharing and oil exports between the Government of Iraq and the Kurdistan Regional Government."[68]

In a book that should be read by those involved in economic reconstruction, James Savage illustrates how imposing unrealistic "benchmarks" may have unexpected consequences. The 17th Benchmark, which raised the Iraqi budget execution as the main measure of CPA's success, resulted in massive waste, corruption, and ineffective policy outcomes. The goal became to spend money quickly – whether American or Iraqi funding – since the fiscal stimulus was believed to support security and stability efforts.[69]

It was thus that efforts at expediency trumped any concern about how money was spent and overwhelmed the CPA and Iraqi government's limited capacity for accountability. Although it was true that the urgency of paying salaries and pensions and other emergency measures rightly outweighed concerns over accountability initially, as had happened in Kosovo earlier, the fact that the CPA could not account for $9 billion in Iraq funds, as assessed by the Special Inspector General for Iraq Reconstruction, was just amazing. This was particularly so since US interveners often accuse the Iraqis, Afghans, and others of corruption.[70]

At the same time, best budgetary practices in industrialized countries may be neither effective nor desirable when applied to countries such as Iraq for the reasons discussed earlier. Despite the technicalities of the budgetary process, Savage makes it clear that the budget is a political process, and much will depend on what is politically feasible in the country.[71] In this regard, as detailed in his book, the US budgetary experts rightly rejected imposing an American model of budget formulation on the Iraqis, relying instead on the basic elements of the existing system because successful institutional changes are highly contingent on aid beneficiary ownership and buy-in. In its absence, the ability of Iraqis to subvert, sabotage, and minimize the effectiveness of foreign-generated rules would have been significant.

Peacebuilding in countries on the agenda of the Peacebuilding Commission

The decision to include two countries on the Commission's agenda in 2006 that had made the transition years before (Burundi in 1998 and Sierra Leone in 2002) was an early harbinger of the problems the Commission would encounter in performing its tasks effectively and without duplication. It also presaged the scarcity of resources and tremendous waste that can result from inadequate institutional arrangements.[72]

Burundi and Sierra Leone had UN integrated peacebuilding operations in place in 2006. Thus, the Commission's mandate to "to bring together all relevant actors, to marshal resources and to advise on and propose integrated strategies for post-conflict peacebuilding and recovery" added yet another layer to the many strategies already in place (for example, at the time of its inclusion, Sierra Leone had three strategies in place, including one on poverty reduction).[73]

Had the Commission really wanted to have an impact from the very beginning to comply with its mandate, it would have tried hard to get, say, Nepal onto its agenda. The country signed the Comprehensive Peace Agreement of 2006 and needed to establish a strategy for reconstruction as soon as possible. This would have given the Commission a purpose early on, namely, to support peacebuilding in countries not on the Security Council agenda or exiting from it. Both Sierra Leone and Burundi had at the time large peacebuilding operations already in place, and the Commission added to the confusion, duplication, and waste in resources. More worrisome, it also strained weak national bureaucracies with increased and often competing demands on their time and resources.

Chapter 5 discussed the folly of including Liberia on the Commission's agenda in 2015. In the case of Guinea, Guinea-Bissau, and the Central African Republic, the Commission could play a more useful role in keeping lacklustre interest in these countries alive among donors.

All six countries on the Commission's agenda have been analyzed recently, and case studies were published in 2015 and 2016.[74] The surprising thing of all of them is the small importance that economic matters play in the analysis of peacebuilding in those countries. Except for a few general allusions to "humanitarian assistance" or "development," no economic issue is discussed with any specificity or depth. This is particularly striking since economic and social conditions in these countries are appalling and certainly have haunted peacebuilding efforts – and will continue to do so. It is all the more surprising since UNDP ranks them all (except Rwanda) among the worst six percent of the 188 countries included in the 2015 *HDI*. Rwanda is ranked in the bottom 13 percent of all countries.

As discussed in Chapter 5, Liberia's lack of inclusive economic policies is a major cause of concern and risk if and when the UN peacekeeping operation finally exits the country after 13 years. Liberia's development model in the post-war period, following that of the past, is based on natural resource exploitation, which generates most of the country's output, foreign exchange and fiscal revenue.[75]

The natural resource sector, driven by economic growth in iron ore and cash crops operating as "enclaves," has greatly benefited foreign investors and domestic elites but has failed to produce many links to other sectors of the economy. More importantly, it has failed to create jobs for the majority of the 75–80 percent of the population living in rural areas who have been excluded from any peace dividend in terms of better livelihoods or services and who hardly survive from subsistence agriculture and petty trading.

In fact, the 2015 *HDI* shows that during the first decade after the peace agreement, roughly 65 percent of the population lived below the national income poverty line, 85 percent if measured by purchasing power parity (PPP) levels of $1.25 a day. How is this possible for one of the two largest recipients of aid in the world? In fact, the percentage living in poverty using the PPP criteria was much higher than in any of the other five countries on the Commission's agenda.

It was indeed ironic but also unfortunate, given the disastrous performance of her country in terms of human development in the seven years she had led it, that Secretary-General Ban Ki-moon appointed Ellen Johnson Sirleaf in 2012, together with the leaders of Indonesia and Britain, to lead a global panel to set new international targets on sustainable development. What kind of example was the Secretary-General trying to set? Was he trying to score on the gender issue[76] by rewarding Johnson Sirleaf for being the first black woman president in Africa, who as a former staffer of the World Bank and UNDP had become the darling of donors? It was precisely the misguided development-as-usual policies in a country torn by civil war, instability, poverty, and appalling human development indicators that made necessary a large UN peacekeeping operation in the country to maintain the peace.

While it is understandable that the UN and other foreign interveners have been desperate for a success story in establishing peace after civil war in Africa, doubts about the growth path adopted by the country have been increasing since 2011. Even the World Bank, which had encouraged and supported Liberia's policies, warned about the continuation of the "growth without development" policies that had in the past led to civil war rather than to middle income status, as many thought it would. The Bank noted that, despite Liberia's success at both stabilizing the macro environment and regaining the confidence of the international community, a lack of "inclusive growth," was creating increasing social conflict. Indeed, the Bank listed the "latent risk of disruption of peace, political and economic stability" as one of the concerns in Liberia going forward.[77]

Presidential and parliamentary elections in October 2011 were also indications of the higher risk. The election, which required a second round in November that was marred by violence and boycotted by the opposition, had created a new sense of urgency. Soon after the election, President Johnson Sirleaf acknowledged having heard "loud and clear" the message from her people of their demand for decent jobs and better services. Her announcement that her second term would focus on national reconciliation, a clearly neglected aspect of her first term, was welcome by many at the time, but critics remained sceptical.

As an article by Silas Siakor and Rachael Knight in the *New York Times* on 20 January 2012 warned, "unbeknown to many outside Liberia, Ms. Johnson Sirleaf's government may now be sowing the seeds of future conflict by handing over huge tracts of land to foreign investors and dispossessing rural Liberians." Silas Siakor, of The Sustainable Development Institute in Liberia, exposed evidence that Liberia President Charles Taylor used the profits of unchecked, rampant logging to pay for the costs of the civil war. This evidence was key to the imposition of UN sanctions on logging in Liberia.

All these and many other issues should have set off alarm bells in the secretary-general's office that perhaps Johnson Sirleaf was not exactly the person to honour with such appointment, particularly if the purpose was to promote issues relating to sustainable development. The model she was using for her people was certainly not working and must not be emulated. As discussed in Chapter 5, the Commission was oblivious to it until SRSG Karin Landgren brought the issue up in a May 2015 meeting.

Conclusions

This chapter picked up on a number of country experiences in which economic factors – or the neglect of them – affected UN peacebuilding efforts, both positively and negatively. Some of these experiences have been repeated over and over in different countries, but both national leaders and foreign interveners have failed to take advantage of lessons learnt.

In putting these case studies together, I was struck by the lack of institutional memory at the UN, particularly in the economics area. Regrettably, the good and bad lessons as well as best practices which emerged from such cases seem to have been forgotten, at a great cost for an organization that has repeated mistakes over and over – and has largely failed to take credit from its many successes.

Going forward, the UN needs to consistently build up a body of evidence of policies that have worked and those that have created problems or derailed peacebuilding efforts. In Chapter 8, I will use these and other experiences discussed throughout the book to synthesize evidence on the economic factors that have affected peacebuilding during the last quarter of a century. I will present evidence in eight general premises that national leaders with the assistance of foreign interveners could analyze and adapt to the national context so that the economics of conflict resolution and the economics of peace can support rather than hinder peacebuilding efforts.

Notes

1 See del Castillo, *Guilty Party*, 166–167.
2 "El papel de los desmovilizados en la construcción de la paz," paper presented at a conference in Nicaragua in 1995 by members of AMODEG (Portuguese acronym of the Mozambican Association of Demobilized Soldiers).
3 For a detailed case study, see del Castillo, *Rebuilding War-Torn States*, Chapter 7.
4 See, for example, Charles T. Call, "Assessing El Salvador's Transition from Civil War to Peace," in *Ending Civil Wars: The Implementation of Peace Agreements*, 383.
5 For a detailed analysis of the program and the challenges, see del Castillo, "Arms-for-Land Deal: Lessons from El Salvador," in *Multidimensional Peacekeeping: Lessons from Cambodia and El Salvador*, Michael Doyle, I. Johnstone and Robert C. Orr, eds. (Cambridge: Cambridge University Press, 1997).
6 El Salvador Peace Agreement (Mexico City: United Nations, 1992).
7 De Soto, "Ending Violent Conflict in El Salvador," in *Herding Cats*, 362 and 379.
8 Rubén Zamora, "Foro: Procesos de Reconstrucción Comparados: El Caso de El Salvador (Guatemala: Flacso, 9 March 1995), 4.
9 De Soto, "Ending Violent Conflict in El Salvador," 379.
10 For details and data, see Graciana del Castillo, "Post-Conflict Reconstruction and the Challenge to the International Organizations: The Case of El Salvador," *World Development*, Vol. 29 (December 2001): 1967–1985. As I joined the secretary-general's office in early 1992, with responsibility for post-conflict reconstruction and as liaison with the BWIs, relations with the Fund were held at a technical level on El Salvador and on other war-torn countries.
11 David Holiday and William Stanley, "Building the Peace: Preliminary Lessons from El Salvador," *Journal of International Affairs*, 46/2 (Winter 1993), 423.
12 Goulding, *Peacemonger*, 241–45.
13 The performance of the economy during the reconstruction plan was impressive. See del Castillo, "Post-Conflict Reconstruction" for details, particularly Tables 1 and 2.
14 Rubén Zamora, "Foro," 9–10.
15 El Salvador Peace Agreement, Chapter V, 5. See also Doyle and Sambanis, *Making War and Building Peace*, 208–209.
16 Ibid.
17 As a member of the "Business and Peace" group at USIP, I questioned the wisdom of focusing exclusively on foreign companies for two reasons: the domestic private sector has much to offer, and its exclusion could lead to suspicion of foreign interveners' intentions.
18 Del Castillo, *Rebuilding War-Torn States*, 134.
19 United Nations, *A More Secure World*, 61.

20 For details, see del Castillo, *Rebuilding War-Torn States*, 127–130.
21 Gunnarson, Agneta et al., *La Cooperación sueca con El Salvador: 1979–2001* (Stockholm: SIDA Evaluation, 04/20, July 2004).
22 See de Soto and del Castillo, *Obstacles to Peacebuilding Revisited*, 221.
23 Personal exchange with Roger Myerson.
24 Michael Doyle, I. Johnstone and Robert C. Orr, Introduction to *Multidimensional Peacekeeping*, 10.
25 Ibid., 16.
26 Cheryl M. Lee Kim and Mark Metrikas, "A Fragile Peace," in *Multidimensional Peacekeeping*, 118 and 124.
27 Philip Shenon, "Cambodia Arms Flow Back to Thailand," *The New York Times* (7 March 1993), cited by Doyle, "Authority and Elections in Cambodia," in *Multidimensional Peacekeeping*, 160.
28 For details see Aldo Ajello and Patrick Wittmann, "Mozambique," in *The UN Security Council: From the Cold War to the 21st Century*, David M. Malone, ed. (Boulder, Colo., and London: Lynne Rienner, 2004), 437–450; Aldo Ajello, "Mozambique: Implementation of the 1992 Peace Agreement," in *Herding Cats*, 619–642.
29 See also Dobbins et al., *The UN's Role in Nation Building*, 104.
30 Paul Collier, "The Economic Causes of Civil Conflict," in *Turbulent Peace: The Challenges of Managing International Conflict*, Chester A. Crocker, Fen O. Hampson, and Pamela Aall, eds. (Washington, DC: United States Institute for Peace Press, 2nd edition, 2001), 158–159.
31 For details see Aldo Ajello and Patrick Wittmann, "Mozambique," 440.
32 For a discussion of problems related to peace implementation in Guatemala, see William Stanley and David Holiday, "Broad Participation, Diffuse Responsibility: Peace Implementation in Guatemala," in *Ending Civil Wars*, 421–462.
33 James Boyce, "Aid Conditionality as a Tool for Peacebuilding Opportunities and Constraints," in *State Failure, Collapse and Reconstruction*, Jennifer Milliken, ed. (Malden, Mass.: Blackwell Publishing Ltd., 2003), 266–289.
34 Guatemala received $1.7 billion in aid over the first five years of the peace process (1997–2001), which amounted to only slightly over 2 percent of GDP annually on average.
35 Stanley and Holiday, "Broad Participation, Diffuse Responsibility."
36 As Juan Carlos di Tata (my classmate at Columbia) told me many times, the Fund had pushed the government in the past to increase tax revenue, but it was always blocked by the strong business association.
37 Gilbert M. Khadiagala, "Implementing the Arusha Peace Agreement on Rwanda," in *Ending Civil Wars*, 463.
38 Ibid., 466, with the author citing Catherine Newbury, "Background to Genocide in Rwanda," *Issue* 23/2 (1995), 12–17.
39 International Monetary Fund, *Rwanda: 2014 Article IV Consultation and Second Review Under the Policy Support Instrument* (Washington, DC: IMF Country Report No. 14/343, 2014), 5.
40 World Bank, 2011 *World Development Report*, 159.
41 Although Collier in particular but other analysts as well have recommended that aid be disbursed to war-torn countries after a few years in the transition so that countries can increase their absorptive capacity and be

able to utilize such aid more productively, this could seriously endanger their capacity to keep the peace in the immediate transition. What might be true from a purely development perspective is certainly not true from an economics of peace point of view where the overriding priority is not to be productive but to ensure that the country does not relapse into war.

42 See Andrew England, "The Task of Rebuilding a Nation"; David White, "Hopes Pinned on Regional Integration to End Aid Dependence"; and Tom Burgis, "A Difficult Name to Sell to the World," *Financial Times*, 5 December 2006, *Special Report on Rwanda*. See also Kevin Whitelaw, "Rwanda Reborn," *US News & World Report*, 23 April 2007. For more details on Rwanda's economy, see P. Crisafully and A. Redmond, *Rwanda, Inc.* (New York: Palgrave Macmillan, 2012).

43 Many have expressed concern not only about Rwanda's undemocratic behaviour but also about its aggressive military actions over time in the DRC. See, for example, Andrew England, "A More Conciliatory Agenda," *Financial Times*, 5 December 2006, *Special Report on Rwanda*.

44 The issue of sequence with regard to different aspects of the transition is discussed in various chapters in Arnim Langer and Graham K. Brown, eds, *Building Sustainable Peace: Timing and Sequencing of Post-Conflict Reconstruction and Peacebuilding* (Oxford: Oxford University Press, 2016).

45 The author was economic policy adviser to the SRSG in Kosovo in the early period of the transition when the economic framework was established.

46 For an analysis of unsuccessful DDR efforts in Afghanistan and for the extensive bibliography on the subject, see del Castillo, *Guilty Party*, 243. For Kosovo, see del Castillo, *Rebuilding War-Torn States*, Chapter 8.

47 For a detailed analysis of economic reconstruction in Afghanistan, see del Castillo, *Guilty Party* (2nd edition), and *Rebuilding War-Torn States*, 166–190. Except where otherwise specified, data and calculations for Afghanistan are from the author's databank used in *Guilty Party*.

48 Ahmed Rashid, *The Taliban: Militant Islam, Oil and the Fundamentalism in Central Asia* (London: I. B. Tauris and Co. Ltd, Kindle Edition), locations 4758–63.

49 Marina Ottaway and Anatol Lieven, "Rebuilding Afghanistan: Fantasy Versus Reality," *Policy Brief* (Washington, DC: Carnegie Endowment for International Peace, January 2002), 7.

50 Cited by Edward Girardet, *Killing the Cranes* (White River Junction, Vt.: Chelsea Green Publishing Company, 2011), 330–331. See also Barnett R. Rubin, *Afghanistan From the Cold War Through the War on Terror* (New York: Oxford University Press, 2013) for more details on the position of this group.

51 World Bank, *World Development Report*, 196.

52 Del Castillo, "Economic Reconstruction and Reforms in Post-Conflict Countries," in *Building Sustainable Peace*.

53 For an update of this vicious circle in Afghanistan in 2014–2015, see *2016 Epilogue* in del Castillo, *Guilty Party* (2nd edition). Data on drugs is compiled by the UN Office of Drugs and Crime.

54 These are well analyzed by the Special Inspector General for Afghanistan. See also del Castillo, *Guilty Party*.

55 Schaper and McKechnie spoke at a conference I organized in October 2009 on "Peace Through Reconstruction" at Columbia University.

56 Ibid.

57 World Bank presentation at Senior Official Meeting (Kabul, 4–5 September 2015), 9.

58 Del Castillo, *Guilty Party*, 235.

59 For detailed case studies on economic reconstruction in Kosovo and Iraq and for an analysis of the resource fund in Timor-Leste, see del Castillo, *Rebuilding War-Torn States*, 137–165, 191–217, and 249–251, respectively.

60 For an excellent analysis of transitional administrations, see Richard R. Caplan, *International Governance of War-Torn Territories: Premise and Reconstruction* (Oxford: Oxford University Press, 2005).

61 In East Timor, the "backward looking" problem was to establish claims dating from the Portuguese and Indonesian administrations. See Caplan, *International Governance of War-Torn Territories*, 149–150. See also del Castillo, *Rebuilding-War Torn States*, 237–238.

62 Ibid., 148–149.

63 See, for example, Doyle and Sambanis, *Making War and Building Peace*, 199.

64 Del Castillo, "Auferstehen aus Ruinen," and *Rebuilding War-Torn States*, 249–251.

65 The World Bank, *2011 World Development Report*, 156, presents the typical development as usual argument for creating such a fund, ignoring the high risk of relapse.

66 Del Castillo, *Rebuilding War-Torn States*, 204–205.

67 Ibid., 195–196.

68 UN, *Report on the Work of the Organization* (New York: UN, 2015), 15.

69 James D. Savage, *Reconstructing Iraq's Budgetary Institutions: Coalition State Building after Saddam* (New York: Cambridge University Press, 2013).

70 Ibid.; see also del Castillo, *Rebuilding War-Torn Countries*, footnote 372.

71 For this reason, he argues that donor agencies that have political clout were more effective in Iraq. Thus, the U.S Treasury, which was privy to political and security decisions, was clearly more effective than USAID in supporting Iraq.

72 Del Castillo, *Rebuilding War-Torn States*, 59–62.

73 Jenkins, *Peacebuilding*, 78–89.

74 See de Coning and Stamnes, *UN Peacebuilding Architecture*; and UN, *The Challenge of Sustaining Peace*.

75 For details on the Liberia economic model, see del Castillo, "Aid and Employment Generation in Conflict-Affected Countries."

76 I would not have objected as much if she had been appointed to some committee on gender issues.

77 World Bank, "Liberia: Growth Diagnostics for Inclusive Growth," paper presented at the High Level National Economic Forum, Monrovia, 12–13 September, 1 and 24.

8 Policymaking premises for effective economic reconstruction

- **Background to the premises**
- **Basic premises**
- **Conclusions**

Despite the specificity of each particular case, both good and bad lessons from the experience in the post-Cold War period have allowed us to identify the special needs and policy constraints of war-affected countries and to propose a number of premises that national policymakers and foreign interveners must consider before engaging in the economics of conflict resolution and in the economics of peace. The premises presented in this chapter are listed in Table 8.1.

Background to the premises

As Boutros-Ghali emphasized in 1992, "the foundation stone of [peacebuilding] is and must remain the State."[1] Although national policy ownership is key to policy success and sustainability, it is understandable that foreign interveners will have an important role in the reconstruction and peacebuilding strategy of poor war-torn countries with weak governance and low levels of human development. It is also understandable that given the low savings capacity of these countries, particularly in the early transition, they will rely on economic aid to carry out reconstruction.

The focus of the discussion on whether aid is good or bad is unwarranted for war-torn countries that generally have a low savings capacity, at least in the short run. The issue is how to make aid more effective and dynamic in creating investment (rather than consumption), and more inclusive and fair, by creating employment and better services for the large majority of the population, including the rural population, which is often large in these countries.

The success of economic reconstruction is not only key to peace-building efforts; it is *sine qua non* for security and political stability and national reconciliation. If it fails, the country will become aid dependent, the economy will not be viable and able to provide services and jobs, and peace will be put at risk.

Each country, however, will end up with a different strategy, at the national and local level, depending on factors that are peculiar to their own economies. These include commitments made in peace agreements; the level of war destruction; the economy's physical resources and human skills; its trade and investment relations with the rest of the world and its connectivity; the level of international support that the country can garner based on geopolitical factors, the availability of natural resources and other assets that can attract foreign investors; and the specific timeframe for reconstruction. Options, of course, will evolve as countries move along the path shown in Diagram 3.1

Some of the premises discussed below are related but have different policy implications.[2] Others may depend on the specific stage in which countries find themselves in the war-to-peace transition. But ignoring these premises has often led to misguided policies, misplaced priorities and wasted aid, which have been directly associated with setbacks and even to the collapse of the peace process in many countries.

This, of course, does not mean that all premises should apply to all situations at all times. Common sense is of utmost importance in applying them. The more informed and the better different stakeholders understand the country, its people, its culture, its security, its politics, its economy, and its idiosyncrasies, the more appropriate for the context the strategy for economic reconstruction will be and the longer peace is likely to last.

Failure at effectively addressing the economics of conflict resolution during peace negotiations, as has often been the case in the past, and the economics of peace during the post-conflict phase continue to be major obstacles to peacebuilding. Peace mediators and special/executive representatives of the secretary-general heading multidisciplinary operations in countries transitioning to peace must have the right kind of expertise to ensure that proper consideration is given to the following premises.

Basic premises

Premise 1: Economic reconstruction is not development as usual

For countries undergoing the multidisciplinary war-to-peace transition, the overarching goal of economic reconstruction – or the economics of peace – must be to promote stability and to avoid a relapse into

Table 8.1 The economics of peace premises for effective reconstruction and peacebuilding

	Because	*It requires that*
Premise 1	Economic reconstruction is not development as usual	• The peace (political) objective should prevail over the development (economic) one at all times; • Because the political objective should prevail over the economic one, optimal (first-best) economic policies are not attainable nor desirable.
Premise 2	Policymaking following crisis is distinctly different from normal development	• Emergency policies be adopted without delay; • Priority be given to crisis-affected groups; • The impact of aid be maximized, avoiding corruption; • National policymakers rein in the international community to ensure policy ownership and sustainability.
Premise 3	Economic policies and institutions must be simple, transparent, flexible, sequenced, and realistic	• Policies and institutions not be too complex as to facilitate inefficiency and corruption and require foreign consultants to operate; • Authorities that lack political legitimacy limit themselves to adopting conflict-sensitive and uncontroversial policies; • Institutions be built reflecting the country's financial conditions; • Frameworks be built with flexibility to engage in expansionary policies when facing delays in aid.
Premise 4	The private sector must be effectively engaged in the peace process	• Economic expertise be part of mediators' teams to analyze the local private sector, how it can best be involved, and what it is willing to provide; • The private sector be effectively involved in post-conflict reconstruction.
Premise 5	The impact of aid must be maximized through effective, integrated, sequenced, and noncorrupt practices	• Large spikes in aid be utilized effectively, minimizing corruption; • Aid be channelled through the national budget to support national ownership and build capacity, to be cost effective, and to ensure project sustainability; • Humanitarian and reconstruction aid not be conflated and that reconstruction aid be disbursed promptly and invested wisely to avoid aid dependency; • Aid be replaced with foreign direct investment and exports as soon as possible.
Premise 6	Peace processes must contemplate a fair use of natural resources	• Peace agreements contemplate a fair use of natural resources and compensation to losers to ensure that those who benefited from the spoils of war can be lured to support the peace process.

	Because	*It requires that*
Premise 7	Rapid growth is not enough; growth must be inclusive, dynamic, and sustainable	• A level playing field be created for the large majority of the population rather than only supporting elites; • The economy move from supporting subsistence agriculture and microenterprises to increasing productivity to make growth more dynamic; • The environment and biodiversity be respected; • Economic activity be made sustainable once aid starts to wither.
Premise 8	Create an appropriate yardstick to measure success	• Because the peace objective should always prevail over the development one and therefore second-best policies are often needed, success should be measured by the "peacebuilding yardstick," where policies and projects are judged more qualitatively by whether they contribute to peacebuilding rather than on purely economic criteria.

conflict. Thus, in addition to the normal challenge of socioeconomic development, countries must accommodate the extra burden of economic rehabilitation of dilapidated infrastructure and services and the critical challenge of national reconciliation following civil wars.

The later includes complex and often difficult-to-finance activities, such as the delivery of emergency aid to former conflict zones (some of which may be outside government control); the rehabilitation of public goods; the reintegration of former combatants, refugees and internally displaced groups into society and productive activities; the rebuilding of houses and other economic assets destroyed during the conflict, and the clearance of mines.

A peace dividend in terms of better basic services, infrastructure, and improved incomes for the large majority of the population have proven key to the effective and sustained implementation of peace agreements. Peace agreements lacking effective programs to rebuild the economy and create productive and inclusive jobs have proved ill-prepared in allowing countries to stand on their own feet and avoid large aid dependencies.

Governments need to establish well-planned and synchronized programs for disarming, demobilization and reintegration (DDR). Reintegration has largely failed mainly because of the temporary and hence unsustainable nature of many of the employment opportunities, particularly through public infrastructure projects (which are not fiscally sustainable) and jobs with foreign agencies. Reintegration is the longest and one of the most costly and difficult-to-finance programs in peace agreements.

The creation of private sector jobs is essential to the success of reintegration policies, and the record is most unimpressive. Foreign interveners have been largely incapable of supporting war-torn countries to create sustainable jobs in the private sector through the promotion of local entrepreneurship and new startups. Active policies to promote such opportunities through subsidies, credit, training, and technical support are imperative. The provision of subsidies directly to firms for the hiring of crises-affected groups could be promising and must be considered.[3]

Because peace-related activities have important economic and financial consequences and should be given priority in budget allocations, the peace (political) and development (economic) objectives often clash during the transition to peace. Effective economic policymaking in war-torn countries must focus on ensuring that the peace objective should prevail at all times during the economics of peace phase.

It should be clear to all that, should the country revert to war – which in our sample has happened more than half the time – there will hardly be any chance for development to take root. Recognizing the political constraint to economic policymaking means accepting that optimal and best-practice economic policies are not attainable – or, indeed, even desirable during this phase.

Premise 2: Economic policymaking following crises is distinctly different from normal development

Economic policymaking in countries coming out of crises – following either conflict, natural disasters, or financial collapse – must be fundamentally different from policymaking under normal development for five main reasons (Table 8.2). The differences arise with respect to the horizon over which economic policies can be planned (short-term vs. medium- and long-term); the amount of aid (sharp spikes vs. low and stable flows); the treatment of different groups (preferences vs. equal treatment for all); the establishment of security and the rule of law (foreign vs. domestic forces); and the involvement of the international community in national affairs (intense and intrusive vs. noninterference in national affairs).

Because the overriding objective of post-crisis situations is to avoid reverting to war or aggravating social tensions, this second premise for effective reconstruction is that economic policymaking should be geared towards:

Table 8.2 Economic policymaking

In countries in normal development	In countries in post-conflict or other crises
Medium- and long-term framework	Distortionary emergency programs required
Low and stable foreign assistance	Sharp spikes in foreign assistance
Application of the "development principle"	Application of the "reconstruction principle"
Government establishes rule of law	Foreign troops and police support rule of law
Political involvement of international community considered interference	Intensive and often intrusive political involvement

Adopting emergency policies without delay

While under normal development, economic policies and programs aimed at addressing economic stagnation, backwardness, weak institutions, poor human resources, poverty, foreign indebtedness, and other pathologies of underdevelopment are planned with a medium- and long-term horizon in mind, no such luxury exists following crises.

As countries come out of crisis, emergency policies must be adopted decisively and without delay to deal with homeless populations, hunger, disease, returnees, displaced populations, and demobilizing fighters as well as all other immediate needs created by the crisis.

Emergency policies often serve a short-term humanitarian, political, or security purpose but often distort and have other unintended consequences on long-term development. Such policies may even conflict with some of the other premises for effective reconstruction, as, for example, the need to channel funding through the government budget since this may significantly delay the process to the point that it may be impossible to prevent disaster.

Delays in approving disbursement of funds in the immediate transition to peace and misguided priorities to wait for the country to have higher absorptive capacity – reflecting the development-as-usual approach of multilateral and bilateral development organizations – have often impeded effective reconstruction and led the country back to conflict.

Giving priority to crisis-affected groups

In post-crisis situations, policymakers often need to put aside the guiding "equity" (or development) principle – that is, treating equally all groups with the same needs – in favour of the "peacebuilding" (or political) principle, which justifies giving special treatment to groups most affected by the crisis, even in the presence of others with similar needs.

Thus, for peace to be long lasting, economic reconstruction policies should be targeted toward decreasing the grievances of those groups most affected by the conflict. Going forward, programs should be carefully designed so as to include women, children, and youth that were involved as combatants and were victims of specific violence against them during the conflict and are often neglected in reintegration and in other programs.

Utilizing aid effectively, reining in the international community and ensuring national policy ownership

Due to the large volume of aid, technical assistance, and foreign troops in the post-conflict context, it is inevitable that the political involvement of the international community in the internal affairs of these countries be intense and intrusive.

Under normal development, such level of foreign political involvement would be considered an unacceptable interference with national sovereignty. At the same time, the large physical presence of the international community in the reconstructing country often creates serious economic distortions.

Moreover, due to the large involvement of foreign interveners, national ownership in the post-conflict context, which is key to the successful implementation and sustainability of reconstruction policies, is difficult to achieve. Policies should not be imposed from abroad or even by unrepresentative elites within the government. It is up to national leaders to design policies, set up priorities, and build up broad support for them at the national and local levels. National ownership, national capacity and ingenuity, and national consensus building are essential elements to sustain the peace. At the same time, national leaders need to ensure support of donors to be able to implement their policies. A difficult balance indeed!

Premise 3: Economic policies and institutions must be simple, transparent, flexible, and realistic

Despite their scarce human resources, technical capabilities, and infrastructure, countries in the transition from war must establish as soon as possible a basic framework for macroeconomic policymaking as well as the microeconomic foundations to create an appropriate legal and regulatory framework for investment, production, and trade. In such circumstances, it is unrealistic and certainly counterproductive to create a framework that is too complex and requires expertise and resources that the country does not have and may not expect to have for a long time.

At the same time, countries should avoid policies that may be optimal for countries during normal development, such as the independence of the central bank and other restrictive monetary or fiscal policies, that will limit options for governments to implement and finance key peace-related programs and to gain legitimacy. Within reason, policies directed towards productive investment, including food production to replace imports, in economies with large excess capacity would not need to be inflationary. Governments need the option to do it through their own domestic resources if need arises to avoid relapse.

Since the establishment of clear and stable property rights is a precondition for investment, policymakers need to address this issue head on. The experience of several conflict-affected countries has illustrated how property rights issues can be very different across countries. In some, the issue is "backward looking," which means that rights have to be established and registries have to be updated, something that requires technical and financial support. In others, the issue is "forward looking" since investors are not sure what will happen when legitimate authorities assume power. Uncertainty about property rights in such cases is normally paramount in discouraging investment.

In the meantime, a weak interim national government, or even more a transitional administration led by the UN or a foreign government, should normally avoid implementing policies such as privatizing natural resources, liberalizing specific sectors, or any other major legal, institutional or regulatory change when doing so may incite political resistance, even in peacetime.

If such interim authority decides to go ahead with privatization anyway, it should evaluate carefully the cost of disposing of national assets at a large discount. Because investors are reluctant to invest in assets for which property rights might change once a legitimate government takes over, they will require an exorbitant discount in the price of the assets to incur such a risk.[4]

Premise 4: The private sector must be effectively engaged in the peace process

During peacemaking, an expert on the economics of conflict resolution in the mediator's team will need to analyze carefully the private sector in the specific country to determine what the sector could bring to the negotiations, design, and post-conflict implementation of the peace agreement. It is clear that, despite not being a party to the agreement, the private sector will be critical to its implementation.

Because the spirit and the letter of peace agreements will either facilitate or impede their implementation, mediators will not be able to design effective and implementable agreements without understanding what type of economy and programs the parties want, and the government and the private sector are willing to support and finance in the post-conflict phase. All three stakeholders must take ownership of the reconstruction process for it to succeed. This is why a mediator's team needs proper economic expertise.

Financing for post-conflict reconstruction and creating sustainable employment are critical issues in this respect that need to be properly addressed. While there is generally uncertainty during peace negotiations about availability of foreign assistance, projections need to be made. Even in countries with strong private sectors that contribute handsomely to government coffers and can create necessary employment, tensions usually arise since economic and peace objectives often compete for limited resources. The situation of countries with weak private sectors is even more challenging.

Many of these countries are rich in natural resources and hence have great potential to attract foreign investment for export in areas such as agriculture, mining, and energy. But exploitation of such resources is often resisted by local communities and other groups. Thus, innovative ways to promote and attract investors while ensuring a fair gain for local communities in particular and for the domestic economy in general is key to avoid future conflicts.

Because in many countries certain investors in the private sector have benefited greatly during the war from the illegal exploitation of natural resources, drugs, or sanctions, those investors often act as spoilers. In poor countries farmers may also become spoilers if drug eradication and interdiction programs take away their means of subsistence.[5]

Moving out as quickly as possible from the underground war economy, which is known to undermine peace, governance, and the rule of law, may require policies which are resisted by the international financial institutions but are used by industrial countries. Such policies may include tax incentives, subsidies, and other price-support mechanisms for improved irrigation, production, and infrastructure development.

Peace mediators can also consider support from the private sector in donor countries. In this regard they could look for support from foundations and other philanthropic organizations that are interested or are already operating in specific war-torn countries. Mediators could also look for support from specialized companies in specific sectors. For example, peace processes can normally benefit from specialized advice on how to bring cleaner and cheaper electricity to cities and rural areas.

Mediators and donors must stay away from decisions on specific sectors that can create suspicions in war-torn countries or that may hint at foreigners' effort to disempower them by giving contracts to foreign contractors and taking over their assets through early efforts at privatization.

Premise 5: The impact of aid must be maximized through effective, integrated, sequenced, and noncorrupt practices

Large spikes in aid are difficult to utilize and manage effectively

Countries coming out of big crises attract large amounts of foreign aid as media attention focuses on the plight of drowned or starving children, raped women, homeless populations, physical destruction, and other such tragedies (Table 6.1). By contrast, aid during normal development fluctuates much less and remains at much lower levels (generally between 1 and 10 percent of GNI). Media frenzies following crises are ephemeral, and with few exceptions aid flows soon ebb back to the lower and more stable levels that characterize normal development.

The large and short-lived spikes in aid, the improvised way in which they are channelled, the low absorptive capacity and the weak institutions of the countries put special pressure on both governments and donors to utilize aid more effectively and to avoid corruption at the time of the transition to peace.

Aid must be channelled through the central government budget

In countries coming out of war or chaos, aid has not only proved to be ineffective but also expensive. By channelling a large part of their aid through their own projects – based on their own agendas and priorities, and utilizing their own contractors and inputs – donors have clearly led to a fragmented and costly strategy in which governments have little ownership. Such strategy has led to unsustainable projects and facilitated corruption.[6]

For reconstruction aid to be effective and cost-efficient it has to be largely channelled through the government budget. Only this would allow for a well-integrated strategy based on national priorities. Officials rely on the budget for providing services and infrastructure without which they would be unable to acquire legitimacy. Channelling aid through the budget would make it possible to build capacity in the civil service. Unless the authorities know how much money enters the country, policymaking decisions will be distorted. Although this should be the general premise, there are emergency situations where there might be no time to go through the normal process. This is why policy and institutional flexibility are so much desired in war-torn countries.

Humanitarian and reconstruction aid must not be conflated

Aid must move quickly from short-term humanitarian purposes – to save lives, feed, and shelter those giving up war – to reconstruction activities aimed at creating investment, productivity growth, food security, and the sustainable employment that will enable those giving up arms to live dignified lives. Weaning countries off humanitarian aid as soon as feasible is necessary to avoid distortions and aid dependencies, a key but much forgotten lesson from the Marshall Plan.

Another key lesson from the Marshall Plan – also included as the third item in Boutros-Ghali's dictum for effective reconstruction and peacebuilding (Chapter 1) – is that humanitarian assistance should go hand in hand with investment and capacity building to avoid long-term dependence.

Donor-imposed policies to liberalize trade have led to cuts in tariffs on rice and other staple products. This, together with food aid and other types of assistance that change relative prices, discourage local production and work. At the time of the 2010 earthquake, President Clinton reckoned that the liberalization policies he championed in Haiti were good for his farmers in Arkansas but destroyed Haiti's rice production and made them import dependent. Such misguided policies have deterred food security and have led to floods of imports in countries like Liberia, Afghanistan, and Haiti that they can ill afford and have to be financed by donors. In addition to food, the provision of health and education should also be put on a sustainable basis as soon as possible.

A pertinent question becomes, what kind of aid will be most effective in creating productive capacity and local capabilities? Only reconstruction (or economic) aid targeting investment opportunities that use local capabilities, land, and natural resources can increase productive capacity. Its economic impact, however, will depend on how productively the aid is invested, whether the investment is sustainable, and the impact it has on the labour market, on income distribution, on the exchange rate, on reactivating production and trade, and on protecting the environment. Since in many war-torn countries, 75 to 85 percent of the population depends highly on the rural sector, reconstruction aid should initially target support for farmers and micro and small enterprises as well as basic infrastructure and services.[7]

Disbursement of reconstruction aid should not be delayed, as is often the practice, waiting for the country to have the right conditions in terms of political leadership, governance, institutions, and human capacity. In the meantime, humanitarian assistance continues to be disbursed, which leads to increasing dependency. At the same time, reconstruction aid should not be allocated to projects that are not likely to survive or be sustainable, as often happens with large infrastructure projects in insecure areas that are sabotaged.

The differential impact between humanitarian and reconstruction aid has become blurred in the present context, with the same agencies, NGOs or military forces often providing both of them and with the two often under the same command in UN and US-led operations.

Aid should be replaced with foreign direct investment and exports as soon as possible

To avoid the aid dependency that afflicts many war-torn countries, national leaders should ensure that flows of foreign exchange resulting from aid should be replaced with those resulting from foreign direct investment and exports. This is easier said than done in war-torn countries, where uncertainty and insecurity are high, property rights are questioned, the business climate is unfriendly to investors, and investment opportunities may not be promising, particularly in countries that are not rich in natural resources.

For these reasons, debate should take place on how to create potentially win-win projects, putting the rural communities, foreign investors, the government, and donors to work together in projects from which all expect to gain. Chapter 9 posits the need to think outside the box to address such overwhelming challenges. Reconstruction zones are recommended as a way to attract foreign direct investment to challenging places while promoting more effective use of aid and domestic resources, all while adopting conflict-sensitive economic policies that will support peacebuilding efforts.

Premise 6: Peace processes must contemplate a fair use of natural resources, including land, mining, water, and forests

Peace agreements that do not contemplate a fair use of natural resources and compensation to losers will make the post conflict transition particularly difficult. Compensation is necessary to ensure that those who benefited from the spoils of war and become "losers" from the peace agreement can be lured away from the illicit and profitable economics of war. Collaboration with the peace process will only take place if losers are given a stake in the political and economic process of the country going forward.

Premise 7: A peacebuilding yardstick must be created to measure success

Given that the peace (political) objective should always prevail over the development (economic) one and that optimal economic policies are not always attainable or desirable in the war-to-peace transition, a different yardstick must be used to measure success.

Success should not be measured in terms of the number of jobs created, the percentage of people taken out of poverty, or by indicators of economic growth and inflation, as it is under normal development. Success should be measured with the "peacebuilding yardstick," where policies and projects are judged more qualitatively by whether they contribute to peace and reconciliation rather than on purely economic criteria.

As an example, we can use the arms-for-land program in El Salvador. If judged with a conventional yardstick (e.g., yield per acre, debt repayment, etc.), this program would not get high marks. But the yardstick should be whether the program contributed to maintaining the ceasefire and to promoting national reconciliation, and whether it allowed beneficiaries to find productive employment that would permit them to make a decent living without resorting to arms. Using the "peacebuilding yardstick," this program was a resounding success (although it proved unsustainable for the reasons discussed in Chapter 7).

An additional problem in measuring success in the conventional way relates to the scarcity of and distortions with the data, which make empirical research, particularly econometric work, difficult given the unreliability of the data itself (and the few times series observations available). In some countries such as Iraq, for example, there was no data from international organizations because of UN sanctions. In Kosovo and East Timor, data on output and other variables were lacking because both were provinces of sovereign governments and macroeconomic and foreign trade data are compiled at the national level. In both cases comparisons of economic performance before and after the conflict were difficult.

Large movements of people and capital also hinder such comparisons. For example, the food situation, housing, services, and other indicators may worsen in some areas during reconstruction in the presence of large numbers of returnees, who were refugees in neighbouring countries or internally displaced during the conflict. Moreover, the behaviour of certain variables can become highly anomalous, complicating economic analysis.

One of the issues that came to the secretary-general's attention in the early 1990s was the fact that Somalia, a country that had no government, no monetary authority, and a failed economy, saw its domestic currency appreciate. This puzzled many UN officials in the country, who failed to realize that it reflected the inability of the country to print domestic currency amid plentiful inflows of international aid. Despite the collapse in government, Somalis had a preference for their national currency, which resulted in significant appreciation of the domestic currency.[8] To analyze data issues and anomalies that will affect reconstruction programs is another reason why adequate economic expertise is necessary for effective peacemaking and peacebuilding.

Premise 8: Peacebuilding requires the application of the T. E. Lawrence dictum

Last but not least, both national authorities and their foreign interveners must apply the T. E. Lawrence dictum that it is better "to let them do it" than it is to "do it better for them" and apply it to all peacemaking and peacebuilding activities. Thus, foreign interveners should let national negotiators, local leaders, and communities determine what their economic needs and priorities are, and the government should let the insurgents determine their preferred venue for reintegration. Unless the participants are empowered and take ownership, programs will not be sustainable, resources will go to waste, and peace will not endure. Foreign interveners, of course, should be there to support whatever needs locals have as they strive for peace, stability, and prosperity.

Conclusions

For the peacebuilding record to improve, these premises must be carefully analyzed before national authorities and foreign interveners embark on new peace processes. Each circumstance is unique and therefore all premises will not apply, or will apply differently, to different circumstances. Policymakers and their supporters will be well served, however, by trying to figure out how these premises – compiled from good and bad experiences and best practices from peacebuilding efforts over the world during the last quarter of a century – could affect or fit their own circumstances.

Some of the premises are related but have different policy implications. Others may depend on the specific stage in which countries find themselves in the war-to-peace transition. But ignoring these premises has often led to misguided policies, misplaced priorities and wasted aid, all of which have been directly associated with setbacks and even to the collapse of the peace process in many countries.

For countries to be able to break out of the vicious circle of violence, insecurity, corruption, unemployment, drug trafficking, and aid dependency in which many find themselves requires revising in fundamental ways what they are doing now. These premises provide a good start for modifying strategies so that peacebuilding efforts can have a more than even chance of success.

Notes

1   Boutros-Ghali, *An Agenda for Peace*, para. 17.
2   Some of these premises were first raised in del Castillo, *Rebuilding War-Torn States*.
3   For some proposals, see Graciana del Castillo and Edmund Phelps, "The Road to Post-War Recovery," *Project Syndicate*, 9 July 2007.
4   The experience of the Democratic Republic of Congo in this regard is relevant. Investments in diamond mines and others were made at very advantageous terms for the investors who took the risk.
5   For an analysis of this issue, see Nico Schrijver, *Development Without Destruction* (Bloomington: Indiana University Press, 2010), 159–188.
6   This has been as much of a problem in Afghanistan and Iraq as it was in Haiti and Liberia. As the US Government Accountability Office and the special inspectors general for Afghanistan and Iraq have well documented, corruption, waste and other inefficiencies are not by any means restricted to local officials or institutions. By contrast, money channelled through the trust funds through which donors finance the government's core operating budget are administered under best international transparency and accountability practices.
7   Many development institutions, including the UNDP, other UN agencies, the World Bank, the regional development banks, and the bilateral development agencies such as USAID can play a critical role as catalysts and coordinators of reconstruction aid. The World Bank and the UNDP also organize donors' meetings, including consultative group meetings and roundtables where donors pledge funds for reconstruction. Even at these donors' meetings, funding for humanitarian and reconstruction purposes are often conflated.
8   See del Castillo, *Rebuilding War-Torn States*, 44–45.

9 Moving forward

Thinking outside the box

- **Reconstruction zones**
- **Conclusions**

If Secretary-General Guterres and his team want to improve the UN peacebuilding record, the organization needs to think outside the box. Doing the same thing over and over as in the past and expecting different results will no longer be forgivable after a quarter of a century of failed experiences and enormous cost in lives and treasure.

Hopefully, this book has provided enough evidence of the importance of the economics of conflict resolution and the economics of peace in peacemaking and in making peace sustainable. Most accumulated evidence, unfortunately, documents how economic factors can derail peace processes if ignored or treated as development as usual instead of adopting conflict-sensitive economic policies. The UN's dismal record with peacebuilding is there for everyone to see. As Nobel Laureate Paul Krugman, would say, "If this surprises you, you haven't been paying attention."[1]

In the spirit of the last chapter, where eight premises were presented based on country experiences discussed in Chapter 7 and elsewhere in the book, this chapter will sketch a minimalist structure for reconstruction zones (RZs), taking into account the basic premises in designing economic policies so as to avoid the major pitfalls in past peace processes.

Reconstruction zones

The RZs that I propose are a way to get different stakeholders in war-torn countries – governments, foreign interveners (including the UN development system and other donors), foreign investors, NGOs and local communities – working together in an integrated manner on a win-win project where everyone could expect to benefit from it. RZs would consist of two distinct but linked areas to ensure synergies between them: a local-production zone (LRZ) producing for domestic consumption, and an export-oriented (ERZ) one producing exclusively for foreign markets.

Any existing export enclave, such as concessions for natural resource exploitation or free-trade zones (assembling operations of low-skilled manufacturing or commercial agriculture), could become the basis of an ERZ. Any new greenfield foreign direct investment could also serve the purpose. While it is normally impossible for governments in war-torn countries to provide basic infrastructure, services, security, and a stable legal and regulatory framework for foreign investors across the country, ERZs make that possible within gated areas. In exchange, investors would commit to train local workers, create employment by purchasing local inputs and services, improve corporate practices and local providers' standards, facilitate the transfer of innovative and productivity-enhancing technologies, and establish links with local technical schools and universities. ERZs could exploit natural resources in the agriculture and mining sectors, process agricultural products, or assemble low-skilled manufacturing goods.

The main purpose of LRZs is to address head on impediments to private sector development in rural areas. By redressing the bias against farmers and other small producers (light manufacturing and services for the RZs) and providing opportunities for the communities, LRZs could lead to more inclusive and sustainable growth. This can only be done with financial and other support from investors in the ERZs as well as with a more effective and integrated use of aid and technical assistance and local government support. In exchange, the communities would ensure that security is maintained in the zones, protecting their own livelihoods while lowering the investment risk that foreign investors face in these countries.

LRZs would focus on integrated rural development of agricultural and livestock products for the domestic market to boost food supplies and reduce dependence on imports, and they can produce light manufacturing and services, including for the ERZs. By providing a level playing field for men and women in the communities in terms of security, social services, infrastructure, credit, and other inputs (such as seeds, fertilizers, and agricultural machinery), the local zones would also help to bolster gender empowerment in the rural areas where the productivity of women is low precisely because they do not have access to these inputs.

Different national leaders, with the support of foreign interveners, will have to build on this minimalist structure, filling in the details according to the country's specific needs and preferences; the investment opportunities in natural resources or other areas; the aid and technical support they can expect to garner; the interest and capabilities in the domestic private sector; the capacity of national and local governments; and other local idiosyncrasies. Once the structure is fully built up in this way it can provide an effective strategy for moving the country forward into a path of peace, stability, and prosperity.

Many of the private sector activities that create growth in war-torn countries, including natural resource concessions and business parks and free trade zones for low-skilled manufacturing, operate as enclaves for export within the country. Enclaves do not have connections with the rest of the economy and often create threats to human security by putting large investors and local communities in confrontation with each other as they are in Liberia, Haiti, and the Niger Delta.

In these places, the investors have displaced families and communities; taken their land and other natural resources; affected their water, food, and other means of support; or exploited labour by paying inadequate wages, providing unacceptable working conditions. This clearly shows that for investment in general and for these zones in particular it is necessary to support conflict-sensitive economic policies in war-torn countries.

I first proposed the idea of RZs in *Rebuilding War-Torn States* in 2008 as part of a five-pronged employment promotion strategy. At the request of the United States Institute of Peace (USIP) and of the World Institute for Development Economics Research of the United Nations University (UNU/WIDER), I first applied the framework to Afghanistan and Haiti, two countries at the top of the U.S. foreign policy agenda in 2011, and then to Liberia in 2012. These three highly-aid-dependent countries needed to replace the fragmented aid policies of the past by adopting an integrated model that would allow them to move toward more inclusive capitalism and self-reliance.

Since the framework and specific applications to these three countries are available,[2] I only provide here a description of the minimalist framework (Table 9.1) and a list of the purposes and what could be achieved from the RZs (Table 9.2).

Although natural-resource-rich countries always find investors greedy for their resources, and other countries may attract them as a result of their cheap labour, such investments are not often accompanied by the creation of employment and other opportunities in sufficient quantities or acceptable quality. As a result, it is necessary to make the investments more desirable and less resisted by the local population, particularly the indigenous communities that are often displaced and their livelihoods threatened.

Table 9.1 Minimalist structure for reconstruction zones

RZs will consist of:	
An export-oriented zone (ERZ) that will benefit the country by:	• Attracting/increasing foreign direct investment (FDI) into natural resource exploitation, manufacturing using low-skilled labour (*maquila*), or investment into any other area attractive to FDI;
	• Representing a source of tax revenue for the government (depending on exemptions granted);
	• Representing a source of foreign exchange (export revenue is partly repatriated to pay for salaries and taxes and to make new investments);
	• Representing an important source of unskilled jobs and potentially some skilled ones in the formal market;
	• Providing a market for the agricultural and food products, services, and light manufacturing produced in the LRZs (see below).
A domestic-production zone (LRZ) that will complement the ERZ by:	• Establishing them next or surrounding existing ERZs, starting with one or two and increasing over time as the experience shows positive results;
	• Establishing local councils in them to make decisions about rural development and business development in the LRZs in an inclusive and participatory way (bottom-up rather than top-down approach);
	• Empowering local governments and institutions to support the LRZs;
	• Focusing on import substitution of agricultural and livestock products so as to minimize dependence on food imports;
	• Promoting livestock production (chicken, goats, cattle, pigs, fish) and their products (eggs, milk, meat, leather) through better nutrition and veterinary care;
	• Producing light manufacturing for domestic consumption in the RZs and elsewhere in the country.
The development of RZs will require:	• Utilizing infrastructure projects already built for/by the ERZs (roads, airports, and railroads), allowing RZs to be established without major infrastructure;
	• Providing inputs in the early phase (improved seeds, fertilizers, cuttings, saplings) and ensuring that in later years the area under cultivation is expanded by using the LRZs' own nurseries and that farmers have access to inputs at subsidized prices as needed;
	• Building adequate small-scale infrastructure to jump start local food production (storage, irrigation and drainage, power, machinery) as needed;
	• Building infrastructure necessary to create a level playing field for small and medium-sized enterprises (SMEs), including subsistence farmers and other microenterprises;
	• Facilitating the registry of SMEs and lowering their cost (since government functions are mostly centralized in capitals);
	• Creating a simple and low cost framework for SMEs to operate in the formal sector (perhaps a flat 5 or 10 percent tax in exchange for government services);
	• Building social infrastructure and telecommunications for the community, including to make it attractive to youth to remain in rural areas (schools, clinics, training centres, community buildings, internet, other) as needed;
	• Involving the local government in the provision of services, including security;
	• Involving technical assistance and aid from all foreign interveners interested in supporting an integrated project.

Table 9.2 Overall objectives of reconstruction zones (RZs) to move countries towards a path of peace, stability, and prosperity

Promote government's legitimacy

- By changing the perception of the people that the government is unresponsive to their needs and that assistance is provided by donors and NGOs;
- By addressing head on the main impediments to inclusive and sustainable growth, essential to consolidate peace, stability, and prosperity;
- By promoting food and nutrition security and basic health systems that would make the country less vulnerable to disease and pandemics;
- By rebuilding the education and training programs to provide today's workers and future graduates with the skills they need to become productive members of the workforce;
- By enforcing a zero tolerance policy for corruption and nepotism.

Promote national reconciliation and peace consolidation

- By reintegrating former combatants and other conflict-affected groups through productive activities;
- By improving the lives and livelihoods and creating opportunities for the large majority of citizens;
- By creating a level playing field for small and medium-sized enterprises (SMEs), including subsistence farmers and other microenterprises;
- By using conflict-sensitive policies that address the grievances of the communities vis-à-vis investors.

Address head on main impediments to inclusive growth

- By transforming the structure of the economy through diversification away from enclave production;
- By promoting integrated rural development (jointly with the development of human capital, infrastructure, business development and credit);
- By increasing import substitution of food and nutrients and basic manufacturing goods to improve unsustainable trade imbalances;
- By providing land tenure security for both the investors and the communities in the RZs;
- By creating a level playing field in infrastructure and financing for SMEs on an equal gender basis;
- By using technical expertise from universities and other specialized schools, both in the country and abroad, to adapt technology and expertise to the specific needs of the RZs;
- By putting the government and donors working together in a specific, comprehensive, well-designed and contained project so that aid effectiveness and accountability can improve

Strengthen local governments and communities

- By promoting decentralization;
- By involving local governments, letting RZs play a key role in strengthening them as well as local institutions;
- By deciding themselves what they want to produce, what type of infrastructure they need, what kind of skills will be necessary and what other needs they have, giving the communities strong policy ownership which will make the RZs sustainable;
- By having donors provide intervention in the areas needed;
- By providing experts on secondment from foreign governments or from specialized organizations for very short periods of time for training purposes, allowing foreign interveners to support capacity building at the local level.

Promote gender equality

- By having gender equity be the guiding principle of integrated rural development in the RZs;
- By providing productive inputs (seeds and fertilizer), tools, credit, training, and access to land to women on an equal basis since lack of access has resulted in women's much lower productivity in the agricultural sector;
- By putting families to work together on an equal footing and by ensuring that women's health issues are addressed appropriately through human development and capacity building.

Promote environmental sustainability and protect biodiversity

---

- By focusing on environmental sustainability as one core component of the rural development strategy;
- By promoting woodlot production and orchards to compensate for deforestation in mining and other areas.

Peace mediators may want to look at the RZs as an overall basic framework to be used in the negotiations between the parties leading to the establishment of the national reconstruction plan. Given that the RZs can be started at a small scale and with investors already in the country, they could create a quick peace dividend for the communities involved. Such positive impact could be used for demonstration purposes in the short run, which would facilitate the early transition at a time when expectations are high and people easily get disillusioned if they do not feel a visible impact in their lives and livelihoods. If it works well, RZs can be expanded to other areas later.

With donors and government support, both at the national and local levels, and an appropriate legal framework, reconstruction zones could help make aid less disjointed and fragmented than in the past, and more effective and better integrated. They can also reduce aid dependency pressure on donors by attracting foreign investment and raising exports. By helping to reactivate the economy in a balanced and inclusive way, the RZs could also become a major policy tool to improve human security, consolidate peace, develop critical natural resources and food security, reintegrate war-affected groups productively, and move war-torn countries more rapidly towards self-reliance.

Conclusions

National governments and foreign interveners should stop trying to build schools for which there are no teachers, or educating women and youth for jobs that do not exist, or create clinics for which there are no doctors and medicines, or service roads for which there is no legal product to transport. They should also stop attracting foreign investors into natural resource exploitations and low-skilled manufacturing where they operate as enclaves without creating productive links with the domestic economy and local communities, often even displacing them and threatening their livelihoods. Such investment not only fails to benefit the war-torn country as it should but creates additional sources of conflict in countries in which the risk is already high.

War-torn countries need to move into a path of peace, stability and prosperity. RZs are just an example of a more integrated framework utilizing conflict-sensitive policies and synergies between local communities, foreign investors, governments, and foreign interveners to facilitate such a move. Without new approaches, such as this one, UN efforts at peacebuilding will continue failing since peacekeepers cannot be kept in the country forever to maintain the peace, and aid cannot continue to finance the basic needs and the resulting often huge fiscal and external imbalances of war-torn countries forever. So sustaining the peace should not be the only goal; countries need to eventually be able to stand on their own feet to avoid permanent dependence.

Notes

1 Paul Krugman, "Worthy of Our Contempt," *The New York Times*, 1 August 2016.
2 See del Castillo, *Rebuilding War-Torn* States, 290–301; del Castillo, *Reconstruction Zones in Afghanistan and Haiti: A Way to Enhance Aid Effectiveness and Accountability* (Washington, DC: United States Institute of Peace, Special Report #292, October 2011); del Castillo, "Aid and Employment Generation in Conflict-Affected Countries: Policy Recommendations for Liberia," Working Paper No. 2012/47, UN/WIDER, Helsinki, 2012; del Castillo, *Guilty Party*, 407–414; and del Castillo, "Natural Resources and Emerging-Country Investors in War-Torn Countries," *Third World Quarterly*, 35 (October 2014), 1911–1926. For an analysis of the legal and regulatory framework for RZs, see del Castillo, "Reconstruction Zones as a Driver of Investment and Inclusive Growth in War-Torn Countries," paper prepared for the Tenth International Conference on Interdisciplinary Social Sciences (Split, Croatia, 11–14 June 2015).

Bibliography

Addison, Tony, ed., *From Conflict to Recovery in Africa* (Oxford: Oxford University Press, 2003). Addison's pioneering contribution shows how broad-based economic recovery does not inevitably follow from peace settlements and discusses how such recovery can and should be achieved to avoid relapse into conflict. Several case studies on Africa provide evidence.

Addison, Tony, and Tilman Brück, eds, *Making Peace Work: The Challenges of Social and Economic Reconstruction* (London and New York: Palgrave Macmillan, 2009). This volume provides case studies on major issues affecting economic and social reconstruction, including the economics of war and natural resources, horizontal inequalities, rebuilding fiscal institutions, physical and social infrastructure development, and entrepreneurship.

Ballentine, Karen, and Jake Sherman, eds, *The Political Economy of Armed Conflict: Beyond Greed and Grievance* (Boulder, Colo.: Lynne Rienner Publishers, 2003). Seminal work on the dynamics of war economies and the challenges these pose for conflict resolution and sustainable peace, with case studies on Burma, Colombia, Kosovo, Papua New Guinea, and Sri Lanka.

Barakat, Sultan, *After the Conflict: Reconstruction and Development in the Aftermath of War* (London: I. B. Tauris, 2005). This book addresses critical issues of reconstruction and development in war-torn countries, including peace agreements, conflictual peacebuilding, aid, humanitarian assistance, land, health, and reintegration of former combatants, and it proposes basic pillars for reconstruction.

Berdal, Mats, "Peacebuilding and Development," in B. Currie-Alder, R. Kanbur, D. M. Malone, and R. Medhora, eds, *International Development* (Oxford: Oxford University Press, 2014). In this influential article, Berdal analyzes peacebuilding as an activity that envisages a major role to economics and development policies and actors, discusses the operational challenges of involving the latter in politically sensitive tasks, and presents key policy priorities of donors and the international financial institutions.

Berdal, Mats, and Achim Wennmann, *Ending Wars, Consolidating Peace: Economic Perspectives* (London and New York: Routledge for The

International Institute for Strategic Studies, 2010). This book addresses how economic factors can positively shape and drive peace processes but often lead to failure with peacebuilding and reconstruction. Key economic reconstruction issues relating to aid, fiscal capacity, the utilization of natural resources, and the role of the Bretton Woods institutions are analyzed.

Berrebi, Claude, and Sarah Olmstead, "Establishing Desirable Economic Conditions," in Paul K. Davis, ed., *Dilemmas of Intervention: Social Science for Stabilization and Reconstruction* (Washington, DC: RAND Corporation, 2011). This important article on economic stabilization and reconstruction draws a clear distinction between post-conflict and other development settings and frames economic and social reconstruction strategies amid the security and political challenges and reform taking place in the country.

Boyce, James K., ed., *Economic Policy for Building Peace: The Lessons from El Salvador* (Boulder, Colo., and London: Lynne Rienner Publishers, 1996). This early and important contribution to the field of economic reconstruction in poor countries coming out of civil war, focuses on how economic policies should be reshaped for their special circumstances and needs so that they can address the root causes of the conflict to avoid relapse.

Boyce, J. K., and M. O'Donnell, eds, *Peace and the Public Purse: Economic Policies for Postwar State-Building* (Boulder, Colo., and London: Lynne Rienner Publishers, 2007). This important book addresses issues that diplomats and peace negotiators often neglect: building a durable peace and avoiding an aid trap requires building a state with the ability to collect revenue, allocate resources and manage expenditures effectively. It provides case studies on countries and issues, including monetary policy and postwar debts.

Caplan, Robert, *International Governance of War-Torn Territories: Premises and Reconstruction* (Oxford: Oxford University Press, 2005). Chapter 6, "Economic Reconstruction and Development," 135–157, provides interesting and cogent arguments on some of the major challenges of economic reconstruction and warns against some neoliberal policies often adopted that are not always suited to countries recovering from war.

Collier, Paul, "Postconflict Economic Policy," Chapter 5 in Charles T. Call, *Building States to Build Peace* (Boulder, Colo.: Lynne Rienner Publishers, 2008). Recognizing that until recently, development organizations did not systematically distinguished post-conflict settings as requiring a distinctive approach, this important article accepts that in fact, post-conflict reconstruction should not be simply development as usual.

De Soto, Álvaro, and Graciana del Castillo, "Obstacles to Peacebuilding," *Foreign Policy*, 94 (Spring 1994); and "Obstacles to Peacebuilding Revisited," *Global Governance*, 22 (April–June 2016). The first article identifies the lack of capacity of the UN to deal with major obstacles to UN peacebuilding efforts posed by restrictions imposed by IMF-sponsored economic programs. The second argues that the UN seems no better prepared today than it was at the end of the Cold War to deal with such obstacles and that the organization continues to neglect the economic aspects of peacebuilding at its own risk.

Del Castillo, Graciana, *Guilty Party: The International Community in Afghanistan* (Bloomington, Ind.: XLibris, 2nd edition, 2016). While most books on the Afghan War cover security and political issues, this book posits that inclusive and sustainable growth rather than war is the answer to extremism, insurgency, drugs, and poverty. It focuses on what went wrong with US-led intervention and what can still be done to bring peace, stability, and prosperity to the country and the region.

Del Castillo, Graciana, *Rebuilding War-Torn States: The Challenge of Post-Conflict Economic Reconstruction* (New York: Oxford University Press, 2008). This book provides a comprehensive analysis of economic reconstruction amid the multipronged transition to peace, arguing that unless the political objective prevails at all times, peace will be ephemeral, while policies that pursue purely economic objectives can have tragic consequences.

Junne, G., and W. Verkoren, eds, *Post-Conflict Development* (Boulder, Colo., and London: Lynne Rienner Publishers, 2005). This book focuses on the need to move beyond emergency relief to create new social and economic structures (including policies, infrastructure, social services, and environmental and financing mechanisms) that can serve as the foundations to lasting peace.

Langer, Arnim, and Graham K. Brown, eds, *Building Sustainable Peace: Timing and Sequencing of Post-Conflict Reconstruction and Peacebuilding* (Oxford: Oxford University Press, 2016). This groundbreaking work covers the timing and sequencing challenges, dilemmas, and tradeoffs of different policy reforms and their consequences for the transition to peace. It also provides evidence that many reforms thought to be critical during the transition are better left for the long-term "development as usual" phase.

Looney, Robert, "Neoliberalism in a Conflict State: The Viability of Economic Shock Therapy in Iraq," *Strategic Insights*, III/6 (June 2004). This excellent analysis covers the controversies between the Bush Administration emphasis on neoliberal policies in the form of "shock therapy" as the solution to Iraq's reconstruction, those in the field facing political constraints and uncertainty who argued for a more step-by-step approach, and Iraqis who perceived US-led policies as a western experiment geared towards benefiting from their oil and other assets.

Myerson, Roger, "Standards for State-Building Interventions," in Robert M. Solow, ed., *Economics for the Curious: Inside the Minds of 12 Nobel Laureates* (London and New York: Palgrave Macmillan, 2014). Nobel Laureate Myerson argues that successful democratic development depends on the availability of leaders that can use public funds responsibly in providing services and good governance. Foreign interveners must create opportunities for political and economic decentralization so that local leaders can develop a good reputation to get elected not only at the local but also at national levels.

Savage, James D., *Reconstructing Iraq's Budgetary Institutions: Coalition State Building After Saddam* (Cambridge: Cambridge University Press, 2013). This book is much more than an excellent case study of the fiscal issues and budgetary process reform – formulation, approval, and execution – in Iraq. It clearly identifies a set of U.S. interagency problems which has affected the impact of U.S. operations and performance in Iraq as they have in other war-torn countries, particularly Afghanistan.

Woodward, S., "Economic Priorities for Successful Peace Implementation," in Stephen J. Stedman, Donald Rothchild, and Elizabeth M. Cousens, eds, *Ending Civil Wars: The Implementation of Peace Agreements* (Boulder, Colo., and London: Lynne Rienner, 2002), 183–214. The article's seminal contribution was to warn of the lack of any systematic analysis by academics and policymaking practitioners of the contribution of economic factors to peacebuilding. The author discusses the necessary economic tasks and barriers to peace implementation and identifies five emerging lessons.

Index

Addison, Tony 68, 92
Afghanistan 5–6, 16–17, 32, 40, 103, 131–3; agriculture 134, 135; Bonn Agreement 131, 132; conflict relapse 3, 36, 103, 108, 134; corruption 103, 109, 135; currency exchange 131, 133; drug production/trafficking 4, 36, 134–136; economic policymaking and the macroeconomic framework 131–4; employment 134; 'expeditionary economics' 25, 33, 136; Indices (AMLI 103–104, 109; *Doing Business Index 2016*: 110; *FSI* 103, 110; *HDI* 3, 103, 109, 110; *Iceland Social Progress Index* 110; IMF 133; *Peace Index* 110, 116; *Terrorism Index* 110); missed opportunities in the drug sector 135; *Operation Enduring Freedom* 36; 'peace through security' strategy 40; policy ownership 24–5; political transition 35; poor governance 49; rural sector 132–133; US-led military intervention 24–5, 131, 136; wrong policy sequence 134; *see also* Afghanistan, aid; UNAMA
Afghanistan, aid 25, 105, 132, 133; aid channelled outside the national budget 132, 135–6; aid dependency 2–3, 9, 108, 109, 130, 134; aid diverted to security forces 136–7; aid trap 134; *see also* Afghanistan; aid

An Agenda for Development 13, 17, 21; basic pillars of development 21; DDR 17; economic aspects of peacebuilding 17; peacebuilding activities 17; *see also* Boutros Ghali, Boutros; peacebuilding
An Agenda for Peace xiii, 14–18, 20, 21, 22, 26, 95; economic aspects of peacebuilding 14–15; peacebuilding activities 14, 16, 26; peacebuilding, definition 14; post-conflict peacebuilding xiii, 14, 16, 18, 20, 81; timing and sequence of peacebuilding 16–17, 26; *see also* Boutros Ghali, Boutros; peacebuilding
agriculture 130, 131, 134, 135, 142, 166; *see also* farmer; rural sector
aid 2–5, 8–9, 15, 24–25, 29–31, 34, 36, 39, 49, 51–56, 94,100, 102, 108–110,118–119, 148–162; aid comparisons (table) 105–06; aid dependency 38, 100, 108, 150, 159, 162, 16; aid in different countries (Angola 105, 108; Cambodia 125; El Salvador 22, 105, 108, 120, 123, 127; Guatemala 105, 108, 127, 145; Haiti 105, 108; Iraq 105, 108; Liberia 74, 94, 105, 108; Liberia, Guinea, Sierra Leone 93; Mozambique 70–71, 106, 108, 119; Rwanda 106, 119, 129; Vietnam 53); aid in RZs 163–169; channelling aid through or outside the national budget 36–7, 132, 157–8;

"orphans" 5, 93, 94, 108; development aid 54; emergency aid 55, 151; food aid 17, 158; humanitarian aid 54, 150, 158–9; reconstruction aid 54, 118, 148, 150, 157, 158–9, 162; *see also* Afghanistan, aid; donors; ODA

Ajello, Aldo 86–7, 126

AMLI (*Anti-Money Laundering Index*) 103–104, 109, 116

Angola 2, 23, 126; aid 105, 108; conflict relapse 3, 101, 103

Annan, Kofi 30–1, 79, 80, 82, 84, 88, 95, 96; *In Larger Freedom* 96, 100–101

Anstee, Margaret Joan 65, 86, 97–8

arms-for-land program 8, 61, 64, 69–70, 119, 120–121, 123, 160

Arnault, Jean 81, 127

Ban Ki-moon 4, 84, 90–1, 95, 142

Barakat, Sultan 57

Berdal, Mats 13, 25, 46–7, 88

Bosnia and Herzegovina 30, 49, 62, 68, 103, 106; Srebrenica 24, 84

Boutros Ghali, Boutros xii–xiii, 26, 62; Boutros-Ghali's dictum for effective reconstruction and peace-building 17–18; integrated approach to human security and development 8, 20–2, 64–6, 79; the State as the foundation stone of peacebuilding 23, 148; *see also An Agenda for Peace*; *Supplement to An Agenda for Peace; An Agenda for Development*

Boyce, James 64, 114, 127

Brahimi, Lakhdar 132

Brahimi Report (*Report of the Panel on UN Peacekeeping*) 16, 88; development-as-usual approach 81, 132

Burundi 87, 103, 105, 111, 113; re-establishment of basic governance 24; UN Peacebuilding Commission 118, 140–1

BWIs (Bretton Woods Institutions) 2, 7–9, 11, 23, 25, 36, 59–75; change in rhetoric 75; conditionality 60, 62, 74; economic reconstruction 60–1; reconstruction/economics of development distinction 59–60, 61, 63–4; economic stabilization 12, 50; evolution of BWIs assistance 60; goals of international assistance to post-conflict countries 60; optimal economic policies 57, 64; ownership 73; pre-eminence of peace over narrow economic objectives 8–9, 64; quasi-legislative functions 60; 'silo' approach 117; supporting the transition to peace 59; UN/BWIs relationship 62, 124, 127 (collision course 8, 15, 62; communication problems 25–6, 81–2); *see also* IMF; World Bank; IFIs

Call, Charles 25

Cambodia 15, 23, 103, 124–5; conflict relapse 103, 108; DDR 124–5; *see also* UNTAC

Camdessus, Michel 72

capacity building 36–7, 133, 135; humanitarian assistance and 18, 26, 158

CAR (Central African Republic) 103, 105, 111, 113, 116; *Iceland Social Progress Index* 110; UN Peace-building Commission 141

Carville, James 92, 98

CEPAL Review: 1995 'Post-Conflict Peace-Building' xiv, 62–3

Chad 110

Chard, Margaret 57

Cheng-Hopkins, Judy 84, 85–6, 93

civil war 1, 7, 11, 29, 101; peace-making after 30–1; *see also* conflict

civilian police 8, 14, 31, 55

Cliffe, Sarah 70

Clinton, Bill 30, 158

Collier, Paul 66, 101, 115, 126, 145–6

Colombia 68

conflict xiii–xv, 1–3, 6–11, 13–21, 24, 29, 31, 34, 37, 39–40, 44–45, 50 ; conflict risk (high risk 19, 80, 101, 134, 134; lower risk 19–20); economic factors that fuel 46–7; *see also* civil war; conflict prevention; conflict relapse conflict prevention 18–20, 91; economic tools for 18–19; international financing for 19; *see also* conflict relapse/recurrence; preventive diplomacy

conflict relapse/recurrence xiii, 1–3, 7–9, 11, 14, 29, 37, 45, 51, 57, 63–64, 70, 80, 84, 101–102, 103–104 (table), 107–108, 118, 149, 155, 162; in different countries (Afghanistan 3, 36, 103, 108, 134; Angola 3, 101, 103; Cambodia 103, 108; East Timor 103, 108, 138, 139; Haiti 103, 108; Iraq 3, 103; Mozambique 70, Rwanda 3, 101, 103)

corruption 4, 9, 33, 49, 55, 162; *Corruption Perception Index* 103–104, 109; in different countries (Afghanistan 103, 109, 135; Iraq 140)

Côte d'Ivoire 103

Cousens, Elizabeth 25

Cristiani, Alfredo 118, 119, 120, 121

decentralization 35–36, 123–4, 167;

DDR (disarming, demobilization, and reintegration) 6–7, 15, 55, 151; *An Agenda for Development* 17; donor's reluctance to finance 25; effective reintegration 17, 20, 25, 26, 41; employment 17, 18, 26, 151; in different countries (Cambodia 124–5; El Salvador 119, 120; Mozambique 70); gender issues 119; importance of 17; NATO 32; a peacebuilding activity 16, 17–18, 26; sustainable peace 54; *see also* reintegration

de Soto, Álvaro xii–xv, 6–10, 14, 22–24, 37, 65, 69, 79–80, 82, 120–1; criticisms to *An Agenda for Peace* 14; economics of conflict resolution in El Salvador 120; *see also* *Foreign Policy*: 'Obstacles to Peacebuilding'; *Global Governance*: 'Obstacles to Peacebuilding Revisited'

demining 16, 17, 27, 45, 48, 55

democracy 107, 123–4; a basic pillar of development 21

development: basic pillars of 21, 26; development aid 54; integrated approach to human security and development 20–2; *see also An Agenda for Development*; economics of development

displaced population 3, 55, 128, 151, 165

distortions 33, 41, 54, 153, 154, 158; Kosovo 138; UN missions 53, 102, 108–109, 158

Dobbins, James 91, 114

donors 2, 4–5, 20, 22–3, 25, 52, 102, 108, 156–7; donor-imposed conditionalities 34; in the economic transition 38–9; political transition 34, 36; security transition 31; *see also* aid; foreign interveners

Doyle, Michael W. 46, 108, 114, 115, 124

DRC (Democratic Republic of Congo) 16–17, 36, 103, 162

drug production/trafficking xiv, 3–4, 31–34, 36, 49, 68, 162; in different countries (Afghanistan 4, 36,135, 135; Guinea-Bissau 107)

East Timor 85, 104, 106, 112, 114, 132, 139, 160; conflict relapse 103, 108, 138, 139; *HDI* 139; IMF 138; NATO 24; property rights 137, 147; UN-led transitional administration 24, 53, 130, 137, 138

Ebola 5, 74, 93

economic expertise xiv, 11, 46, 150, 155–56, 161; importance of 121–122 (El Salvador), 125 (Cambodia), 128 (Guatemala)

economic growth 46, 70–72, 92, 103–104, 108–109, 160; 'growth without development' 94, 142; inclusive growth xiv, 21, 73–74, 87, 129, 151, 164, 167; sustainable growth xiv, 40, 54, 75, 87, 151, 164, 167

economic policy/policymaking 37, 40, 43, 47, 54, 60, 69, 132–135 (Afghanistan); conflict-sensitive economic policies 45, 56, 122, 150, 159, 163, 165, 167, 169; in normal development and in crises economic 138, 150, 152–4; first-best (optimal) policies 45, 57, 62–64, 67, 72, 134, 150, 152, 155, 160; second-best (suboptimal) policies 45, 63–64, 67, 72, 151; sequence 2, 13–15, 23, 43–45, 91, 95, 131, 134, 150, 157

economic reconstruction 29, 31, 33, 40–1, 44–46, 49–54, 56–57; BWIs 59–61; *development-PLUS* challenge 54–56; evolving context from the Marshall Plan to the post-Cold War period 51–3; humanitarian relief/reconstruction conflation 44, 50, 159, 162; humanitarian relief to development continuum 65; similarities between countries in post-conflict reconstruction and fragile countries in normal development 53–6, 67–8, 80; success of 149; UN 60–1; *see also* economic reconstruction, basic premises for effectiveness; economics of peace

economic reconstruction, basic premises for effectiveness 11, 17, 143, 148–62, 150 (table); private sector 150, 155–7; *see also* economic reconstruction

economic transition 1, 10, 30, 34, 38–40, 43–45, 50, 63; *see also* economics of peace, economic reconstruction, political economy of peace

economics of conflict resolution (peacemaking) xiv, 1, 11, 20, 44–46, 56, 118, 144, 148, 155–156; in different countries 121–22 (El Salvador), 125 (Cambodia), 128 (Guatemala)

economics of development 1, 44; challenges and policies 45; development-as-usual approach 18, 26, 49, 61, 62, 68, 72, 81, 123, 132, 134, 142, 153; economics of peace/economics of development conflation 11, 43, 50–1, 54, 60–1, 81, 82, 110, 132; from economics of war directly into economics of development 2, 107, 129, 133, 134; a

long-term and open-ended proposition 51; peace objectives should prevail over development objectives 8–9, 60, 65, 80, 150, 160; *see also* development

economics of peace xii, 1–2, 9–11, 15, 20, 31–32, 43–46, 48–49, 53, 56–57, 59, 61, 81,117, 134, 144, 149 ; basic premises 148–162 (table 150–151); exiting to the economics of development 122–123; creating employment opportunities 44, 52, 151; interrelations and differences with the economics of war, the economics of conflict resolution and the economics of development 45 (diagram); *also* economic reconstruction; economic transition; political economy of peace; conflict relapse/recurrence

economics of peacemaking *see* economics of conflict resolution

economics of war xiv, 1–2, 9, 11, 32, 43–45, 48–49, 56, 125, 160; difficulty of moving away from the economics of war 118; *see also* illicit activities

economy: a basic pillar of development 21, 26; contribution of economic factors to peacebuilding 82; economy and peace 72; four distinct economic phases of transition 44, 56; *see also* economic growth; economic policy; economics of conflict resolution; economics of development; economics of peace; economics of war

El Salvador 3, 7, 15, 16, 23, 37, 61, 68, 103, 118; 1992 Peace Accord/Chapultepec Agreement xii–xiii, 7–8, 122, 123 ('economic and social questions' 120–1); aid 22, 105, 108, 120, 123; DDR 119, 120; employment 122; 'exit' from economics of peace to economics of development 122–3; gender issues 119; *HDI* 103, 108; IMF 7–8, 60, 61, 62, 72 (obstacles to peacebuilding created by IMF-sponsored economic programs

7–8, 119–20, 121); impartiality 82; National Reconstruction Plan 62, 122; political and economic decentralization 123–4; reintegration 61, 120–1, 123; role of the private sector in peacemaking and peacebuilding 121–2; UNDP 123; World Bank 61, 70; *see also* MINUSAL; UNUSAL; arms-for-land program
election 26, 39, 102, 132; Liberia 142–3; local election 36, 37, 124; national election 37, 107, 124
employment 148; Afghanistan 134; DDR 17, 18, 26, 151; economics of peace 44, 52, 151 conflict-sensitive employment policies 56; effective reintegration 17, 18, 26, 102; El Salvador 122; IMF 73; poor education and 53; private sector 21, 122, 152; World Bank 68–9, 70; youth 52, 73; *see also* livelihood; unemployment
environmental issues 5; RZ, environmental sustainability and biodiversity 168
EU (European Union) 4, 138
Eurodad (European Network on Debt and Development): *Conditionality Watch* 74
expeditionary economics 25, 33, 136

FARC (Revolutionary Armed Forces of Colombia) 33
farmers 49, 143, 156; economic reconstruction 52, 133–4; private sector 47; reintegration 18; *see also* agriculture; rural sector
FMLN (Spanish acronym for the Farabundo Martí National Liberation Front) 7, 61, 120–1, 124
food 49, 72, 122, 167; *An Agenda for Development* 17; food aid 17, 158; food production 17, 155, 166; Rwanda 129, 130
foreign interveners 2, 9, 12, 29, 52–3, 102, 135, 148, 161; peacebuilding costs 2, 35; political transition 34–5; *see also* donors; foreign intervention

foreign intervention 4, 24, 34–35, 57; political transition 34–5; reining in foreign interventions 154; *see also* foreign intervener
Foreign Policy: 1994 'Obstacles to Peacebuilding' xiii, 6, 8, 15, 21, 22, 23, 65
fragile country 54, 55, 56, 66, 67; IMF 73; similarities between countries in post-conflict reconstruction and fragile countries in normal development 53–6, 67–8, 80
FSI (Failed States Index) 103–104, 109, 110
FUNDS (Future United Nations Development System) 20, 91–2; *Peacebuilding Challenges for the UN Development System* 92

gender issues/rights 31, 34, 39, 41, 46, 119; RZs and gender equality 168
Ghani, Ashraf 133
Global Governance: 2016 'Obstacles to Peacebuilding Revisited' xiii, 9–10, 82
governance: poor/weak governance 4, 9, 32, 36, 49, 148; re-establishment of basic governance 24, 35–6; *see also* government; insurgency; political aspects of peacebuilding
government: centralized government 35–6, 107; corruption 6, 9; interim leader 35; legitimacy 35–6, 37, 167; provision of services and infrastructure 36; RZs 163, 167, 168, 169; *see also* governance
Guatemala 23, 68, 103, 126–8; aid 105, 108, 127, 145; gender issues 119; IMF 127, 128
Guéhenno, Jean-Marie 36, 42
Guilty Party: 2016 *The International Community in Afghanistan* xiv, 117
Guinea 5, 74; UN Peacebuilding Commission 141
Guinea-Bissau 103, 105, 107, 111, 113; UN Peacebuilding Commission 141
Gunnarson, Agneta 123

Guterres, António 3, 18, 83, 95, 110, 163; 'It's the Economy, Stupid' 92; UN Peacebuilding Architecture 92, 95

Haiti 49, 73, 103, 111, 113, 158, 162, 165; aid 105, 108; conflict relapse 103, 108
HDI (Human Development Index) 103–104; Afghanistan 3, 103, 109, 110; East Timor 139; El Salvador 103, 108; Liberia 3, 103, 109, 118, 142; Mozambique 70, 103, 108, 109; Rwanda 103, 141; *see also* UNDP
High-Level Panel on Threats, Challenges and Change 122–3
Hoffman, Peter 49
Holiday, David 121, 127
Howard, Lise M. 85
human rights 9, 14; an integral part of development 21; national reconciliation 37; respect for 31, 41; violation of 37, 130
humanitarian assistance 103, 107; capacity building 18, 26, 158; humanitarian aid 54, 150, 158–9; humanitarian crisis 24; humanitarian relief/reconstruction conflation 44, 50, 159, 162; humanitarian relief/reconstruction distinction 65; investment 18, 26, 158
humanitarian intervention 24

Iceland Social Progress Index 110
IFIs (international financial institutions) 12, 23, 108; *see also* BWIs; IFM; World Bank
illicit activities 3, 9, 31, 38, 44, 45, 49, 109, 125, 160; extortion 3, 33; smuggling 3, 49; *see also* drug production/trafficking; economics of war; insurgency; money laundering; terrorism
ILO (International Labour Organization) 69
IMF (International Monetary Fund) 2, 7, 12, 62, 72–4; constraints imposed by IMF economic programs 15, 118, 120; economic

reconstruction/economics of development distinction 59–60, 61, 63–4, 72; El Salvador's arms-for-land program 8, 121; obstacles to peacebuilding created by IMF-sponsored economic programs 7–8, 119–20, 121); employment 73; fragile country 73; IEO 74; neo-liberal policies 74; prevention of economic crises is more effective than crisis resolution 19; recon-struction and growth 50; reports on different countries (Afghanistan 133; East Timor 138; El Salvador 7–8, 60, 61, 62, 72; Guatemala 127, 128; Rwanda 128, 129); *see also* BWIs; IFIs
impartiality xii, 61, 64, 82
inequality 2, 6, 40, 71, 74, 107
Institute of Economics and Peace: *Global Peace Index* 6, 109, 110, 116
insurgency 9, 32–3, 68, 107; Afgha-nistan 33; causes of 120; econom-ics of war 49; illegal activity 32–3, 135; weak governance 32, 36
integrated approach to human secur-ity 8, 10, 13, 20–22, 26, 30, 64, 79, 89, 117; integrated approach to development 20; to human security (or peacebuilding) and develop-ment 13, 20–22, 26
International Colloquium on Post-Conflict Reconstruction Strategies, Austria 65
investment 5, 107, 130, 168–9; aid targeting investment opportunities 158; economics of peace and reac-tivation of investment 44, 52; for-eign investor, benefit for 107, 144 (spoiler 156); humanitarian assis-tance 18, 26, 158; private sector 18, 47–8, 156; property rights 155; RZ 165, 168; RZ and foreign direct investment 159, 164, 166, 168; sustainable investment 37
Iraq 6, 16–17, 53, 103; 2003 US-led military intervention 6, 24; aid 105, 108; conflict relapse 3, 103; CPA 137, 139; corruption 140;

currency exchange 131, 139; 'expeditionary economics' 25, 33, 136; mistakes in 139–40; *Peace Index* 110, 116; 'peace through security' strategy 40; poor governance 49; property rights 137; reintegration 131; *Terrorism Index* 110; unemployment 139; US-led transitional administration 130

Jenkins, Rob 85, 87
Johnson Sirleaf, Ellen 142–3
Jones, Gareth 68–9

Kagame, Paul 118, 119, 129, 130
Karzai, Hamid 132–3
Keynes, John M. 8, 30
Khadiagala, Gilbert 128
Khmer Rouge 125
Kim, Jim Yong 71; *Dying for Growth: Global Inequality and the Health of the Poor* 71
Knight, Rachael 143
Korea 7, 52
Kosovo 6, 49, 103, 131; currency 131, 133; distortion 138; NATO 24; property rights 137; SRSG 137; UN-led transitional administration 24, 53, 130, 137
Krugman, Paul 163

Lagarde, Christine 73–74
Landgren, Karin 94, 143
Lawrence, T. E. 161
legitimacy 119; government 35–6, 37, 167
Liberia 5, 32, 40, 93–4, 103; aid 74, 94, 105, 108; aid dependency 2–3, 108, 109, 130; elections 142–3; 'growth without development' policies 94, 142; *HDI* 3, 103, 109, 118, 142; poor governance 49; poverty 142; PPP 142; recreating policies and institutions of the past 50, 141; rural sector 142, 143; UN Peacebuilding Commission 93–4, 141–3; UN troops in 3, 74, 108, 141, 142; see also Johnson Sirleaf, Ellen
Lieven, Anatol 131

livelihood 32, 54, 70, 94, 107, 130, 133, 165, 169; peacebuilding 11, 38, 92; RZ 164, 167, 168; sustainable peace 48; *see also* employment

Malone, David 46–7
Marshall Plan 7, 43, 51, 62, 158
McAskie, Carolyn 84, 87, 88
McKechnie, Alastair 135–6
MDGs (Millennium Development Goals) 70
Meyer-Knapp, Helena 37
military intervention 3, 6, 48, 53, 103–104, 117; US-led military intervention 24–5; *see also* peacebuilding following military intervention
MINUSAL (UN Mission in El Salvador) 123; *see also* El Salvador
money laundering 49, 109, 116; AMLI 103–104
A More Secure World: Our Shared Responsibility 96, 101
Mozambique 3, 23, 103, 125–6; aid 71, 106, 108; aid dependency 109, 119; DDR 70; economic growth 70–1; gender issues 119; *HDI* 70, 103, 108, 109; MDGs 70; reintegration 126; SRSG 125, 126; World Bank 70; *see also* UNOMOZ
multidisciplinary transition to peace 1, 6, 10, 12, 29, 31, 40–1, 49, 61, 63, 82, 118, 137; case studies on UN multidisciplinary operations, literature on 110, 111–14; economic transition 10, 29–30, 31, 38–9; interrelation between all aspects of transition 10, 29, 30, 39–40, 41, 117; irreversible transition 29; political transition 10, 29, 31, 34–7; reverse causality 39, 40, 117; security transition 10, 29, 30–4; 'silo mentality' 10, 30, 115; social transition 10, 29, 31, 37–8; UN, ill prepared to deal with 22, 102, 110, 117; *see also* economics of peace; national reconciliation; political aspects of peacebuilding; security
Myerson, Roger 34–6, 37, 123–4, 132

Nadiri, M. Ishaq 5
Naim, Moisés 6
Namibia 102
nation-building 23, 50, 57–8
national reconciliation 7, 9, 31, 39, 40, 143, 151; human rights 37; most challenging and expensive proposition 52; reintegration 31, 38; Rwanda 129; RZ 167; *sine qua non* to preserving peace and stability 39; social transition 10, 29, 31, 37–8
NATO (North Atlantic Treaty Organization) 24, 32, 135
neoliberalism 71, 74, 130
NGO (non-governmental organization) 2, 36, 71, 159, 163, 167
North Korea 109

Obama, Barack 5, 71
ODA (OECD Official Development Assistance) 56, 58, 105–106; *see also* aid
ONUSAL (UN Observer Mission in El Salvador) 123; *see also* El Salvador
organized crime 4, 33
Ottaway, Marina 131
ownership 34, 90, 130, 154; Afghanistan 24–5; BWIs 73; importance of 73, 161; policy ownership 23–5, 37, 148

Pakistan 5, 6, 110
peace: a basic pillar of development 21; peace as political objective of peacebuilding 8–9, 60, 64, 65, 80, 150, 152, 160; *see also* sustainable peace
peace agreement 34, 46, 103–104, 108; different agreements (Afghanistan, Bonn Agreement 131, 132; Cambodia, Paris Agreement 124–5; El Salvador, Chapultepec Agreement xii–xiii, 7–8, 120–1, 122, 123; Rwanda, Arusha Agreement 3, 128); compensation to losers 150, 159–60; economic aspects of 21–2, 151; economic expertise 155–6; effective peace agreement 46–47; fair use of natural resources 150, 159; peacebuilding following peace agreements 118–30; reintegration and gender 151
Peace Index 6, 109, 110, 116
peace mediator 11, 21, 46, 149, 156–7; economic expertise 21, 155–6; RZs 168
peace negotiation xiv, 1, 29, 46, 47, 53, 118, 122, 128, 149; *see also* economics of conflict resolution
peacebuilding, aim of 63, 90; costs 2, 94; conceptual framework definition 14, 25, 50, 90–1; failures at 2, 23, 40, 80, 84, 100–101, 115; international financing of 22–3; obstacles to xiii–xiv, 1, 6–10; peace as political objective of 8–9, 60, 64, 65, 80, 150, 152, 160; peacebuilding activities 14, 16, 17–18, 26, 81, 91; peacebuilding strategy xv, 46; post conflict peacebuilding 16, 20, 79–80, 81, 90; pre-eminence of peace over economic objectives 8–9, 60, 64, 65, 80, 150, 152, 160; preventive peacebuilding 16, 20, 81, 90; sequence and timing 15–16, 26, 131, 134; transition to peace, stability, and prosperity 1, 2, 44, 83, 107, 110, 115, 138; UN capacity to deal with 1, 10, 26; UN critical role in xii
peacebuilding, difficulty in integrating the political and economic aspects of 8–9, 15; failure at addressing economics of conflict resolution 1, 149; failure at addressing economics of peace 1, 117, 148; international financing 126; *see also* peacebuilding record
peacebuilding, in the aftermath of military intervention 48, 118, 130–40; *see also* Afghanistan; East-Timor; Iraq; Kosovo; military intervention
peacebuilding, political aspects of 61, 65–6, 67, 81, 97–8; economics of peace/economics of development distinction 60, 61, 63–4, 66–7;

political conditionality 127; political dimension of conflict 60; political nature of peacebuilding activities 65; political objective: peace 8–9, 60, 64, 65, 80, 150, 152, 160; political transition 10, 29, 31, 34–7, 39 (developing a participatory and inclusive government 31, 36; donor-imposed conditionalities 34; foreign intervention 34–5; promoting respect for the rule of law and rights 31, 41); *see also* governance; peacebuilding

Peacebuilding, record of xv, 2–4, 9, 11, 15, 30, 41, 66, 84, 88, 91, 93, 100–15; aid dependency 100; conflict relapse 84–5, 103–104, 107, 115; corruption 9; data, information on 102; global indices 109–10; ineffective aid 9; lack of economic expertise 11, 21; lack of integrated, operational, cost-effective approach 21; lack of productive opportunities for reintegration 15; misguided policies 2, 9, 23, 40, 134, 135; misplaced/lack of priorities 9, 23, 25, 134, 135; *see also* peacebuilding

peacebuilding, yardstick to measure success 9, 64, 151, 160–1

peacekeeping xiii; dependency on peacekeeping operations 2, 9, 34; failure xv, 169; success 14, 15, 16

peacemaking xiii; economic action that could help peacemaking 20; success 14, 15, 16; *see also* economics of conflict resolution

Pérez de Cuéllar, Javier xiii

Phelps, Edmund S. 3, 75

political economy of peace 1, 31, 44–45; *see also* economic transition; economics of peace; economic reconstruction

Ponzio, Richard 84, 88

post-conflict xiv, 1; sequence of policies 2–3

post-conflict peace-building xiii–xiv, 14, 17; versus preventive diplomacy 14, 16, 18–20; *see also*

post-conflict reconstruction xiii, failure at effective 3,

poverty: as cause of insurgency 120; economic policies/poverty/social unrest relationship 72; Liberia 142; poverty alleviation 60, 107; Rwanda 129

preventive diplomacy xiii, 10, 14, 16, 19, 90; preventive diplomacy/ peacebuilding distinction 16; preventive diplomacy vs. post-conflict peacebuilding 18–20

private sector 7, 21, 31, 36, 45, 47–49, 69,107, 121–122, 150, 152, 155–7; domestic private sector 45, 47, 144, 165; in conflict resolution 45; employment 21, 122, 152; *see also* SME

privatization 134, 137, 155, 157

property rights 37, 41, 55, 155, 159; 'backward looking 119, 137, 155

provision of services and infrastructure 129; economics of conflict resolution 48; economics of peace 38, 44, 52, 151; government 36; insurgency 32; terrorism 4

PRT (Provincial Reconstruction Team) 33 41

Rashid, Ahmed 131

Rebuilding War-Torn States xiii, 3, 75, 165

reconciliation *see* national reconciliation

refugee 3, 55, 104, 124, 125, 151, 161; refugee crisis 4

regime change 3, 29, 48, 53, 103

reintegration 7, 18, 38, 41, 151, 154, 167; El Salvador 61, 120–1, 123; employment and effective reintegration 17, 18, 26, 102; Iraq 131; Mozambique 126; national reconciliation 31, 38; reintegration into productive activities 15, 48; UN, lack of preparation 102; *see also* DDR

RENAMO (Mozambican National Resistance) 126

Renewing the United Nations: A Programme for Reform 80

reverse causality 39, 117
Roberts, Nigel 68, 77
Rodgers, Dennis 68–9
RPF (Rwandan Patriotic Front) 128, 129
Rubin, Barnett 132
rule of law 9, 31, 34, 38, 39, 82, 134, 152, 153, 156
rural sector 31, 37; economic reconstruction 36, 148, 157, 159, 167, 168; in different countries (Afghanistan 132, 133; Liberia 142, 143; Rwanda 130), inclusive growth 129; LRZs 164, 166, 167; *see also* agriculture; farmer
Russia 6
Rwanda 2, 103, 118, 128–30; aid 106, 119, 129; Arusha Agreement 3, 128; conflict relapse 3, 101, 103; food 129, 130; gender issues 119; genocide 3, 128, 129; *HDI* 103, 141; IMF 128, 129; national reconciliation 129; poverty 129; re-establishment of basic governance 24; rural sector 130; UN Peacebuilding Commission 118, 141; World Bank 128, 129
RZ (reconstruction zone) 11, 163–9; benefits of 168; conflict-sensitive economic policies 159, 165, 167, 169; development in rural areas 164, 166, 167; donor 163, 167, 168; environmental sustainability and biodiversity 168; ERZ (export-oriented zone) 164, 166; foreign direct investment 159, 164, 166, 168; gender equality 168; government 163, 167, 168, 169; investment 165, 168; LRZ (local-production zone) 164, 166; minimalist structure for 164–5, 166; objectives of 167; private sector 164, 165

Sambanis, Nicholas 46, 108, 115
Savage, James 140
Schaper, Herman 135
security: creating/improving security institutions 32; donor and 31; importance of 31, 39; improving

security 30–1 (cost of 32); local actors 32; NATO 32; 'peace through security' strategy 40; public security 31–2; security stabilization 10, 49, 133; security transition 10, 30–4
Siakor, Silas 143
SIDA (Swedish International Development Cooperation Agency) 123
Sierra Leone 5, 85, 87, 103, 106, 111, 113, 118, 140–1
Skoog, Olof 91
SME (small and medium enterprise) 18, 26, 52, 159, 166, 167
Somalia 2, 103, 106, 116, 161
South Sudan 103, 106, 110, 112, 114, 116, 161
sovereignty 19, 23–5, 34, 124, 154
spoiler 31, 45, 46, 56, 156
SRSG (Special Representative of the Secretary-General) 12, 24, 81, 85, 86–7, 125, 126; duplication 86
stabilization 34, 50, 54, 55, 63; economic stabilization 8, 9, 12, 50; local actors 32; security stabilization 10, 49, 133; successful stabilization 35
Stanley, David 121, 127
state 34–5; failed state 3, 24; as foundation stone of peacebuilding 23, 148; *see also* fragile country; *FSI*; policy ownership
statebuilding 50, 57–8, 112
Strauss-Kahn, Dominique 72, 73
subsidy 133, 152, 156
Supplement for An Agenda for Peace 15, 20, 22, 24, 90; economic aspects of peacebuilding 15; preventive/post-conflict peacebuilding 16, 90; timing and sequence of peacebuilding 1, 16; *see also An Agenda for Peace*; *An Agenda for Development;* Boutros Ghali, Boutros
sustainable peace 17, 82, 83, 89, 90, 91, 94; DDR 54; diverting attention from the UN's lack of operational capacity 95; employment 48
Syria 6, 110, 116

T. E. Lawrence dictum 161
the Taliban 4, 20, 33, 131, 132, 135
Taylor, Charles 143
terrorism 3, 4, 32; 9/11 attacks 24;
    drug trafficking 4, 135; economics
    of war 49; recruit of members by
    providing services and infra-
    structure 4; *Terrorism Index* 109,
    110; *see also* the Taliban
Tett, Gillian 117
Timor-Leste *see* East Timor
transition *see* multidisciplinary tran-
    sition to peace
transparency 55, 116, 162
Transparency International 104, 109
Tschirgi, Neclâ 82, 84, 88

UCDP-PRIO (Uppsala Conflict
    Data Program; International Peace
    Research Institute, Oslo) 102, 115
UN (United Nations) xii, 2, 12, 74–5;
    failures 2, 23, 40, 80, 84, 100–101,
    115; ill prepared to deal with mul-
    tidisciplinary transition to peace
    22, 102, 110, 117; lack of institu-
    tional memory 16, 88, 120, 143;
    mediation of internal conflict xiii;
    operational capacity 110, 115; sanc-
    tions 143, 160; 'silo mentality' 10, 30,
    89, 115, 117; thinking outside the
    box xv, 125, 159, 163–9; UN/BWIs
    relationship 62, 124, 127 (collision
    course 8, 15, 62; communication
    problems 25–6, 81–2); *see also the
    entries below for* UN
UN Department of Economic and
    Social Affairs 65, 81; *Inventory of
    Post-Conflict Peacebuilding
    Activities* 65
UN Department of Peacekeeping
    Operations 3
UN Department for Political Affairs
    3; peacebuilding 65–6, 80–1, 85;
    UN Peacebuilding Architecture 89
UN General Assembly 83, 91,
    95, 96
UN Peacebuilding Architecture xiv,
    5, 10–11, 82, 83–8; 2010 inter-
    governmental review of 88–9; 2015
    The Challenge of Sustaining Peace

89–90, 91, 92, 94, 98, 101; assess-
    ment 88–92; impact on peace-
    building 89, 92; lacking
    operational mandate/capacity 82,
    83, 84, 85; shortcomings xiv–xv,
    10, 85–6, 95, 123; sustained peace
    82, 90, 91, 94; *see also* UN
    Peacebuilding Commission; UN
    Peacebuilding Fund; UN Peace-
    building Support Office
UN Peacebuilding Commission 5, 83,
    85, 87, 91; CSC 84; purposes 84,
    89, 141; shortcomings xiv–xv, 84,
    88, 89, 92, 93–5; UN Security
    Council 88, 89, 95; *see also* UN
    Peacebuilding Architecture; UN
    Peacebuilding Commission,
    countries on the agenda
UN Peacebuilding Commission,
    countries on the agenda of 118,
    140–3; Burundi 118, 140–1; CAR
    141; Guinea 141; Guinea-Bissau
    141; *HDI* 118, 141; lacking coun-
    try diversity 93, 141; lacking
    inclusive economic and social
    policies 118, 141; Liberia 93–4,
    141–3; Sierra Leone 140–1;
    Rwanda 118, 141
UN Peacebuilding Fund 84, 87; *see
    also* UN Peacebuilding
    Architecture
UN Peacebuilding Support Office 84,
    85, 88, 89, 91, 93, 94, 95; *UN
    Peacebuilding: An Orientation* 16;
    see also UN Peacebuilding
    Architecture
UN peacekeeper xv, 53, 108, 122–3, 169
UN Secretary-General 22, 26, 63;
    ERSG 85; goals of international
    assistance to post-conflict coun-
    tries 60; impartiality 61;
    operational capacity to deal with
    war-torn countries 79, 80; *see also*
    Annan, Kofi; Ban Ki-moon;
    Boutros Ghali, Boutros; Guterres,
    António
UN Security Council 6, 7, 95; coun-
    tries exiting from 87, 93, 122–3,
    141; goals of international assis-
    tance to post-conflict countries 60;

UN Peacebuilding Commission 88, 89, 95
UNAMA (UN Assistance Mission in Afghanistan) 132; *see also* Afghanistan
UNDP (UN Development Programme) 21, 50, 60, 61; economic reconstruction/economics of development distinction 61, 64, 65, 123; El Salvador 123; goals 26; impartiality, lack of 61, 82; peacebuilding 80, 81, 82, 96; reconstruction aid 162; *see also HDI*
unemployment 128, 139, 162; *see also* employment
UNODC (UN Office on Drugs and Crime) 4
UNOMOZ (UN Operation in Mozambique) 125, 126; *see also* Mozambique
UNTAC (Transitional Authority in Cambodia) 124, 125; *see also* Cambodia
UNU/WIDER (UN University/ World Institute for Development Economics Research) 115, 165
URNG (Guatemalan National Revolutionary Unity) 127
US (United States) 109, 115; Afghanistan 24–5, 131, 136; *Counterinsurgency Field Manual* 32–3; 'expeditionary economics' 25, 33, 136; Iraq 6, 24, 130; 'peace through security' strategy 40; US-led military intervention 24–5; US/ Russia polarization 6; 'war on terror' 24
USAID (US Agency for International Development) 50, 80, 147, 162
USIP (US Institute of Peace) 165

Van Beijnum, Mariska 89
Venezuela 19, 86

Vieira de Mello, Sergio 86
Vietnam 7, 52, 53

war-to-peace transition *see* multidisciplinary transition to peace
weapons, destruction of 14, 16
Weiss, Thomas 6, 49
Williams, Brian 125
Wolfensohn, James 76
Wood, Elizabeth 64
Woodward, Susan 68, 73, 82
World Bank 2, 7, 11, 50, 59–61, 64, 66–75; WDR *Conflict, Security, and Development* 67–70, 71–2, 89, 101; Afghanistan 135; arms-for-land program 61, 70; *Breaking the Conflict Trap* 66; conflict insensitive approach 69; *Doing Business Index 2016*: 110; economic growth 70–1; economic reconstruction/ economics of development distinction 59–60, 61, 66–8, 123; employment 68–9, 70; Mozambique 70; peacebuilding 80, 81; policy change 72, 76; post-conflict reconstruction 50; reconstruction aid 162; Rwanda 128, 129; State and Peace-Building Fund 67; *see also* BWIs; IFIs
WDR *Conflict, Security, and Development* WDR *Conflict, Security, and Development* 67–70, 71–2, 89, 101
Word Summit Outcome (2005) 82, 96
World War I 8, 30
World War II 51

Yemen 6, 110, 116

Zamora, Rubén 120, 122
Zoellick, Robert 66–7

Routledge Global Institutions Series

127 The Politics of Expertise in International Organizations (2017)
edited by Annabelle Littoz-Monnet (The Graduate Institute of International and Development Studies, Geneva)

126 Obstacles to Peacebuilding (2017)
by Graciana del Castillo (Ralph Bunche Institute for International Studies, Graduate Center, City University of New York, CUNY)

125 UN Peacekeeping Doctrine in a New Era (2017)
Adapting to stabilization, protection and new threats
edited by Cedric de Coning (Norwegian Institute of International Affairs), Chiyuki Aoi (Aoyama Gakuin University), and John Karlsrud (Norwegian Institute of International Affairs)

124 Global Environmental Institutions (2nd edition, 2017)
by Elizabeth R. DeSombre (Wellesley College)

123 Global Governance and Transnationalizing Capitalist Hegemony (2017)
The myth of the "emerging powers"
by Ian Taylor (University of St Andrews)

122 Human Rights and Humanitarian Intervention (2016)
Law and practice in the field
by Elizabeth M. Bruch (University of Washington Tacoma)

121 UN Peacebuilding Architecture (2016)
The first 10 years
edited by Cedric de Coning (Norwegian Institute of International Affairs) and Eli Stamnes (Norwegian Institute of International Affairs)

120 Displacement, Development, and Climate Change (2016)
International organizations moving beyond their mandates
by Nina Hall (Hertie School of Governance)

119 UN Security Council Reform (2016)
by Peter Nadin

118 International Organizations and Military Affairs (2016)
by Hylke Dijkstra (Maastricht University)

117 The International Committee of the Red Cross (2nd edition, 2016)
A neutral humanitarian actor
*by David P. Forsythe (University of Nebraska–Lincoln) and
Barbara Ann J. Rieffer-Flanagan (Central Washington University)*

116 The Arctic Council (2016)
Governance within the Far North
by Douglas C. Nord (University of Umeå)

115 Human Development and Global Institutions (2016)
Evolution, impact, reform
*by Richard Ponzio (The Hague Institute for Global Justice) and
Arunabha Ghosh (Council on Energy, Environment and Water)*

114 NGOs and Global Trade (2016)
Non-state voices in EU trade policymaking
By Erin Hannah (University of Western Ontario)

113 Brazil as a Rising Power (2016)
Intervention norms and the contestation of global order
*edited by Kai Michael Kenkel (IRI/PUC-Rio) and
Philip Cunliffe (University of Kent)*

112 The United Nations as a Knowledge System (2016)
by Nanette Svenson (Tulane University)

111 Summits and Regional Governance (2016)
The Americas in comparative perspective
*edited by Gordon Mace (Université Laval), Jean-Philippe Thérien
(Université de Montréal), Diana Tussie (Facultad Latinoamericana de
Ciencias Sociales), and Olivier Dabène (Sciences Po)*

110 Global Consumer Organizations (2015)
by *Karsten Ronit (University of Copenhagen)*

109 Expert Knowledge in Global Trade (2015)
edited by *Erin Hannah (University of Western Ontario), James Scott (King's College London), and Silke Trommer (University of Helsinki)*

108 World Trade Organization (2nd edition, 2015)
Law, economics, and politics
by *Bernard M. Hoekman (European University Institute) and Petros C. Mavroidis (European University Institute)*

107 Women and Girls Rising (2015)
Progress and resistance around the world
by *Ellen Chesler (Roosevelt Institute) and Theresa McGovern (Columbia University)*

106 The North Atlantic Treaty Organization (2nd edition, 2015)
by *Julian Lindley-French (National Defense University)*

105 The African Union (2nd edition, 2015)
by *Samuel M. Makinda (Murdoch University), F. Wafula Okumu (The Borders Institute), David Mickler (University of Western Australia)*

104 Governing Climate Change (2nd edition, 2015)
by *Harriet Bulkeley (Durham University) and Peter Newell (University of Sussex)*

103 The Organization of Islamic Cooperation (2015)
Politics, problems, and potential
by *Turan Kayaoglu (University of Washington, Tacoma)*

102 Contemporary Human Rights Ideas (2nd edition, 2015)
by *Bertrand G. Ramcharan*

101 The Politics of International Organizations (2015)
Views from insiders
edited by *Patrick Weller (Griffith University) and Xu Yi-chong (Griffith University)*

100 Global Poverty (2nd edition, 2015)
Global governance and poor people in the post-2015 era
by David Hulme (University of Manchester)

99 Global Corporations in Global Governance (2015)
by Christopher May (Lancaster University)

98 The United Nations Centre on Transnational Corporations (2015)
Corporate conduct and the public interest
by Khalil Hamdani and Lorraine Ruffing

97 The Challenges of Constructing Legitimacy in Peacebuilding (2015)
Afghanistan, Iraq, Sierra Leone, and East Timor
by Daisaku Higashi (University of Tokyo)

96 The European Union and Environmental Governance (2015)
by Henrik Selin (Boston University) and
Stacy D. VanDeveer (University of New Hampshire)

95 Rising Powers, Global Governance, and Global Ethics (2015)
edited by Jamie Gaskarth (Plymouth University)

94 Wartime Origins and the Future United Nations (2015)
edited by Dan Plesch (SOAS, University of London) and
Thomas G. Weiss (CUNY Graduate Center)

93 International Judicial Institutions (2nd edition, 2015)
The architecture of international justice at home and abroad
by Richard J. Goldstone (Retired Justice of the Constitutional
Court of South Africa) and Adam M. Smith (International Lawyer,
Washington, DC)

92 The NGO Challenge for International Relations Theory (2014)
edited by William E. DeMars (Wofford College) and
Dennis Dijkzeul (Ruhr University Bochum)

91 21st Century Democracy Promotion in the Americas (2014)
Standing up for the Polity
by Jorge Heine (Wilfrid Laurier University) and
Brigitte Weiffen (University of Konstanz)

90 BRICS and Coexistence (2014)
An alternative vision of world order
edited by Cedric de Coning (Norwegian Institute of International Affairs), Thomas Mandrup (Royal Danish Defence College), and Liselotte Odgaard (Royal Danish Defence College)

89 IBSA (2014)
The rise of the Global South?
by Oliver Stuenkel (Getulio Vargas Foundation)

88 Making Global Institutions Work (2014)
edited by Kate Brennan

87 Post-2015 UN Development (2014))
Making change happen
edited by Stephen Browne (FUNDS Project) and Thomas G. Weiss (CUNY Graduate Center)

86 Who Participates in Global Governance? (2014)
States, bureaucracies, and NGOs in the United Nations
by Molly Ruhlman (Towson University)

85 The Security Council as Global Legislator (2014)
edited by Vesselin Popovski (United Nations University) and Trudy Fraser (United Nations University)

84 UNICEF (2014)
Global governance that works
by Richard Jolly (University of Sussex)

83 The Society for Worldwide Interbank Financial Telecommunication (SWIFT) (2014)
Cooperative governance for network innovation, standards, and community
by Susan V. Scott (London School of Economics and Political Science) and Markos Zachariadis (University of Cambridge)

82 The International Politics of Human Rights (2014)
Rallying to the R2P cause?
edited by Monica Serrano (Colegio de Mexico) and Thomas G. Weiss (The CUNY Graduate Center)

81 Private Foundations and Development Partnerships (2014)
American philanthropy and global development agendas
by Michael Moran (Swinburne University of Technology)

80 Nongovernmental Development Organizations and the Poverty Reduction Agenda (2014)
The moral crusaders
by Jonathan J. Makuwira (Royal Melbourne Institute of Technology University)

79 Corporate Social Responsibility (2014)
The role of business in sustainable development
by Oliver F. Williams (University of Notre Dame)

78 Reducing Armed Violence with NGO Governance (2014)
edited by Rodney Bruce Hall (Oxford University)

77 Transformations in Trade Politics (2014)
Participatory trade politics in West Africa
by Silke Trommer (Murdoch University)

76 Rules, Politics, and the International Criminal Court (2013)
by Yvonne M. Dutton (Indiana University)

75 Global Institutions of Religion (2013)
Ancient movers, modern shakers
by Katherine Marshall (Georgetown University)

74 Crisis of Global Sustainability (2013)
by Tapio Kanninen

73 The Group of Twenty (G20) (2013)
by Andrew F. Cooper (University of Waterloo) and Ramesh Thakur (Australian National University)

72 Peacebuilding (2013)
From concept to commission
by Rob Jenkins (Hunter College, CUNY)

71 Human Rights and Humanitarian Norms, Strategic Framing, and Intervention (2013)
Lessons for the Responsibility to Protect
by Melissa Labonte (Fordham University)

70 Feminist Strategies in International Governance (2013)
edited by Gülay Caglar (Humboldt University, Berlin), Elisabeth Prügl (the Graduate Institute of International and Development Studies, Geneva), and Susanne Zwingel (the State University of New York, Potsdam)

69 The Migration Industry and the Commercialization of International Migration (2013)
edited by Thomas Gammeltoft-Hansen (Danish Institute for International Studies) and Ninna Nyberg Sørensen (Danish Institute for International Studies)

68 Integrating Africa (2013)
Decolonization's legacies, sovereignty, and the African Union
by Martin Welz (University of Konstanz)

67 Trade, Poverty, Development (2013)
Getting beyond the WTO's Doha deadlock
edited by Rorden Wilkinson (University of Manchester) and James Scott (University of Manchester)

66 The United Nations Industrial Development Organization (UNIDO) (2012)
Industrial solutions for a sustainable future
by Stephen Browne (FUNDS Project)

65 The Millennium Development Goals and Beyond (2012)
Global development after 2015
edited by Rorden Wilkinson (University of Manchester) and David Hulme (University of Manchester)

64 International Organizations as Self-Directed Actors (2012)
A framework for analysis
edited by Joel E. Oestreich (Drexel University)

63 Maritime Piracy (2012)
by Robert Haywood (One Earth Future Foundation) and Roberta Spivak (One Earth Future Foundation)

62 United Nations High Commissioner for Refugees (UNHCR) (2nd edition, 2012)
by Gil Loescher (University of Oxford), Alexander Betts (University of Oxford), and James Milner (University of Toronto)

61 International Law, International Relations, and Global Governance (2012)
by Charlotte Ku (University of Illinois)

60 Global Health Governance (2012)
by Sophie Harman (City University, London)

59 The Council of Europe (2012)
by Martyn Bond (University of London)

58 The Security Governance of Regional Organizations (2011)
edited by Emil J. Kirchner (University of Essex) and Roberto Domínguez (Suffolk University)

57 The United Nations Development Programme and System (2011)
by Stephen Browne (FUNDS Project)

56 The South Asian Association for Regional Cooperation (2011)
An emerging collaboration architecture
by Lawrence Sáez (University of London)

55 The UN Human Rights Council (2011)
by Bertrand G. Ramcharan (Geneva Graduate Institute of International and Development Studies)

54 Responsibility to Protect (2011)
Cultural perspectives in the Global South
edited by Rama Mani (University of Oxford) and Thomas G. Weiss (The CUNY Graduate Center)

53 The International Trade Centre (2011)
Promoting exports for development
*by Stephen Browne (FUNDS Project) and
Sam Laird (University of Nottingham)*

52 The Idea of World Government (2011)
From ancient times to the twenty-first century
by James A. Yunker (Western Illinois University)

51 Humanitarianism Contested (2011)
Where angels fear to tread
*by Michael Barnett (George Washington University) and
Thomas G. Weiss (The CUNY Graduate Center)*

50 The Organization of American States (2011)
Global governance away from the media
by Monica Herz (Catholic University, Rio de Janeiro)

49 Non-Governmental Organizations in World Politics (2011)
The construction of global governance
by Peter Willetts (City University, London)

48 The Forum on China-Africa Cooperation (FOCAC) (2011)
by Ian Taylor (University of St. Andrews)

47 Global Think Tanks (2011)
Policy networks and governance
*by James G. McGann (University of Pennsylvania) with Richard
Sabatini*

**46 United Nations Educational, Scientific and Cultural Organization
(UNESCO) (2011)**
Creating norms for a complex world
by J.P. Singh (Georgetown University)

45 The International Labour Organization (2011)
Coming in from the cold
*by Steve Hughes (Newcastle University) and
Nigel Haworth (University of Auckland)*

44 Global Poverty (2010)
How global governance is failing the poor
by David Hulme (University of Manchester)

43 Global Governance, Poverty, and Inequality (2010)
*edited by Jennifer Clapp (University of Waterloo) and
Rorden Wilkinson (University of Manchester)*

42 Multilateral Counter-Terrorism (2010)
The global politics of cooperation and contestation
by Peter Romaniuk (John Jay College of Criminal Justice, CUNY)

41 Governing Climate Change (2010)
*by Peter Newell (University of East Anglia) and
Harriet A. Bulkeley (Durham University)*

40 The UN Secretary-General and Secretariat (2nd edition, 2010)
by Leon Gordenker (Princeton University)

39 Preventive Human Rights Strategies (2010)
*by Bertrand G. Ramcharan (Geneva Graduate Institute of International
and Development Studies)*

38 African Economic Institutions (2010)
by Kwame Akonor (Seton Hall University)

37 Global Institutions and the HIV/AIDS Epidemic (2010)
Responding to an international crisis
by Franklyn Lisk (University of Warwick)

36 Regional Security (2010)
The capacity of international organizations
by Rodrigo Tavares (United Nations University)

**35 The Organisation for Economic Co-operation and Development
(2009)**
by Richard Woodward (University of Hull)

34 Transnational Organized Crime (2009)
by Frank Madsen (University of Cambridge)

33 The United Nations and Human Rights (2nd edition, 2009)
A guide for a new era
by Julie A. Mertus (American University)

32 The International Organization for Standardization (2009)
Global governance through voluntary consensus
by Craig N. Murphy (Wellesley College) and
JoAnne Yates (Massachusetts Institute of Technology)

31 Shaping the Humanitarian World (2009)
by Peter Walker (Tufts University) and
Daniel G. Maxwell (Tufts University)

30 Global Food and Agricultural Institutions (2009)
by John Shaw

29 Institutions of the Global South (2009)
by Jacqueline Anne Braveboy-Wagner (City College of New York,
CUNY)

28 International Judicial Institutions (2009)
The architecture of international justice at home and abroad
by Richard J. Goldstone (Retired Justice of the Constitutional Court of
South Africa) and Adam M. Smith (Harvard University)

27 The International Olympic Committee (2009)
The governance of the Olympic system
by Jean-Loup Chappelet (IDHEAP Swiss Graduate School of Public
Administration) and Brenda Kübler-Mabbott

26 The World Health Organization (2009)
by Kelley Lee (London School of Hygiene and Tropical Medicine)

25 Internet Governance (2009)
The new frontier of global institutions
by John Mathiason (Syracuse University)

24 Institutions of the Asia-Pacific (2009)
ASEAN, APEC, and beyond
by Mark Beeson (University of Birmingham)

23 United Nations High Commissioner for Refugees (UNHCR) (2008)
The politics and practice of refugee protection into the twenty-first
century
*by Gil Loescher (University of Oxford), Alexander Betts (University of
Oxford), and James Milner (University of Toronto)*

22 Contemporary Human Rights Ideas (2008)
*by Bertrand G. Ramcharan (Geneva Graduate Institute of International
and Development Studies)*

21 The World Bank (2008)
From reconstruction to development to equity
by Katherine Marshall (Georgetown University)

20 The European Union (2008)
by Clive Archer (Manchester Metropolitan University)

19 The African Union (2008)
Challenges of globalization, security, and governance
*by Samuel M. Makinda (Murdoch University) and
F. Wafula Okumu (McMaster University)*

18 Commonwealth (2008)
Inter- and non-state contributions to global governance
by Timothy M. Shaw (Royal Roads University)

17 The World Trade Organization (2007)
Law, economics, and politics
*by Bernard M. Hoekman (World Bank) and
Petros C. Mavroidis (Columbia University)*

16 A Crisis of Global Institutions? (2007)
Multilateralism and international security
by Edward Newman (University of Birmingham)

15 UN Conference on Trade and Development (2007)
*by Ian Taylor (University of St. Andrews) and
Karen Smith (University of Stellenbosch)*

**14 The Organization for Security and
Co-operation in Europe (2007)**
by David J. Galbreath (University of Aberdeen)

13 The International Committee of the Red Cross (2007)
A neutral humanitarian actor
*by David P. Forsythe (University of Nebraska) and
Barbara Ann Rieffer-Flanagan (Central Washington University)*

12 The World Economic Forum (2007)
A multi-stakeholder approach to global governance
by Geoffrey Allen Pigman (Bennington College)

11 The Group of 7/8 (2007)
by Hugo Dobson (University of Sheffield)

10 The International Monetary Fund (2007)
Politics of conditional lending
by James Raymond Vreeland (Georgetown University)

9 The North Atlantic Treaty Organization (2007)
The enduring alliance
*by Julian Lindley-French (Center for Applied Policy, University of
Munich)*

8 The World Intellectual Property Organization (2006)
Resurgence and the development agenda
by Chris May (University of the West of England)

7 The UN Security Council (2006)
Practice and promise
by Edward C. Luck (Columbia University)

6 Global Environmental Institutions (2006)
by Elizabeth R. DeSombre (Wellesley College)

5 Internal Displacement (2006)
Conceptualization and its consequences
*by Thomas G. Weiss (The CUNY Graduate Center) and
David A. Korn*

4 The UN General Assembly (2005)
by M. J. Peterson (University of Massachusetts, Amherst)

3 United Nations Global Conferences (2005)
by Michael G. Schechter (Michigan State University)

2 The UN Secretary-General and Secretariat (2005)
by Leon Gordenker (Princeton University)

1 The United Nations and Human Rights (2005)
A guide for a new era
by Julie A. Mertus (American University)

Books currently under contract include:

The Regional Development Banks
Lending with a regional flavor
by Jonathan R. Strand (University of Nevada)

Millennium Development Goals (MDGs)
For a people-centered development agenda?
by Sakiko Fukada-Parr (The New School)

The Bank for International Settlements
The politics of global financial supervision in the age of high finance
by Kevin Ozgercin (SUNY College at Old Westbury)

International Migration
by Khalid Koser (Geneva Centre for Security Policy)

The International Monetary Fund (2nd edition)
Politics of conditional lending
by James Raymond Vreeland (Georgetown University)

The UN Global Compact
by Catia Gregoratti (Lund University)

Institutions for Women's Rights
*by Charlotte Patton (York College, CUNY) and
Carolyn Stephenson (University of Hawaii)*

International Aid
by Paul Mosley (University of Sheffield)

Coping with Nuclear Weapons
by W. Pal Sidhu

Global Governance and China
The dragon's learning curve
edited by Scott Kennedy (Indiana University)

The Politics of Global Economic Surveillance
by Martin S. Edwards (Seton Hall University)

Mercy and Mercenaries
Humanitarian agencies and private security companies
by Peter Hoffman

Regional Organizations in the Middle East
by James Worrall (University of Leeds)

Reforming the UN Development System
The Politics of Incrementalism
by Silke Weinlich (Duisburg-Essen University)

The International Criminal Court
The Politics and practice of prosecuting atrocity crimes
by Martin Mennecke (University of Copenhagen)

BRICS
by João Pontes Nogueira (Catholic University, Rio de Janeiro) and
Monica Herz (Catholic University, Rio de Janeiro)

The European Union (2nd edition)
Clive Archer (Manchester Metropolitan University)

Protecting the Internally Displaced
Rhetoric and reality
Phil Orchard (University of Queensland)

For further information regarding the series, please contact:

Nicola Parkin, Editor, Politics & International Studies
Taylor & Francis
2 Park Square, Milton Park, Abingdon
Oxford OX14 4RN, UK
Nicola.parkin@tandf.co.uk
www.routledge.com